# WHAT IS CHRISTIANITY?

D1595968

# OTHER RELATED TITLES

In addition to *What is Christianity?* we are delighted to offer the following titles by J. Gresham Machen . . .

## NOTES ON GALATIANS edited by John Skilton

The chief feature of this volume is that it makes available in convenient form the "Notes on Biblical Exposition" which Dr. J. Gresham Machen published in the earlier 'Christianity Today' from January 1931 to February 1933. Students at Westminster Seminary have made profitable use of these Notes on Galatians 1:1 - 3:14 by following them, with minor inconvenience, through bound periodical volumes; but for many others who might greatly benefit from them, they have long been inaccessible. Here you will find a master exegete opening up important and essential material to help understand the import of the great Apostle on this vital portion of Scripture.

## THE VIRGIN BIRTH OF CHRIST

"Years ago I was tasked with a paper on the incarnation of the Son of God. My professor suggested some books that either approached the topic from a naturalistic standpoint or exalted Mary in the whole process. As I browsed the card catalog topically (yes, before computer cataloging!), I came across a book from the 1930s. It hadn't been checked out for several years. It was Machen. My soul was excited, revived, and my mind expanded. In an age where many books become dated, quickly, it is not so with Machen. Not so especially with 'The Virgin Birth.' Read it for the first time or read again. Just read it! Then pass it on." - **Dr. C.N. Willborn**

## THE ORIGIN OF PAUL'S RELIGION

"J. Gresham Machen not only believed, practiced, and proclaimed Paul's gospel, he was also able to defend its authenticity at the highest scholarly level. Because 'The Origin of Paul's Religion' penetrates to the heart of the matter it continues to speak to contemporary controversies over the nature of the gospel and the Christian faith." - **Sinclair Ferguson**

## BIBLICAL & THEOLOGICAL STUDIES: *Commemorating the 100th Anniversary of Princeton Theological Seminary*

"Biblical & Theological Studies is an overlooked gem in the world of reprints. I'm grateful it is finally being brought back into circulation. The chapters on seminary training and homiletics are timeless, as is Warfield's moving testimony on Christ's emotional life. This is a must read for seminary students and ministers, and will be of great value to thoughtful believers."- **Joel R. Beeke**

# WHAT IS CHRISTIANITY?

*A Selection of Notable Addresses*
*By a Noble Defender of the Faith*

By
J. Gresham Machen

Edited by
Ned B. Stonehouse

Solid Ground Christian Books
Birmingham, Alabama USA

Solid Ground Christian Books
PO Box 660132
Vestavia Hills AL 35266
205-443-0311
mike.sgcb@gmail.com
www.solid-ground-books.com

WHAT IS CHRISTIANITY?
*A Selection of Notable Addresses by a Noble Defender of the Faith*
J. Gresham Machen (1881-1937)
Edited by Ned B. Stonehouse (1902-1962)

First published in 1951 by Wm. B. Eerdmans, Grand Rapids, MI

First Solid Ground edition published in May 2013

Cover design by Borgo Design
Contact them at borgogirl@bellsouth.net

ISBN- 978-159925-287-2

# CONTENTS

# Special Dedication of this New Edition

## to

## *Rev. Frank Barker, PhD.*

Solid Ground Christian Books is honored to dedicate this new edition of *What is Christianity?* to Rev. Frank Barker, of Birmingham, Alabama. Rev. Barker first read Machen while serving a church in Oxford, Alabama as he was in seminary and training for the ministry. Machen spoke directly to his heart and he later had the privilege of studying the man and his writings in a seminary course. This was a turning point in his ministry. It was Rev. Barker's personal copy of a 1951 first edition of *What is Christianity?* that led to this new reprint. Thus it was felt that the best way to honor him at this time is to dedicate the book to him.

Rev. Harry Reeder, current pastor of Briarwood Presbyterian Church, said the following about the man he succeeded at the church:

"Frank Barker has been a model and a mentor for me as a Christian man and as a Pastor for almost the entire span of my life in ministry. Now, to enjoy the privilege of continuing that relationship in the context of a collegial relationship at Briarwood where he serves as *Pastor Emeritus* is only an added blessing. Frank exemplifies an unstoppable commitment to fulfill the Great Commission by 'making disciples of all the nations' through our Lord's church, the Body and Bride of Christ. His walk in the Lord and for the Lord have consistently exemplified a quiet security in the saving the grace of Christ. At the same time, he manifests the transforming grace of Christ by his unabashed love for Christ, his relentless commitment to learn of Christ from His Word and his submission through the practice of persistent intercessory prayer continually exalts Christ and multiplies his faithful effectiveness in serving Christ."

IN MEMORY OF

ARTHUR W. MACHEN

# INTRODUCTION

This volume contains a selection of the most notable addresses delivered by J. Gresham Machen during the last twenty five years of his life. A few utterances prepared directly for the printed page rather than for the public platform are also included as adding substantially to our knowledge of his point of view on various questions. Thus this collection of addresses and articles — together with *God Transcendent,* the volume of sermons published in 1949 — supplements the rich literary legacy constituted by the books which were published on Dr. Machen's own initiative. As the Introduction to *God Transcendent* has recalled, he was a singularly effective spokesman for Christianity for more than a score of years before his death on New Year's Day, 1937. Though his own books constitute the most significant record of what he had to say, they do not tell the complete story. Especially the public phases of his career as preacher, teacher, educator and citizen are illumined by the contents of the two volumes of sermons and addresses which are now made available to the general reader. The present volume particularly discloses the rich diversity of his interests and activities as a Christian man and minister.

The first address, "What is Christianity?" supplies a not unsuitable title for the entire collection, and serves to introduce a group of addresses delivered on various public occasions. In substantially the form presented here it was spoken before the General Assembly of the Free Church of Scotland on May 30th, 1927. There is evidence from correspondence, clippings and other data that this theme was frequently utilized at Bible conferences, in addressing college students, and on other occasions. This observation, as a matter of fact, also applies to several other addresses which are noted as having been given on particular occasions.

The following three addresses (II-IV) were delivered in London on June 10th, 1927, under the auspices of The Bible League of Great Britain, and under the general title, "Is the Bible Right About Jesus?" After having been issued by The Bible League in pamphlet form, they were revised by the author for *The Evangelical Student,* and published in successive issues beginning in October, 1928. It is their revised form that is published here.

The addresses on the Virgin Birth and the Resurrection of Christ (V, VI) are splendid examples of discourses presented at Bible conferences conducted at Stony Brook, Winona Lake and Grove City, as well as at various churches and institutions. After having been given at a conference at the National Bible Institute in New York City, they were published in the journal of that institution, *The Bible Today,* between December, 1924, and April, 1925.

The occasion of the address that follows (VII) was distinctive since it was not delivered under Christian auspices, but at a public meeting of The Fellowship of Reconciliation held in New York City, on October 29th, 1924. Yet the occasion was not altogether unique, for Dr. Machen was rather frequently invited to represent the position of orthodox Christianity in the forum of public discussion. That he accepted such invitations, and yet did not accommodate his message to curry favor, is evidence of the fearless and fervent faith that dominated his career.

"The Importance of Christian Scholarship" was the general title for the next three addresses (VIII-X) which were delivered in London on June 17th, 1932. Like the addresses given there in 1927, they were held under the auspices of The Bible League, which had invited him to visit England for the purpose.

"The Christian View of Missions" (XI) was an address presented as a part of the "Church of the Air" program of Station WCAU, Philadelphia, on May 7th, 1933, and was published in *Revelation* for June of that year. It reflects Dr. Machen's intense concern with foreign missions, and is of especial interest in connection with the controversy concerning the conduct of foreign missions which followed upon the publication of *Rethinking Missions* in 1932 and in which he took a leading part.

There follow a group of addresses and papers which relate to Dr. Machen's career in the field of theological education. While these materials accordingly are somewhat academic in character, none of a technical character is included, and hence the generally popular character of the volume is maintained. "Christianity and Culture" (XII) is one of his earliest printed addresses, having been given on September 20th, 1912, at the opening of the 101st session of Princeton Seminary. The following discourse (XIII) constitutes the address delivered on the occasion of his inauguration as Assistant Professor of New Testament in Princeton on May 3rd, 1915, and hence marks an important milestone in his career. "The Modern Use of the Bible" (XIV) is the only review republished in this volume, and is selected from scores of longer and shorter reviews contributed to theological and religious journals and newspapers. These three items were published in *The Princeton Theological Review* in the issues, respectively, of January 1913; July, 1915; and January, 1925.

"The Christian and Human Relationships" (XV) was prepared as a talk to students at Princeton Seminary, and appears to have been adapted for sermonic purposes later on. It has been prepared for publication from a manuscript written in longhand about 1915. "The Church in the War" (XVI) is the substance of an address delivered before the alumni of the Seminary on May 6th, 1919, soon after the return of the author from thirteen months of service as a Y. M. C. A. Secretary with the armed forces in France and Belgium during World War I. "Facing the Facts Before God"

(XVII) was published in *The Evangelical Student,* October, 1931, and was addressed to the student movement known as The League of Evangelical Students, with which he was intimately associated for many years.

The last three addresses in this group center about Westminster Theological Seminary, to the establishment and advancement of which Dr. Machen gave unstintingly of his richly varied resources and in which his hopes for the revival of the Reformed Faith in America were largely centered. The first one (XVIII) was the historic address delivered on the occasion of the opening of the new Seminary on September 25th, 1929. The brief addresses which follow (XIX, XX) were messages to the graduating classes of 1931 and 1934.

A final group of articles brings together several utterances on public questions of the day, with two essays indicating his love of nature added for good measure. The first four articles furnish further proof of the eminent position occupied by Dr. Machen as a spokesman for orthodox Christianity. The article, "Does Fundamentalism Obstruct Social Progress?" (XXI), was written in response to the invitation of the editors of *Survey Graphic,* and was published in that journal in its issue of July, 1924.. Professor Machen upheld *the negative* in a discussion in which the *affirmative* was presented by Professor Charles F. Fagnani of Union Theological Seminary, New York. About a year later *The New York Times* accorded him similar recognition when he was invited, as the celebrated Scopes trial in Dayton, Tenn., was approaching, to state the case against Evolution. At the same time Vernon Kellogg, Zoologist and Permanent Secretary and Chairman of Educational Relations of the Natural Research Council was asked to write on "What Evolution Stands For Now." Dr. Machen declined indeed to discuss Evolution as such on the ground that he was not an expert concerning it, but the article, "What Fundamentalism Stands For Now" (XXII), which he prepared, dealt nevertheless in a basic way with the underlying issue. This article, together with that of Mr. Kellogg, was published on the front page of the Special Features Section of the *Times* on June 21st, 1925.

"Christianity and Liberty" (XXIII) was contributed to *Forum* magazine, March, 1931, and is presented here in a somewhat fuller text than the editors found it practicable to publish. The next item (XXIV) was an address prepared in response to an invitation of The American Academy of Political and Social Science to participate in a discussion of the topic, "The Responsibility of the Church in Our New Age." The meeting was held on November 11th, 1932, and the other speakers were Whiting Williams and Rabbi William H. Fineshriber. "The Necessity of the Christian School" (XXV) is offered as the most representative single treatment of the subject of education in general and Christian education in particular. The subject of education was, appropriately enough, of intense concern to Professor Machen. And his utterances concerning it were so frequent that it has proved difficult to choose from several printed articles and addresses and from a number of manuscripts used at college commencements. The address published here was delivered at the Educational Convention of the National Union of Christian Schools held in Chicago in August, 1933.

The closing articles disclose Dr. Machen's passionate love of mountains and the exhilaration he received in climbing them. Though these topics did not lie at the very heart of his view of Christianity, nevertheless his conception of true religion, resting as it did upon the Christian view of the origin and nature of the world, was so broad as necessarily to comprehend within it both his love of nature as God's gift and his wonder at the glories of the creation. The first of these two articles (XXVI) was a paper read before a group of ministers in Philadelphia on November 27th, 1933; the second (XXVII) was contributed to a column entitled, "The Changing Scene and the Unchanging Word," appearing in *The Presbyterian Guardian,* and was published on August 3rd, 1936.

Acknowledgement is hereby made to publishers and editors who have kindly given permission for the republication in this volume of several of the items reproduced. These include J. Oliver Buswell, D. D., of *The Bible Today* for V and VI; Donald Grey Barnhouse, D. D., of *Revelation* for XI; Survey Associates, Inc., for XXI from *Survey Graphic; The New York Times* for XXII; *Forum* magazine for XXIII; Thorsten Sellin of *The Annals* of The American Academy of Political and Social Science for XXIV; John A. Van Bruggen, Ph. D., of The National Union of Christian Schools for XXV; Jarvis S. Morris, Th. D., of *The Presbyterian* for XVI and XVIII and Samuel G. Craig, D. D., of *Christianity Today* for XX and XXVI.

As in the case of the volume of sermons, I am indebted to Miss Margaret S. Robinson for aid in preparing copy and to my wife and the Rev. Leslie W. Sloat for assistance in proofreading. My hearty thanks for their valued help is hereby expressed.

To my sorrow, as a consequence of the recent passing of Arthur W. Machen, the form of dedication has had to be revised since it was first formulated, and it is no longer possible to acknowledge publicly to him my deep appreciation of his sympathetic interest in the preparation of this work. But it is a privilege to be able still to recall his kindness in granting me access to the files of his brother and his encouragement of my effort to make available in book form a selection of addresses and articles which will most significantly supplement Dr. Machen's own published books.

May the publication of this volume serve, at least in a small way, to stimulate men to be concerned with the greatest of questions, to mark the line where the truth lies, and to kindle love of the truth that they may be saved!

N. B. S.

# WHAT IS CHRISTIANITY?

# I

# What Is Christianity?

IN THE trials and conflicts which prevail at the present time one blessing has been given us. It is the blessing of a renewed and closer Christian fellowship with those with whom we are really agreed. As I sit in many of the councils and meetings of the Church at the present day, I have the strange feeling that the deeper things of the heart are being kept in the background, and that we are living merely on the surface of life. It is refreshing, therefore, to be in the company of those with whom one does not need to guard one's every word, but is conscious of the warmth of Christian fellowship which prevails. You — the Free Church of Scotland — have stood for two things. You have stood for liberty of conscience; and you have stood for the Reformed Faith, the system of doctrine which is taught in the Scriptures, which are the Word of God. You are a city set on a hill which cannot be hid. Your example has been an encouragement to those all over the world who are facing the same issue which you, by the grace of God, were enabled to face so nobly.

The question for our discussion, "What is Christianity?", has in recent years actually emerged from the seclusion in which it was formerly kept, and has now attained a place upon the front pages of the newspapers and in the popular magazines. A great many persons, indeed, resent our raising of this question. "If you raise this question," they say in effect, "you will actually interfere with the efficiency of the Church." But, after all, "efficiency" simply means doing things, and the important question is whether the things that are being done are good or bad. It is not enough to know that the Church is going somewhere, but it is also necessary to know where it is going. More important than all questions as to methods of preaching is the basic question what it is that is to be preached. If the agencies of the Church are propagating the gospel of Christ, then it is important that they should be just as well organized as possible; but if they are propagating some other gospel, then the worse organized they are, the better it seems to me to be. We cannot, therefore, avoid the basic question what it is that the Church is in the world to do, or. in other words, what Christianity really is.

But how shall we obtain the answer to this question? It does seem to me to be a matter of simple common sense that we can do so only by taking a look at Christianity as it has actually existed in the world. If I were called upon to give a description of the city of Edinburgh, I should not go out somewhere into the central part of the United States and evolve a description of this city out of my own inner consciousness, but I should travel to the city, look at it the best I could, and then try to give some sort of account of it as it actually is. To say that Christianity *is* this or that is very different from saying that it *ought* to have been this or that, or that the ideal religion, whatever its name, *would* be this or that. Christianity is an historical phenomenon like the State of Pennsylvania or the United States of America or the Kingdom of Prussia or the Roman Empire, and it must be investigated by historical means. It may turn out to be a good thing or it may turn out to be a bad thing — that is another question — but if we are to tell what it is we must take a look at it as it has actually existed in the world.

No doubt we cannot tell all that it is by any such merely historical method as that: we cannot tell all that it is by looking at it merely from the outside. In order that we should tell all that it is, we must ourselves be Christians; we must know Christianity in our own inner lives. But the Christian religion has never been an esoteric type of mysticism; it has always presented itself in the open air; and there are some things about it which should appear to friend and foe alike.

But how shall we take a look at it? It has existed through some nineteen centuries and in a thousand different forms; how can we possibly obtain a common view of it, so as to include in our definition of it what it is and exclude from our definition what it is not? To what point in the long history of Christianity should we turn in order to discover what it really is? Surely the answer to that question is perfectly plain. If we are going to determine what any great movement is, surely we must turn to the beginnings of the movement. So it is with Christianity. We are not asserting at this point in our argument that the founders of the Christian movement had a right to legislate for all subsequent generations. That is a matter for further investigation. But what we are asserting now is that the founders of the Christian movement, whoever they were, did have an inalienable right to legislate for all those subsequent generations that should choose to bear the name "Christian." Conceivably we may change their program; but if we do change their program, let us use a new name. It is misleading to use the old name to designate a new thing. That is just a matter of common sense. If, therefore, we are going to tell what Christianity at bottom is, we must take a look at the beginnings of Christianity.

Now the beginnings of Christianity constitute a fairly definite historical phenomenon, about which there is a certain measure of agreement even between historians that are themselves Christian and historians that are not. Christianity is a great movement that originated a few days after the death of Jesus of Nazareth. If someone should say that it originated at an earlier time, when Jesus first gathered His disciples about Him in Galilee, we should not be inclined to quarrel with him; indeed we might even say that in a sense Christianity originated still farther back, in Old Testament times, when the promise was first given concerning a salvation to come. But if Christianity existed before the death of

Jesus it existed only in a preliminary form. So at least the matter appears to the secular historian, from his superficial and external point of view. Clearly there was a strange new beginning among the disciples of Jesus soon after Jesus' death; and at that time is to be put the beginning of the great world-movement which is commonly called Christianity.

What then was Christianity at that time when it began? We can answer the question with more intelligence, perhaps, if we approach it with the fashionable modern answer to it in our mind and ask whether that answer is right or wrong. Christianity, according to that fashionable modern answer, is a life and not a doctrine; it is a life or an experience that has doctrine merely as its symbolic intellectual expression, so that while the life abides the doctrine must necessarily change from age to age.

That answer of course involves the most bottomless skepticism that could possibly be conceived; for if everything that we say about God or about Christ or about the future life has value merely for this generation, and if something contradictory to it may have equal value in some future generation, then the thing that we are saying is not true even here and now. A thing that is useful now may cease to be useful in some future generation, but a thing that is true now remains true beyond the end of time. To say, therefore, that doctrine is the necessarily changing expression of religious experience or religious life is simply to give up the search for truth altogether.

Was Christianity at the beginning really such a bottomless skepticism? Was it really a life as distinguished from a doctrine?

Now we want to be perfectly plain about one thing; we desire to guard ourselves just as carefully as we can from what would be the most serious possible misunderstanding of our position. We are certainly not asserting that Christianity at the beginning was not a life. On the contrary, it certainly *was* a life: the early Christians were living lives quite different from the lives of the people about them; and without that distinctive Christian life there could be no Christianity then, as without that life there can be no Christianity now. Christianity at the beginning certainly was a way of life.

But how was that Christian type of life produced? There we come to the crux of the whole question. If one thing is clear to the historian it is that that type of life was not produced merely by exhortation or merely by the magic of personal contacts; if one thing is clear to the historian it is that the earliest Christian missionaries did *not* go around the world saying: "We have been living in contact with a wonderful person, Jesus; contact with Him has changed our lives; and we call upon you our hearers, without asking puzzling questions, without settling the meaning of His death, without asking whether He rose from the dead, simply to submit yourselves to the contagion of that wonderful personality." That is perhaps what many modern men might have expected the first Christian missionaries to say, but to the historian it is clear that as a matter of fact they said nothing of the kind.

What they did say is summed up in a few words in the fifteenth chapter of the First Epistle to the Corinthians, where, as is admitted even by historians of the most skeptical kind, Paul is giving nothing less than a summary of what he "received" from the very first disciples of Jesus in the primitive Jerusalem Church. "Christ died for our sins according to the Scriptures; He was buried; He rose again the third day according to the Scriptures" — there we have in brief compass what the first Christian missionaries said.

But what is that utterance that we have just quoted? Is it not an account of facts? "Christ died, He was buried, He rose again" — that is a setting forth of things that happened; it is not an exhortation but a rehearsal of events, a piece of news.

The facts that are rehearsed are not, indeed, bare facts, but facts with the meaning of the facts. "Christ died" is a fact; but to know merely that fact never did any good to anyone; it never did anyone any good to know that a Jew who was called Christ died on a cross in the first century of our era. But it is not in that jejune way that the fact was rehearsed by the primitive Jerusalem Church; the primitive message was not merely that Christ died, but that Christ died *for our sins.* That tells not merely that Christ died, but why He died, what He accomplished when He died; it gives not merely the fact but the meaning of the fact.

But when you say "fact with the meaning of the fact" you have said "doctrine." We have already arrived, then, at the answer to our question. Christianity at the beginning, we have discovered, was not a life as distinguished from a doctrine or a life that had doctrine as its changing intellectual expression, but — just the other way around — it was a life founded upon a doctrine.

If that be so, if the Christian religion is founded upon historical facts, then there is something in the Christian message which can never possibly change. There is one good thing about facts — they stay put. If a thing really happened, the passage of years can never possibly make it into a thing that did not happen. If the body of Jesus really emerged from the tomb on the first Easter morning, then no possible advance of science can change that fact one whit. The advance of science may conceivably show that the alleged fact was never a fact at all; it may conceivably show that the earliest Christians were wrong when they said that Christ rose from the dead the third day. But to say that that statement of fact was true in the first century, but that because of the ad-vance of science it is no longer true — that is to say what is plainly absurd. The Christian religion is founded squarely upon a message that sets forth facts: if that message is false, then the religion that is founded on it must of course be abandoned; but if it is true, then the Christian Church must still deliver the message faithfully as it did on the morning of the first Easter Day.

For our part, we adopt the latter alternative. But it is a mistake to think of us merely as "conservatives"; it is a mistake to think of us as though we were holding desperately to something that is old merely because it is old and as though we were inhospitable to what is new. As a matter of fact, we are looking not merely to a continuance of conditions that now prevail, but to a burst of new power. The Spirit of God will in God's good time again enable men to see clearly, and when they see clearly they will be convinced that the Christian message is true. We long for the coming of that time.

Meanwhile, let us be faithful — as your Church has been gloriously faithful — in our witness-bearing. And let us pray God that He may honor not the messengers but the message, that sinful men may be enabled by the gracious power of the Holy Spirit to embrace Jesus Christ as He is offered to us in the gospel.

## II

# What the Bible Teaches About Jesus

THE SUBJECT which I have been bold enough to propose for the three addresses which I shall have the privilege of attempting to deliver is this: "Is the Bible Right About Jesus?" And, after all, that is the real test of the authority of the Bible. If the Bible is really right about Jesus, the probability is that it is right about other things as well. But before we discuss that question it does seem to me to be important to discuss what the Bible teaches about Jesus. If you are going to determine whether the Bible is right in what it says, it does seem to be important that you should first ask yourself what it says. In other words, I am old-fashioned enough — I know it is quite out of date — to think that it is important to examine a thing before you begin to express an estimate or criticism of it. So it does seem to me that we should first ask ourselves what the Bible teaches about Jesus before we ask ourselves whether that which the Bible teaches is true or false.

In the prologue to the Third Gospel we have words which, literally translated, are approximately as follows: "Forasmuch as many have taken in hand to draw up a narration concerning those things which have been fulfilled among us, just as those who from the beginning were eye-witnesses and ministers of the word have delivered them over to us, it has seemed best to me also, having followed from the beginning all things accurately, to write to thee in order, most excellent Theophilus, in order that thou mightest know, concerning the things in which thou hast been instructed, the certainty."

It is a very wonderful sentence from the point of view of style; the sense is held in abeyance until the very end; it is like a wave gradually forming on the shore until it reaches its climax in those words "the certainty." The man who wrote that sentence was a man gifted from the point of view of style, especially when we observe in the passage that follows, where he was dealing with the delicate details of Palestinian life, that he did not there attempt a classical Greek style, but was possessed of taste enough to catch the wonderful spirit of those Semitic narratives which came to him upon Palestinian ground.

But more interesting than the style of the passage is its content. I do not know that there is any passage in the whole of the Scriptures which needs to be taken to heart more earnestly just now than these words. That Theophilus, to whom the Third Gospel and the Book of Acts are dedicated, was probably an immature Christian: one at least who needed intellectual guidance; in whose case intellectual difficulties needed attention. It is very interesting to learn how the author of a very large portion of the whole New Testament deals with the intellectual needs of such a man. In the first place, there is no evidence that the author treated of the doubts or difficulties that Theophilus may have had as being necessarily sinful. There, I think, he provides a lesson for us when we try to lead people today. But still more important is it to observe that he did not treat those intellectual questionings as though they were a matter of no moment. He did not adopt the modern slogan that "it makes no difference"; that men can be equally close to Jesus no matter what they think of Jesus. But he plainly recognized what is recognized in the whole of the New Testament: that the Christian religion is founded squarely upon a body of facts. In other words, the method of this writer in dealing with intellectual difficulty is, first of all, to get the matter straight.

That is a method which has gone out of fashion at the present time. If there is one thing in the Church in America, and, if what I read is correct, also in the Church elsewhere in the world — if there is one thing that is characteristic of the Church of the present day, it is the alarming growth of plain stark ignorance. Suppose you are leading a Bible Class that is dealing with the Kingdoms of Judah and Israel. It may be well to begin with a little review. Suppose you say: "Now let us get this matter straight. Who was the first King of the united Israel?" There will perhaps be an eloquent silence for a little while, and then there will be various suggestions. Solomon, perhaps, will be a prominent candidate for the position. Finally, a grey-haired gentleman, the oldest member of the congregation, product of a better day in education, may suggest that it was Saul. You will say that that is correct, and that Saul did not exactly make a go of it. And then you will say that the next one was David, and the next Solomon, and then the kingdom was divided. When you get through, they will come up and say: "We never heard anything like it." Try that method in teaching a class. You may make a great hit! It is an entirely new notion to some people just to get the Bible straight. .

Now I had it fairly straight when I was very young, not by attendance at any sort of school, not by the operation of elaborate schemes of pedagogy, but by half-an-hour with my mother on Sunday afternoons at home. I could tell you the kings of Israel and Judah in order. The kings of Israel are easy, because they were all bad. But I could tell you just which ones of the kings of Judah were good and which bad, at a very tender age. But, it may be asked, what is the use of it? What is the use of learning all those mere details? There is a great deal of use of it, I think. For if you get the notion that there was a true progress of history in Old Testament times, then you come to have a certain conviction that is entirely absent from the minds of many persons who try to be good Christians at the present day — the conviction that when our Lord Jesus came into this world for our salvation, He came at a definite point of time, and that if we had been living there we could have seen Him; that like the author of the Fourth Gospel we could have touched Him with our hands, seen Him with our eyes, and heard Him with our ears. In other words, you have formed the fundamental conviction that, unlike other religions, the Christian religion is founded squarely upon a body of historical fact. Very well, it is rather important, I think, for us to try to get straight in our minds what the Bible says about Jesus.

But it is quite impossible to understand what the Bible says about Jesus unless you know also some of the things that the Bible says about other matters as well; and so if you will begin to read your Bible, you will find at least two important things in the Old Testament. At the very beginning, of course, you find the doctrine of Creation, that doctrine that is so much despised today: "In the beginning God created the heavens and the earth." You have there a clear view of a personal God, the Creator and Ruler of the world. Unfortunately that view of a personal God is lost in large sections of the modern Church. Men say that the doctrine of creation is a matter of metaphysics without importance for the Christian. We cannot solve the problem, it is said, as to how the world came into being; those things do not belong to the sphere of religion at all. Our God, men say, is a God of love, and we are indifferent to the question whether there is a God of power. Well, of course, there are many objections to such a way of thinking. A God who is only a God of love and has no power to act is not a person; and a God who is not a person but merely an abstraction is not a God who can love us and whom we can love. But of course the Christian heart negates this lack of interest in the question of the Creator and Ruler of the world. As for us, we say still, as we contemplate the "woodlands robed in the blooming garb of spring," or dark mountains capped with dazzling white: "This is God's world; its majesty and its beauty came from Him."

One thing that is to be regretted in the religious life of the present day is the decline in natural religion. But as for me, I am bound to say that I will not yield to the pantheists in my sense of the friendliness of nature; and when I toil up upon one of our mountains in America — for there we have to pay for our view,

we have not the bare mountains you have in Britain — when I
toil up, and the trees, as I ascend, become smaller and smaller
until the prospect bursts upon my view, as I am far away from
the troubles of the valley below, sometimes I have a feeling of the
friendliness of nature, the friendliness of nature as over against
the hostility of man, which is somewhat in the spirit of the pantheists of all ages, except that in our case it is a far deeper thing;
for as we come thus into contact with nature we can think of that
holy and living Person who has provided its majesty and its
beauty because of His love for us.

And then at the very beginning of the Bible you have also the
other great presupposition of what the Bible tells us about Jesus —
namely, the awful fact of sin. The consciousness of sin is deepened
all through the Old Testament; in the teachings of our Lord, too,
and all through the New Testament. It is deepened by a proclamation of the law of God. The law is the school-master to bring
us to Christ; and unless by learning the lesson of the law we come
to have the consciousness of sin, I fear we shall never come to
Jesus as our Saviour.

On that point I desire not to be misunderstood. I do not mean
for one moment that all Christian experience is alike. I do not
mean that every one, when he comes to Christ, has to go through
a prior period of agony of soul until he comes into the joy of
acceptance of the gospel. I remember a very interesting meeting
that I attended some years ago. It was a meeting of an evangelical
type, an experience-meeting; and the persons who were there
present were asked to say where they were born the first time,
and when and where they were born the second time. One person
said that he was born the first time in such and such a city, and that
he was born the second time on a railway train at such and such
a moment, of such and such an hour, and on such and such a day.
It was a very interesting record of the truest Christian experience,
and God forbid that we should say aught against it. But then
one lady rose to her feet in a very modest way and said something

to the effect that she was born the first time in such and such a place, and she could not tell when she was born the second time because she had grown up in a Christian home. I do not remember her exact words, but the notion was that as she had come to the consciousness of sin she had come also to the consciousness of Jesus as her Saviour. That was a true Christian experience too, and we should never disparage it. My friends, do not misunderstand me. I do believe that there is a definite instant when the wonderful event occurs in the life of every one who becomes a Christian — the wonderful event when he or she is born again; but I do believe also that there are many who cannot tell when that instant was; it is known to God, but not to them. There are many Christians who cannot give the day and hour of their conversion, who do not pass through prior agonies of soul. Certainly such Christian experience is not at all inferior to the experience of those who could give the very day and hour of their conversion. Both kinds of Christian experience, it seems to me, are true forms of Christian experience; and God forbid that we should deprecate either of them. But even in the case of those who grow up in Christian homes and are children of the Covenant from tender years, there is logically connected with their acceptance of Christ as Saviour, the consciousness of the fact that without Him they are lost in sin. So those are the two great presuppositions of the Christian message; the awful holiness, the awful transcendence of God, and the terrible separateness of sinful man from the Holy God.

Then, after the preparation for the coming of our Lord under the old dispensation, at last the fulness of the time had come. In what wondrous fashion the Savior, according to the New Testament, came into this world! He who was so great did not despise the virgin-womb; He was content to be born as a man and to lie as a babe in a manger and to be subject to earthly parents. How wondrous the story is! How different from anything that could have been expected, yet how full of a divine majesty!

In the New Testament there is the record of the life of our Lord upon this earth. And even in the days when He was on earth, He manifested His glory. The writers of the New Testament are conscious of the fact that even when our Lord was subject, in His human nature for the most part, to the petty limitations of human life, yet the glory of the incarnate Word shone forth. With what a trembling wonder the author of the Fourth Gospel says that "the Word became flesh . . . and we beheld His glory!"

At that point, of course — in our dependence upon the Bible for the facts with regard to Jesus — we meet the opposition of many modern men. A great many persons are telling us that we should emancipate ourselves from the slavish dependence upon a Book, and that our true authority is Christ alone. So they tell us that every race and every generation must interpret Christ for itself. We think, in this connection, for example, of that beautiful but harmful little book, *The Christ of the Indian Road*, by E. Stanley Jones, where truth is mixed with error in such a way as to lead many astray. The notion seems to be that every race may interpret Christ for itself.

If that meant simply that every race has its contribution to make to the rich store of our understanding of what God has told us in His Word, then we could no doubt agree. If it meant that the Indian race could understand some aspects of what the Bible says better than other races, in order that when that race had seized some aspects of the truth about Jesus it might share that newly discovered truth with us — if that were what is meant we might agree. But I fear that something very different is meant or, if not consciously meant, at least logically involved in what is said; I fear that what is involved is that the interpretation of Christ which every race attains is an interpretation that is valid for that race alone — as when it is often said, in accordance with the pragmatist scepticism of the day, that "Western creeds" must not be forced upon the "Eastern mind." When you arrive at that point — when you hold that every race may interpret Christ for itself — you are in great danger of substituting just the imagination of your own heart for contact with the real person, Jesus of Nazareth, whom God has presented to all nations in the whole of His Word, not only in the four Gospels, but also, just as truly, in the Epistles of Paul.

I do believe, indeed, with all my heart, that there is a direct contact of the risen Christ with the human soul. But I also believe that if that were all, the whole coming of our Lord upon this earth would have been in vain, and that it is for us when we come into contact with Jesus not to despise the plain record of what He said and did.

There is the first aspect, then, of what the Bible tells us about Jesus. The Bible tells us what manner of person Jesus was and is, and the part of the Bible that tells us that is contained particularly in the four Gospels. But if that were all that we knew about Jesus, we should be of all men most miserable. If we knew only what sort of person Jesus was and is, we should look with hopeless envy upon those who, when He was on earth, pushed in through the crowd where He sat amidst scribes and Pharisees, and had the wonderful experience of looking upon His face. We should be conscious, as we read about that experience, of a wealth of glory from which we should be forever shut out. No, there is something else that we need also to know, how we of the twentieth century can come into contact with Him. And surely that is not such a very simple thing. We cannot observe Him as we go through our busy streets. We are separated from Him by nineteen centuries. How is the wonder to be accomplished that we who live in the twentieth century should have personal contact with One who lived so long ago?

If you will read the religious writers of the present day, you will constantly observe that they assume it as an axiom that we ought to return to the experience of those who came into contact with our Lord in Galilee. I do not believe for one moment that they are right. In book after book, in sermon after sermon, it seems to be assumed that we ought to take the first disciples in Galilee as our models today. "They did not know anything about the Nicene and Chalcedonian doctrine of the person of our Lord," it is said in effect; "and so therefore these things are matters of indifference to us." Such is the argument. But do you not see that if we are to have contact with One who lived in the first century we must know far more about Him than was known by those who came into direct contact with Him when He was on earth? We need to know, for one thing, that He has risen from the dead, and that He is still alive; and then we need also to know how if He is still alive we can come into His presence.

There is where the other great division of what the New Testament says about Jesus Christ comes in; and that other great division is found especially in the Epistles of Paul. The Gospels tell us what manner of person Jesus was and is; and the Epistles tell us—what it is equally important for us to know—how we can come into contact with Him. Do not misunderstand me. The division is not an absolute one. The Epistles tell us not only how we can come into contact with Jesus, but also what sort of person He was and is; the great Christological passages in the Epistles enrich greatly and clarify our knowledge of the person of our Lord. And the Gospels, on the other hand, tell us not only what sort of person Jesus was, but also, by way of prophecy, how future generations could come into contact with Him. But after all, it is not surprising that the full explanation of our Lord's redeeming work should be made known only after the redeeming work was done, and so I have little sympathy with those who regard the words of our Lord when He was on earth as somehow more necessary for our needs than the words of the Holy Spirit that are found, for example, in the Epistles of Paul. You could summarize what we need to know about Jesus by saying that we need to have first, the record of Jesus' life in the Gospels to tell us what sort of person Jesus is, and then we need to have the eighth chapter of Romans and the rest of the Epistles of Paul to tell us how it is that He can become our Saviour today.

What is it that our Lord did, not merely for the men of long ago but for us today? The answer of the whole New Testament, of the whole Bible indeed, is abundantly plain. For us He did more than heal our bodily infirmities. For us He died upon the Cross. There is the point of contact between Jesus and our souls. I do not think that what the New Testament says about the Cross of Christ is particularly intricate. It is, indeed, profound, but it can be put in simple language. We deserved eternal death; the Lord Jesus, because He loved us, died in our stead upon the Cross. It is a mystery, but it is not intricate. What is really intricate and subtle is the manifold modern attempt to get rid of the simple doctrine of the Cross of Christ in the interests of human pride. Of course there are objections to the Cross of Christ, and men in the pulpits of the present day pour out upon that blessed doctrine the vials of their scorn; but when a man has come under the consciousness of sin, then as he comes into the presence of the Cross, he says with tears of gratitude and joy: "He loved me and gave Himself for me."

Men have objections in plenty. The Christian doctrine of the Cross, as it is found in the Bible, is objected to, in the first place, because it depends upon history. But of course it must depend upon history if it is to be a gospel; for "gospel" means "good news"; and news means an account of something that has happened. With regard to the same objection, we might say also that though this way of salvation begins in history it proceeds to present experience. When we read the blessed record, we can take it to our souls and come into contact now with our risen Lord. Men exalt "experience" at the present day, and set it in opposition to the Word of God; but why do they not attend to that Christian experience which testifies that the Word of God is true?

Then men say, in the second place, that it is absurd that one man should die for another man's sins. Of course, it is absurd. Certainly one man cannot die for another man's sins; and the human analogies that have been proposed for the atonement made by Christ usually just show how totally unable the natural man is to understand the doctrine of the Cross. When men appeal to the sacrifice of individuals at the present time as though that were in any full sense analogous to the gift of the Lord Jesus on the Cross, they show that they have never come into any real contact with the Cross of Christ; for when a man comes into contact with the Cross, he is impressed, not with the similarity between that act of self-sacrifice and other acts of self-sacrifice, no matter how noble they may be, but he is impressed with the profound difference; and so he says:

> *There was no other good enough*
> *To pay the price of sin,*
> *He only could unlock the gate*
> *Of heaven, and let us in.*

Because one mere man cannot suffer for another man's sins, it does not follow that the Lord Jesus could not suffer for our sins. And that is why we cling, with all our souls, to the Christian doctrine of the deity of our Lord; for if He be not God, then He cannot be our substitute.

But men say: "What a low view it is of the love of God if you represent an angry God as though He were waiting coldly for a sacrifice to be made!" It is really astonishing to me how preachers of the present day, who are able to read, who have some sort of contact with the Christian literature of all the centuries, should so misrepresent the Christian doctrine of the Cross. Of course I need not point out to you where the error lies. The very point of the Christian view of the Cross is that God does not wait for someone else to pay the price of sin, but in His infinite love has Himself paid the price of sin for us — God Himself in the person of the Son, who loved us and gave Himself for us; God Himself in the person of the Father, who so loved the world that He gave His only-begotten Son.

It is a strange thing that when men talk about the love of God they show by every word that they utter that they have no conception at all of the depths of God's love. If you want to find an instance of true gratitude for the infinite grace of God, do not go to those who think of God's love as something that cost nothing, but go rather to those who in agony of soul have faced the awful fact of the guilt of sin, and then have come to know with a trembling wonder that the miracle of all miracles has been accomplished, and that the eternal Son has died in their stead.

Thus if we put what the Bible says about Jesus together, we can even now have contact with Him. I am bound to say that there was a time when I was greatly troubled in my faith by the defection of the modern world from Jesus of Nazareth as He is set forth in the Scriptures; but as I observe what is becoming of the world when the contact with Jesus is broken, my faith is no longer so much troubled by the argument from modern authority, and I have come to wonder whether, after wandering in devious ways, we shall not be forced to come again, as little children, to the Lord Jesus Christ as He is set forth in the Holy Scriptures and offered to us in the gospel.

Let us unite in a word of prayer:

Almighty God, our Heavenly Father, we give Thee thanks for the wonder of Thy grace in the gift of Christ our Lord and Saviour. How can we ever find words which shall not seem vain as we think of His love for us? How can we, without shame, try to give Thee thanks for that grace of Christ our Saviour who died for us, the Just for the unjust? And how can we think, without shame, of the ill way in which we have requited Thee for Thy love? But we rejoice in the knowledge that when by Thy Holy Spirit we have been united to Christ through faith we are His forever. We pray Thee that thus we may be kept safe by One stronger than we are. And we pray with all our souls for those who have not found Christ as Saviour, that they may be led through the mists of error and doubt into the clear shining of the light of faith: that when they have sought other saviours and their souls are still restless, they may, through Christ, find their rest in Thee. And all that we ask is in the name of Christ Jesus, our Lord and Saviour. Amen.

# III

# The Witness of Paul

W E ARE considering the question whether the Bible is right about Jesus. This morning we considered, in a necessarily very brief and summary way, what the Bible says about Jesus; because obviously it is necessary to determine what the Bible says before we can consider the question whether what the Bible says is true. Certainly what the Bible says about Jesus contains many mysteries; but the distinctive features of it at least can be put almost in a word. Jesus of Nazareth, according to the Bible, was no product of this world, but a Saviour come voluntarily into this world from without. His entrance into the world was a stupendous miracle. While He was on earth He manifested a wondrous control over the forces of Nature. His death was no mere holy martyrdom, but an event of cosmic significance, a sacrifice for the sins of the world. His resurrection was no mere vain aspiration in the hearts of His disciples, but a mighty act of God. That is what the Bible says about Jesus.

That account, in practically all of the larger Churches today, is faced by an alternative account. According to that alternative account Jesus of Nazareth was the fairest of the children of men. He lived a life of wonderful purity and unselfishness. He was conscious of a wonderful closeness to God. He felt that He had a mission to bring others to that closeness of relationship with God that He Himself had. In order to express His sense of that mission He was unfortunately forced to use the categories of thought that prevailed in His day, and so He made the claim to be the Jewish Messiah. At first He won the favor of the crowd, but since He would not be the kind of leader that they desired He fell under their condemnation. He fell a victim, finally, to the hostility of the leaders of His people and the cowardice of the Roman governor, and died the common death of the criminals of that day upon the cross. After His death, His disciples were utterly discouraged. Even when He had been with them they had been far inferior to Him in spiritual discernment and in courage, and now that He was taken from them what little power they might have had seemed to be gone. They fled from Him in cowardly flight in the hour of His dire need. But then after His death they began to meditate upon His life with them, and as they mused thus upon their intercourse with Him, the impression that His person had made upon them was too strong for them to believe that He had perished. Predisposed psychologically in that way they experienced certain hallucinations — experiences in which the optic nerve is really affected, but affected by a pathological condition in the subject himself, not by something in the external world. They thought they saw Him; and perhaps they thought they heard a word or two of His ringing in their ears. These pathological experiences were the means by which the influence of Jesus was continued upon the earth; they were the means by which those weak, discouraged disciples were changed into the spiritual conquerors of the world! It was really, we are told, just the personal influence of Jesus; but the personal influence of Jesus made itself felt, according to this account, in that pathological form.

The really great question in the modern Church is this: Which of these two accounts of Jesus is correct? People often obscure this issue, and tell us that we should not pay too much attention to theological controversy. Let us just be good Christians, we are told, and have faith in Jesus, and not bother our heads about the theological issue of the present day! Of course, such a way of thinking ignores the central question at issue. The central question is whether Jesus of Nazareth was such a one as that faith in Him for men of the twentieth century is absurd, or whether He was such a One as the Bible presents to us, in whom we can have confidence for this world and for the world to come.

How shall we as historians investigate this all-important question? It is customary in modern discussion of the question to begin with certain interesting documents which have come down to us from the first century of our era. I refer to the Epistles of Paul. There we have a fixed starting-point in all controversy. All serious historians of the present day, whether they are Christians or not, are agreed that most of the Epistles of Paul, to say the least, were actually written by the man whose name they bear. There we have at least a fixed point in controversy.

Now, if you will examine the Epistles of Paul, you will discover, even on the basis of those Epistles alone, quite apart from the Gospels, and quite apart even from the Book of Acts (though the general outline of the life of Paul in the Book of Acts is generally accepted even by sceptical historians of the present day), that the Paul who wrote those letters was actually a contemporary of the Jesus of Nazareth whose life we are studying today. He speaks in one of the universally accepted Epistles of having come into contact with the brother of this Jesus (namely, in Gal. 1:19). So Paul was a contemporary of Jesus, a man of the first Christian generation, a man who according to his own testimony had been in direct contact with the brother of Jesus and with Peter, the chief of the intimate friends of Jesus.

The testimony of such a man with regard to the all-important question of the origin of our religion, which is also the question of the truth of our religion, is certainly of the utmost value.

If you will examine the Epistles of Paul you will discover one fact at least — you will discover that Paul was a man who had among his other gifts a remarkable gift of self-revelation. It is perfectly true that we know comparatively little of the details of his life; even if we use all the sources of information which are contained in the New Testament long years of his life are a complete blank. During a large part of his life we cannot trace his movements; we are left entirely in the dark. Despite that fact, however, we are given in the Epistles such intimate contact with the man himself that it is a true word which, I believe, has somewhere been spoken, that Paul is probably the best known man of antiquity.

There are men whom one never comes to know. There are men with whom I have had contact day after day and year after year, and whom yet I have never come to *know*. There are other men into communion with whom I can come by the briefest intercourse. So it is with the Apostle Paul. Without a touch of morbid introspection, without vanity, in the most natural and genuine way, he has allowed us a glimpse into his very inmost soul. He has revealed to us the depths of his life; he has revealed that which makes him great in the history of the world, namely (if I may use the fashionable modern term), his wonderful "religious experience."

As it is looked at thus from the outside by modern historians, the religion of Paul is a matter about which there can be some agreement. The religion of Paul, it is discovered, is distinctly a religion of redemption. It is a religion of redemption in that it begins with the most thoroughgoing pessimism with regard to the condition of humanity that could possibly be imagined. You may understand the difference between a religion of redemption and what is not a religion of redemption by comparing the religion of Paul with the religion of the Modernist Church. The religion of the Modernist Church is a distinctive example of a religion which is *not* a redemptive religion. It begins with optimism as to the present condition of humanity. It begins with what a famous preacher in America has designated as an article which should certainly be put into our creed, namely, "I believe in man." That is not a religion of redemption.

But the religion of Paul — as is recognized just as clearly, in some instances at least, by modern historians who do not at all accept that religion for themselves, as it is by conservative scholars — the religion of Paul is distinctly a religion of redemption. It begins with the most radical pessimism with regard to the present condition of mankind that could possibly be imagined. Such pessimism of course, fills with digust and horror the modern historians of whom I have spoken; but they must recognize the fact that whether they themselves like it or not such was the religion of Paul. Paul believed that the human race is lost in sin, and that a divine event took place outside the walls of Jerusalem when Jesus of Nazareth died apparently as a criminal upon the Cross — that there an event took place which put a new face upon the world, an event of cosmic significance that brought about a revolution in those who were affected by it so far as their relation to God is concerned.

Of course, that character of the religion of Paul as a redemptive religion involves necessarily a certain view of the One by whom redemption was wrought. It is inconceivable that a mere man could by his death thus effect something of cosmic significance. So it is not surprising that Paul held a very peculiar view of this Jesus of Nazareth. It is perfectly plain — I mean on the basis of the Epistles alone — that Paul separated Jesus from ordinary humanity, and placed Him on the side of God. It is indeed disputed, though I think wrongly, by modern historians whether he ever applied to Jesus the Greek word which we translate by the word "God" in our English Bible. According to any commonsense interpretation of Romans 9:5, he certainly did; and the fact is recognized even by some whose general view of the religion of Paul might make another interpretation to them more agreeable. But that is a question of minor importance, because it is perfectly plain, at any rate, that Paul constantly applies to Jesus the Greek term which is translated "Lord"; and that term is the term which is used in the Greek Old Testament, that Paul used, to translate the word "Jehovah," the most awful and holy name of the God of Israel.

Moreover, it is interesting to observe that just the most recent research has demonstrated, or thinks it has demonstrated, the fact that even in the pagan world of that day that word "Lord" was distinctly a term of divinity. Hence it is a case where "a little learning is a dangerous thing" when some modern preachers never use the word "Lord" in reference to Jesus, but use only the word "Master." It is perfectly true that the Greek word *kyrios* ("Lord") is used to designate "master" in ordinary human relationship; but it is also perfectly clear that its connotation as it is used in the New Testament is entirely different. Modern men sometimes use the word "Master" predominantly with reference to Jesus with the notion that they need a simple word used in ordinary life. But as a matter of fact they should not seek an ordinary word if they are to translate the word *kyrios;* but they should seek a highly specialized word; and such a word is the word *kyrios* in the Epistles of Paul. Paul's terminology for the Trinity is this: *theos,* "God"; *kyrios,* "Lord"; *pneuma,* "Spirit."* But it is just the same Trinity of three Persons in one God as that which is designated by "God the Father, God the Son, and God the Holy Ghost."

So the terminology bears out the fact that Paul regards Jesus as clearly on the side of God. But we do not need to depend upon the terminology; because the thing itself is perfectly plain. At the beginning of the Epistle to the Galatians, we have these truly stupendous words — to modern sceptical historians they seem to be most extraordinary, however familiar they may have become to us — "Paul, an apostle not from men nor through a man, but through Jesus Christ, and God the Father, who raised Him from the dead." There we have a separation of Jesus Christ from ordinary humanity and the placing of Him on the side of God!

It is true that Paul elsewhere speaks of Jesus as a man. He speaks elsewhere of "the man Christ Jesus." But if you will examine those passages you may discover that Paul speaks of Jesus as a man as though it were something strange, something wonderful that He should be a man; and at any rate the prevailing way in which he speaks of Jesus involves a clear separation of

---

* See Warfield, *The Lord of Glory,* 1907, p. 231.

Jesus from ordinary humanity and a placing of Him on the side of God.

But you do not need to appeal to individual passages, because the outstanding fact is that Paul stands everywhere in a religious relationship to Jesus Christ. The religion of Paul does not consist merely in having faith in God like the faith which Jesus had in God, but it consists essentially in having faith in Jesus Christ. Modern sceptical historians again may be our teachers here; for they regard that as the supreme problem in the history of the Church. The supreme problem to these historians is the problem how in the world a faith in God like the faith which Jesus had in God and which these historians regard Jesus Himself as having inculcated in His disciples can ever have given place, by a stupendous, a momentous change, upon which nineteen centuries of history have been based, to a faith in Jesus Himself. And that change took place before the time of Paul. That is a fact which cannot be denied — Jesus was for Paul not primarily an example for faith but an object of faith.

Of course, if you hold, as most of us here present no doubt hold, that Jesus was truly God, then this attitude of Paul is cause for no surprise. But far different is it if you occupy the position of modern historians who regard Jesus as a mere man. In that case, you have Jesus, a mere man; and then you have Paul, one of His contemporaries, according to the Epistles whose genuineness everyone admits, separating this Jesus from ordinary humanity and placing Him on the side of God. If that be the way in which we are to look at it, what we have here is an extraordinary instance of deification, the attribution of deity to a mere man on the part, not of later generations, but of one of His contemporaries.

I have often quoted (for I think it is significant) the admission of a man who, I suppose, was the typical representative of that view of Jesus which regards Jesus as a mere man, namely, the late H. J. Holtzmann. Holtzmann said that for this extraordinary deification of the man Jesus as it appears in the Epistles of Paul

he was able to cite no parallel in the religious history of the race.*
Oh, you may say, how about the deification of the Roman Emperors, either at their death or during their lifetime? But that is
totally different in its lack of seriousness, and far more important
than all that, it is totally different from this deification of the
man Jesus because it is found in a polytheistic environment. If
Paul had been a polytheist who could believe in many gods, then
perhaps he might have added Jesus to the gods that he already
worshipped. But Paul was clearly a monotheist; for if the Phari-
saic Judaism of the first century was anything it was an enthusiastic monotheism. I suppose its insistence upon monotheism
was not exceeded even by the Mohammedanism of the present
day. Monotheism was the very center and core of their belief —
a horror of many gods, and a separation of God from the world.
Yet it was this monotheist, sprung from a race of monotheists,
who in his Epistles everywhere places the man Jesus, who had
lived a short time before, and had died a shameful death, clearly
on the side of God, and pays to Him homage that is due to God
alone.

If we went no further we should be led to ask who this Jesus
was who could thus be raised to deity by one of His contemporaries. But our surprise as historians reaches its height when
we observe this curious fact — that Paul does not argue about
this strange view of Jesus. Paul does not seem, in his earlier
Epistles at least, where he is dealing with Palestinian Judaism,
to regard this lofty view of Jesus as a thing about which one word
of argument was needed. "Oh," you may say, "Paul, of course,
was not in the habit of arguing!" Well, was he not? When it came
to matters about which there was a dispute in the churches of his
day, we may thank God that Paul was not a man who was averse
to argument or controversy, because if Paul had been a man averse
to controversy, as many leaders of the Modernist Church say that

* Holtzmann, in *Protestantische Monatshefte*, iv, 1900, pp. 465f, and in
*Christliche Welt*, xxiv, 1910, column 153.

they are, we should have no Christianity today — I mean, when we look at the thing from the human point of view. God might have raised up another instrument; but as a matter of fact it was through the Apostle Paul and men like him that our Christianity was preserved.

No, Paul certainly was in the habit of arguing. He argues about the place of the law, for example, and the all-sufficiency of faith, and the like; but when it comes to this truly stupendous view which he has of Jesus he seems to assume that his view is also the view even of his bitter opponents like the Judaizers attacked in the Epistle to the Galatians. Nowhere does there appear to have been in the early apostolic age any color of support for disagreement with the view held by Paul of the person of Christ.

One can hardly avoid the conclusion, on the basis of a study of the Epistles of Paul, that when Paul does not argue about this matter it is because no argument was needed, because Paul's view was accepted as a matter of course. That involves this stupendous conclusion, that Peter and the very brother of Jesus, men who had walked and talked with Jesus on earth, who had seen Him subject to the petty limitations of human life — that these men actually agreed with this stupendous view of Jesus as a supernatural Person, an object of worship, as He is presented in the Epistles of Paul.

On the basis of the Epistles alone, therefore, we should ask ourselves; "Who was this Jesus? What manner of Person was He that He could thus be raised to divine dignity, not by later generations, but by His own intimate friends?"

The religion of Paul is a phenomenon of history that requires an explanation, and the modern historians have been willing to accept the challenge. The central problem, I suppose, which has confronted modern historians who have tried to construct the origin of Christianity without building it upon a supernatural Christ, is the problem of the origin of this religion of Paul. Four hypotheses with regard to it may be distinguished.

The first is the simple one that Paul's religion was founded upon the real Christ; that Paul came to believe Jesus to be a supernatural Person for the simple reason that as a matter of fact Jesus was a supernatural Person; in other words, that Paul's religion is founded upon the actual descent of a supernatural Person into this world for its redemption, whose death was an event of cosmic significance, and whose resurrection followed as the completion of His redeeming work. That is the supernaturalistic hypothesis, and if that be accepted the whole problem is solved.

But there are other explanations which have been proposed in recent years, and they are alike in denying the entrance into this world of any creative act of God in distinction from the use by God of the forces of nature. The first of these explanations is the "Liberal" or Ritschlian view, which has been dominant in many quarters in the Church for a good many years. There are some indications that among scholars this reconstruction is tottering to its ruin, but still in America, and I believe in this country as well, it dominates the popular presentation of Christianity from the modern naturalistic point of view. According to this explanation, Paul was a true disciple of Jesus in his religious experience, but Paul's theology was the mere temporary form in which in his day that religious experience had to be expressed. That is the hypothesis. You must distinguish the kernel from the husk, it is said. Paul was really affected by the lofty moral life of the real human person, Jesus of Nazareth; but he had to express what he owed to Jesus in the (now outworn) categories of his time — the notion of the atoning death of Christ and the like. It is the business of the modern Christian, according to that view, to discard the husk in order to retain the precious kernel. Paul's religion, according to that formula, comes from the real Jesus, and is a permanent possession of the human race, while Paul's theology, being the mere temporary husk to preserve that kernel, was derived from other sources, and may now safely be discarded by the modern Church.

That hypothesis has been set forth in dozens or hundreds of brilliant books. But in 1904 it suffered a most extraordinary attack, not from a conservative scholar, but from a radical historian, namely William Wrede of Breslau, who pointed out that the whole separation between Paul's religion and Paul's theology, is quite unhistorical, that the religion of Paul is intimately connected with his theology, and that in the Epistles of Paul you do not find quotations of the words of Jesus and citations of His example, but what you do find is the reiteration again and again of the cosmic significance of His death and resurrection.

Of course it was easy for the "Liberal" or Ritschlian historians to point out the excesses of Wrede's view. It was perfectly easy for them to show that Wrede was wrong in supposing that Paul knew little or nothing about the details of the words and deeds of Jesus. It was easy to show that Paul tells in his Epistles more than Wrede supposed, and that he knew far more than in the Epistles he has chosen to tell. The incidental way in which he refers to the institution of the Lord's Supper, for example, seems clearly to show that his information was taken from a fund of further information which was given to the Churches in the beginning. "The Lord Jesus, the night in which He was betrayed" — do you not see that it presupposes a whole account of the events connected with the betrayal? We know what is meant because we have read the story in the Gospels, but it would be a riddle if we did not know about the betrayal by Judas. And elsewhere, as well as in this passage, it is easy to see that Paul had evidently told the Churches far more than in the Epistles he has found occasion to repeat. And indeed that is altogether natural; because if these people in the Churches were asked to take a man who had lived but a few years before as their Saviour, the object of their adoration, questions would have to be asked and answered as to what manner of Person this was.

Wrede's opponents in the camp of modern Liberalism were able to point out the defects of his reconstruction, but they utterly failed to refute him at the central point; it is perfectly clear, as

Wrede observed, that the very center of Paul's religious life is
found just in those things which the Liberal historians had rejected or had minimized as a mere temporary expression of some
deeper experience, namely, the significance of the Cross of Christ,
and so on. Where does the current of Paul's religious life run full
and free? Surely it is in the great theological passages of the
Epistles — the second chapter of Galatians, the fifth chapter of
II Corinthians, the eighth chapter of Romans. Those are the passages in which you have the very center of Paul's life; and so
much, at least, Wrede observed, even though he himself did not
believe for himself one word of what Paul teaches in these matters.
Never was Wrede really refuted by his opponents in the Liberal
camp. According to Wrede, Paul's religion and his theology go
together; and if his theology came from somewhere else than the
real Jesus, his religion came from somewhere else too. So Wrede
ventured on the assertion that Paul was the second founder of
Christianity, a more powerful influence in historic Christianity,
perhaps, though not a more beneficent influence, than Jesus Himself. If you hold that Jesus was a mere man, do you not see
the justification for that view? Liberal historians had produced
a Jesus who had really little in common with the Apostle Paul,
and the radical view of Wrede was the nemesis to which they were
naturally subjected. So a vast literature on the subject sprang
up. But you have a feeling, as you read the works of the Liberal
historians, that in refuting Wrede they get nowhere. They refute
him in detail, but they do not touch the central point.

What would the solution be? It is perfectly plain. The Liberal
theologians were quite right as over against Wrede in holding
that Paul knew much more about the details of the life of Jesus
than Wrede supposed. There the Liberal historians were right.
But Wrede was entirely right as over against them in holding
that the Jesus upon whom Paul's religion was based was not the
reduced Jesus of modern naturalism, but the stupendous Person
who is presented in the Epistles themselves. What, then, is the

solution? It is perfectly simple, as I have said. It is simply that Paul's religion was based upon the Jesus whose death and resurrection were events of cosmic significance, that that Jesus was the real Jesus, that there was not that amazing break between the man Jesus and the One whom Paul, with abundant opportunity of acquainting himself with His life, presented in his Epistles, that the Jesus of the Epistles of Paul was the real Jesus who walked this earth.

But then, if you reject this supernaturalistic solution, and hold, with Wrede, that Paul's religion was not based upon the real Jesus, whence did it really come? Wrede said that it came from pre-Christian Judaism, that Paul had a lofty idea of the Messiah before he was converted, and that no essential change was wrought by his conversion except that he came to believe that this Messiah had come to this earth. But that view has been generally felt to break down; there are few who hold it today. It must be rejected for many reasons, and particularly for the reason that the loftiest view of the Messiah which you find in the apocalyptic books that are thought to preserve for us the doctrine upon which Paul is supposed to be dependent falls far short of the view which Paul holds of Jesus.. There is no doctrine of the deity of the Messiah in those Jewish apocalyptic books, and no trace of the warm religious relationship between the believer and the Messiah. So you would be obliged to come to this extraordinary conclusion, that when the lofty Messiah of pre-Christian Jewish speculation was identified with a mere human being, that identification with a mere human being, instead of drawing down this pre-Christian Jewish notion of the Messiah, lifted it far beyond men's wildest dreams.

The last of the naturalistic hypotheses is that Paul's religion and theology came essentially from the religion of the contemporary pagan world. But that hypothesis is faced with many difficulties with which we have not here time to deal—the difficulty, for instance, of answering the question how contemporary paganism could ever have influenced the life of Paul at the centre either before or after his conversion, and the difficulty found in the fact that the supposed parallels on examination really break down. Therefore, I think, we may say that unless Jesus be the kind of person that is presupposed in the Epistles of Paul, the attempts which have so far been made to explain in some other way the origin of the religion of Paul have not yet attained success. In the Epistles we discover a problem which leads us on beyond our easy complacency in a naturalistic view of the world toward what modern men think of with antipathy as the abyss of supernaturalism; and then we are led to the question whether the stupendous Saviour who is presented in the Epistles of Paul was not truly One who came to this earth for our redemption, and in whom we may have confidence alike for this world and for the world to come.

Let us unite in a word of prayer:

We thank Thee for the witness of the Apostle Paul who was Thy chosen messenger. We rejoice in the glory of these matchless books which have enabled men to live lives of victory over sin and have stayed their souls. And we pray that this great Apostle may again be heard, that the darkness may be dispelled, and that men may find here the great charter of Christian liberty, that without merit of their own, but through the blood of Christ, they may be free for evermore. Amen.

# IV

## The Witness of the Gospels

TODAY we have been considering the question: "Is the Bible Right about Jesus?" This afternoon we considered the witness of Paul. We observed that in the Epistles of Paul we have a fixed starting-point in all the controversy of the present day, since the genuineness of these Epistles is not denied by any serious historian — at least the genuineness of the chief of them. In the Epistles of Paul, we have Jesus presented clearly as a supernatural person, not primarily as an example for religious faith, but as the object of religious faith. We observed further that that stupendous presentation of the person of Jesus which is found everywhere in the Epistles of Paul is so presupposed as a matter beyond debate that the historian can hardly avoid the extraordinary conclusion that that lofty view of Jesus was also the view of those with whom Paul had come into contact, namely, the intimate friends of Jesus who had lived with Him when He was upon this earth.

Therefore as we examine the phenomenon of the religion of Paul, which is a fact of history that no serious historian denies. this question arises in our minds: Who was this Jesus who thus could be raised to divine dignity, and that not by later generations, but by His own contemporaries in the first Christian generation— so raised even by those who had seen Him subject to all the limitations of human life in their intercourse with Him while He was upon this earth? Even if the historian possessed only the Epistles of Paul as sources of historical information about Jesus, he would have enough to give him pause. But as a matter of fact we have

51

other sources of information about Jesus; for in the four Gospels
we find an extended picture of Him, an extended account of His
life upon earth.

I shall not stop here to consider certain very important questions with regard to the Gospels, namely, questions of literary
criticism with regard to the date and authorship of these books,
except to say just in passing that the evidence for the authorship of
one of these books—the Gospel according to Luke—is of such a
singularly cogent kind that to the astonishment of the learned
world it has within recent years convinced some scholars whose
view as to the origin of Christianity is just as much out of
accord with the traditional view of the authorship of these books
as could possibly be imagined. You have the extraordinary
phenomenon that scholars like Professor von Harnack, of Berlin,
whose view as to the origin of Christianity is of a thoroughly
naturalistic kind, as far removed as possible from that which is
present in the Lucan writings, have been so much impressed by
the argument from literary criticism that they have actually come
to the traditional view that the Gospel according to Luke was
written by Luke the physician and companion of Paul, who was in
Palestine in the year A. D. 58, and was there in A. D. 60, and
probably during the interval (these dates being pushed back a few
years if another chronology is adopted), so that he actually came
into direct contact with James, the brother of this Jesus whom
we are studying tonight.

I might point out, too, with regard to all of the Gospels, that
there is a certain self-evidencing quality in their narrative. Personal testimony is a very subtle thing; and when you face a witness on the witness-stand the credence which you will give to his
testimony is dependent very often upon the subtle impression that
you obtain of the person testifying. That sort of evidence, which
often attains a high degree of value, has a larger place in the
production of Christian conviction than often is supposed. If
you are troubled with doubts about the truth of this extraordinary

narrative which you have in the four Gospels, I should commend to you the exercise of reading one of the Gospels through from beginning to end with something like the rapidity which you apply every morning to the morning newspaper or to any book of the day. At other times study the Gospels, but for once just *read* the Gospels. I sometimes think that perhaps that is the reason why God has given us one Gospel which is so short as the Gospel according to Mark—that at one sitting we might easily read the whole book through. In the Gospel according to Mark you are not asked to sit quietly at the feet of Jesus and listen in an extended way to His teaching. You are not taken into the intimacy of His circle as is the case in the Gospel according to John. But you are asked to look at Him with something of the wonder which was in the minds of those first observers in the synagogue at Capernaum. It is a Gospel that makes a first impression; and I tell you, when you read it, if you will brush out of your mind everything you have read about it, and will let the total impression of it be made upon your mind, there will come to you an overpowering impression that that witness is telling the truth.

So it is also with the Gospel according to John. It has been my business for a great many years to read a great many things that have been said against the trustworthiness of the Gospel according to John, and sometimes, as I have read, I have been impressed with the plausibleness of much that is said; but at other times, after filling my mind with what is said about the Gospel according to John, I have just conceived the notion of reading, not what is said *about* the book, but the book itself, and when I have done that the impression has been overpowering. It does seem perfectly plain that the author of this book is claiming to be an eye-witness of the wonderful events that he narrates. There is no writer of the New Testament who lays greater stress upon the plain testimony of the senses than he, and the keyword of the Gospel, I think is found in the words: "And the Word was made flesh, and dwelt among us, and we beheld His glory." You cannot sublimate those words into meaning merely that we human beings have heard about the incarnate Word, but they spring from the wondering gratitude of a man who himself had had the inestimable privilege of touching with his hands and hearing with his ears and seeing with his eyes the incarnate Word of God. When you read the book you have the overpowering impression that the author is telling the truth; and the hypothesis to which you are logically forced if you hold that the book is not true—the hypothesis that this writer is engaging in a refined bit of deception by subtly making the false impression of being an eye-witness when he was no eye-witness at all—this hypothesis becomes, when you become acquainted with the man by reading his narrative for yourself, a monstrous hypothesis indeed.

Tonight I propose not to examine these questions of literary criticism in detail, but just to take for a moment the total picture of Jesus that is provided in the Gospels. And I may say at the start that that picture is a picture of just the kind of person that is presupposed in the Epistles of Paul. Yet there does not seem to be the slightest evidence of any dependence of the writers of the Gospels upon the Epistles. In the Epistles of Paul there is presupposed everywhere a Jesus who was a supernatural person and yet lived a life upon this earth; and you have just such a person presented in all the Gospels.

There are three things that need to be said about the modern reconstruction of Jesus as distinguished from the Jesus who is presented to us in the Gospels. In the first place, that reconstruction involves the elimination of the supernatural from the life of Jesus; because the Jesus of all the Gospels is clearly a supernatural person. It used to be held, perhaps, that you have a difference in the Gospels in this respect; at one time, perhaps, the divine Christ of John was contrasted with the human Christ of Mark. But modern criticism of the Gospels has tended powerfully against any such distinction as that; and it is admitted by the dominant school of criticism today that in the Gospel according to Mark as well as in the Gospel according to John you have presented to you not a mere teacher but a supernatural person whose death had some sort of redeeming significance, not a teacher of righteousness merely, but a Saviour, essentially the sort of supernatural Christ that is presented in the Epistles of Paul.

Here is a strange problem: the Jesus of the Gospels is a supernatural person; He is plainly a real person who lived upon this earth; and yet from the point of view of modern naturalistic criticism a supernatural person can never be real, because by such criticism the supernatural has been eliminated from the pages of history.

Perhaps it may be well to say a word in passing as to what we mean by the "supernatural," what we mean by a "miracle." It is true, there is nothing more unpopular in the discussion of religious questions at the present day than this humble matter of the definition of terms; many persons are very angry when they are asked to check the flow of their thought by so humble a thing as a definition! Many definitions of the word "miracle" have been proposed, but I confess that the only one of them that seems to me satisfactory is one which I learned many years ago. "A miracle," according to that definition, "is an event in the external world that is wrought by the *immediate* power of God." That does not mean that while other events are not wrought by God a miracle is wrought by Him. But it means that in the case of other events God uses means, whereas in the case of a miracle He puts forth His creative power just as truly as in that mighty act of creation which underlies the whole process of the world.

When you adopt that definition of a miracle you have based all your thinking upon a certain very definite philosophy, and that definite philosophy upon which you have based your thinking is called theism—if you will pardon a technical term for a very simple thing. It is the view of the world which Jesus of Nazareth held, as well as the view of the world which has been held by many philosophers. In a truly theistic view of the world it is almost as necessary to assert the real existence of an order of nature as it is to assert the real existence of a personal God. People say nowadays that we who hold to a belief in miracles are doing away with the possibility of science — science which seeks to set forth the orderly course of this world. As a matter of fact, we are being much more kind to science than science is kind to itself; because we are asserting that the order of nature has a real objective existence, a thing which, as I understand it, the scientists of the present day, from the scientific point of view, do not find it necessary to assert at all. We assert that there is such a thing as a really existent order of nature, created by God, upheld at every moment by God, not a machine set going by God and let alone, but something that is under God's control and yet a really existent thing. And what is meant from that point of view as a miracle is the entrance of the *creative* power of God at some point in the course of the world. I do not see how if you really believe in creation at all—and I do not see how unless you believe in creation you can hold to a theistic view of the world—you can have any objection of principle to the entrance of creative acts of God within the course of the world.

So much for the definition of miracle. From that point of view, it is clear that the miracles of the New Testament have a stupendous significance. Some one will say: "What a degrading thing it is that we should suppose that this order of nature had to be broken into. You are requiring us to suppose that there have been unaccountable and meaningless events and our reasonable view of the world is gone!" Not at all, my friends. A miracle from the Christian point of view is not a disorderly thing, but it springs from the source of all the order that there is in the world—namely, the will of God.

Very well, in the New Testament you have Jesus presented as a supernatural person, and you have in the New Testament an account of miracles. At that point many persons enter upon a very peculiar line of thought. Many devout persons nowadays,

even persons who believe in the fact of the miracles, will tell you
that while miracles used to be an aid to faith, now they are a hindrance to faith; that people used to believe in Jesus because of the
miracles, but that now when they already believe in Him on other
grounds they may then come to a belief in miracles, so that although the miracles may be a hindrance that can be overcome,
still they are not an aid to faith, but a hindrance; that people used
to believe in Jesus *because* of the miracles, but now they believe
*in spite* of the miracles. Such a way of thinking involves a very
curious confusion. Of course, it is perfectly true from one point
of view that miracles are an obstacle to faith—but who ever denied
it? The more commonplace a narrative is, the easier it is to believe. If I told you that as I walked the streets of this city I met
several of my fellow-beings, my narrative would be very much
superior to the narrative of the New Testament in one particular;
it would certainly be far easier to believe. But then it is not likely
that anyone would be very much interested in it. So, without
miracles, the narrative of the Gospels would certainly be far
easier to believe; but, do you not see, it would not be worth believing. Without the miracles, the thing that you would be believing would be a totally different thing from that which you are
believing now. Without the miracles, you would have in Jesus a
teacher and example; but with the miracles you have a Saviour
from your sins.

So the Jesus presented in the Gospels is a supernatural person.
But from the point of view of the presuppositions of Modernism
a supernatural person never existed upon this earth. What is
the conclusion? It would seem to be that this Jesus never lived
at all. There have been here and there a few who have held that
view—Kalthoff and Drews in Germany, and W. B. Smith in
America. These men have held that there was no real person corresponding to the Jesus of the Gospels at all. But that view is not
held by really important historians. It is perfectly plain that we
have here an account of a real person living at a definite time upon

this earth, and that if the whole picture is to be regarded as fictitious then there is no way in the sphere of history of distinguishing
truth from sham.

So this Jesus was a real person; He was a supernatural person;
and yet, according to Modernist historians, a supernatural person
is never real! What is the solution from the Modernist point of
view, The solution proposed is that you have two elements in
the Gospels: first a picture of the real, the purely human Jesus;
and, secondly, a defacement of that picture by miraculous ornamentation: and that it is the duty of the modern historian to recover the picture of the true human Jesus; it his duty to remove
the coating of the supernatural which in the Gospels has almost
completely defaced the portrait, to tear away from Jesus these
tawdry trappings of the supernatural, in order that the true presentation of the man Jesus may burst upon the world.

It seemed at first, from the naturalistic point of view, to be a
very hopeful task. You might say, of course, that the way to do
it would be to claim that while the Gospels as we have them are
full of the supernatural, if you get back to the original sources it
would not be so at all. But the trouble is that in the earliest
sources reconstructed, rightly or wrongly, by modern criticism
you have similar supernatural elements. So you have to go to
work in some other way. All you can do is simply to go through
the Gospels and just take the supernatural out. So a hundred
years ago men went very hopefully to work. They said that the
events narrated in the Gospels were historical, but not really
supernatural; that the first observers put a false supernaturalistic
interpretation upon events that were really perfectly natural.
When, for example, it is said in the first chapter of Luke that
Zacharias went into the temple, certainly it was true that a man
of that name went into the temple, and that in the dim religious
light he saw the smoke of the incense rising up, and thought in
the solemnity of the moment that it was an angel, and that as he
had been thinking about certain things he thought that the angel

spoke words to him. That is an example of what is called technically the rationalizing method of dealing with the miracle narratives.

The most powerful critic, perhaps, of the rationalizing method was not an orthodox theologian; but it was David Friedrich Strauss. The famous *Life of Christ* of Strauss appeared in 1835. It was directed against two opponents. In the first place, it was directed against the supernaturalistic view of Jesus, which takes these stories of the miracles at their face value and believes that they are sober fact. Strauss directed all the power of his attack against that view of the believing Christian about the miracles in the Gospels. And I should like to say that if you want a really powerful criticism of the Gospel narratives on the negative side, a really powerful attack against their truthfulness, you cannot do better than go back to the original *Life of Christ* by Strauss, because you will find that most of those who deal with the matter today are far inferior to Strauss in acumen and in the other qualities that are necessary to the task.

But Strauss also attacked the rationalizing method to which I have just referred. He pointed out how ridiculous it is, when the thing for which the whole narrative exists is the miracle in it, to take away the miracle and think you have anything left. No, said Strauss; the whole reason for which these narratives were formed is found in the miracles that they contain; and if the miracles are not historical the thing to say is that nothing is historical and that these miracle narratives are just the clothing of some religious idea in historical form.

That is the mythical view of Strauss—that the narratives are to be taken as a whole and are to be regarded as the clothing in historical form of a religious idea. So if you are to get the miracles out of the Gospels, you have to go to work much more subtly than was thought necessary by Paulus and the early rationalizers. It is clear that you cannot just take out the miracles and leave the rest, but that if you are going to take out the miracles, you must also take a great deal of the rest of the narrative which exists simply for the sake of the miracles.

Here, then, is the phenomenon that has appeared in the modern criticism of the Gospels. You proceed to take the miracles out; in doing so you find to your consternation that great shreds of the rest have to come out also. It is like pulling a pound of flesh out of a living body. Very naturally, therefore, there is a tendency in recent criticism to approach nearer and nearer to the absurd view that it is *all* unhistorical. That is the first difficulty in reconstructing your purely human Jesus—the difficulty of separating the miracles from the rest—because the whole picture is not an agglomeration, but an organism.

Then there is a second difficulty. Suppose you have taken the miracles out of the Gospels and have got a purely human Jesus. It cannot be done, but let us suppose it could be done — you have your human Jesus who never worked miracles (except miracles that you could explain away, such as faith-healing and the like, which are not miracles at all). It would look as though, from the naturalistic point of view, you were in a hopeful condition. At last you have the real Jesus whom we moderns can accept. But the trouble is that when you have reconstructed your purely human Jesus, you find that he is an entirely unbelievable figure. He is not only a person who never *did* exist, but he is one who never *could* have existed. He has a moral and psychological contradiction at the root of His being. That moral and psychological contradiction arises from the stupendous fact of the Messianic self-consciousness of Jesus. It is a fact that the Jesus of the Gospels really did hold that He was the Messiah; and that He held that He was the Messiah, not in some lower political sense, as though it meant merely that He was a King of David's line, but in the stupendous sense that He was actually to sit on the throne of God and be the instrument in judging the earth.

Jesus called Himself the Son of Man. There is much misinterpretation of the term, "Son of Man," on the part of the readers of the Gospels; but it seems perfectly plain that the term does not set forth the human nature of Jesus as over against the divine nature at all, but is a reference to the tremendous scene in the seventh chapter of Daniel, in which one like unto a son of man is represented as being present with the Ancient of Days. The term, "Son of Man," is perhaps a more lofty, a more stupendous, a more supernatural designation of Jesus in the Gospels than the term, "Son of God," at least as that term might be understood in the minds of the people.

People sometimes say: "We are not interested in theology and metaphysics and all that; we are not interested in the doctrine that the creeds set forth about the person of our Lord. It is sufficient for us to read the Sermon on the Mount and try to do what Jesus there says and get rid of all theology." Well, the Sermon on the Mount contains a most stupendous theology; and it contains a stupendous theology just in its presentation of the person of Jesus. If there is one passage in the whole of the New Testament which is loved by the Modernist Church it is the passage in which Jesus represents the scene at the last judgment, where it is said: "Not every one that saith unto me, Lord, Lord, shall enter into the kingdom of heaven; but he that doeth the will of my Father which is in heaven." But just in that very passage you have the stupendous notion presented by Jesus Himself that *He* is to be the one who will sit on the throne of God at the final judgment and be the judge of human beings who have lived in all the periods of history. Why, it is a perfectly stupendous theology, a perfectly stupendous presentation of the majesty of the person of Jesus. What would you think of a mere man who should look out upon his contemporaries and say that *he* was to be the one who was to determine their eternal destiny at the last judgment? You would say he was unbalanced or insane. Some persons are saying that about Jesus today. They have written long and learned books to show the particular kind of insanity with which Jesus was afflicted. It does not worry me a bit. Indeed, I think it is a hopeful sign of the times that these alienists should be investigating the case of a mere man who thought he was divine. At the time when there were emperors of China it used to be thought a pretty sure sign of insanity for a man to declare that he was emperor of China; but, you know, if actually the emperor of China had declared that he was *not* the emperor but someone else, that would have been an equally sure sign of insanity. So these alienists are investigating the case of a man who thought he was divine and was *not* divine; but against one who thought He was divine and *was* divine they have, obviously, nothing to say.

In other words, you have here in modern form the old problem of the stupendous claims of Jesus. How could Jesus have made these claims if they were not true? Some have held that Jesus never really made the claims, that He never claimed to be the Messiah at all. But that view has been held by comparatively few modern scholars, because it is faced by such an overpowering weight of contrary evidence. It was the claim to be the Messiah that cost Jesus His life. That claim is thus deeply rooted in the narrative. Usually, therefore, modern scholars pursue a different policy. They say that Jesus did not know how to express His sense of a mission except in the (somewhat unsatisfactory) category of Messiahship. Sometimes they have held that it was at the baptism that He came to think that He was the Messiah. Very interesting popular presentations of some such view have appeared in modern times. When I was a student in Germany, about twenty years ago, everyone was reading Frenssen's *Hilligenlei*, a novel which incidentally brings in a very interesting psychological reconstruction of Jesus. Jesus is represented as thinking about the Saviour that was to come, and at last He comes to the conclusion that He is that Saviour Himself. It is a very dramatic representation of the way in which He came to that conclusion— and it is also totally unconvincing. It does not make one bit of difference whether you put this acceptance of Messiahship at the baptism, or as many modern scholars have done, at some later time; whether you put it late or early it does—unless the claim was really justified—put a moral stain upon the character of Jesus. And that means putting a moral stain upon the character of a stainless One. Even modern men are forced to admit that as a whole the character of Jesus was totally inconsistent with any lack of mental balance. Thus at the very center of the being of the reconstructed, purely human Jesus, there is a hopeless contradiction. The reduced Jesus of modern naturalism is a monstrosity, whereas the Jesus presented in the Gospels, though He is full of mystery, is yet a person whom a man can love, and a person who might, by the wonderful grace of God, really have lived upon this earth.

That, then, is your second difficulty—your reconstructed Jesus is an unbelievable figure. Then there is a third difficulty. It is found when you raise the question how your purely human Jesus ever could have become a divine Jesus in the belief of the Church. Certainly that step must at least have been taken at a very early time. It is a very extraordinary thing how people can tell us in the modern Church that we have to take a reverse step, that we have to go back from the apostolic Church to Christ Himself. These modern men admit that in the early apostolic Church Jesus was made not merely the example for faith, but the object of faith. But it is said that Jesus did not present Himself in that way; He did not present Himself as an object of faith; and we have to reverse the step which was taken by the primitive apostolic Church and get back to the real Jesus! It does seem to be an extraordinary thing that you have the Christian Church appealing to Jesus of Nazareth and yet that the whole thing is found to be a total mistake, that the mistake was made at the very beginning, and that the whole power of the Church comes from that mistake! We have got to go back, we are told—back from the gospel which sets forth Jesus as Redeemer to the gospel which Jesus Himself preached. It is strange how people who say that seem to think they are bringing us nearer to Jesus. Constantly we hear it asked: "Why should we trouble ourselves with all this puzzling theology about the death of Christ and the resurrection? It is a barrier between us and Jesus. Even such of it as is presented by Paul and by the primitive Jerusalem Church must be wiped out; we must preach the gospel *of* Jesus instead of the gospel *about* Jesus."

But the gospel *of* Jesus, if that is all you have, does not mean that you have any close touch with Him. You can have a gospel of D. L. Moody, but not a gospel about him; a gospel of Paul, but not a gospel about him. "Was Paul crucified for you?" When we say we have a gospel about Jesus we mean that we have a gospel of which Jesus is not the mere author or proclaimer, but the very substance. Jesus proclaimed not only a gospel, but a gospel which had His own person in the center of it. When you read the Gospels a little closer, you will find that everywhere Jesus presented Himself as a Saviour, not merely as a teacher or an example. If He did not present Himself as a Saviour, then His teaching is the most gloomy teaching that there ever was in this world. You may talk about the thunderings of Sinai. But what are they compared with the terrifying law of the Sermon on the Mount? How much higher, how much more terrible that is than the law that is set forth in the Old Testament! How shall we stand if only such persons as those whom Jesus there describes can come into the Kingdom of God? When you read the Sermon on the Mount, you are led straight to the foot of the Cross; if such be the law of God, you need Christ not merely as a Teacher but as a Saviour.

When we come to the Lord Jesus, let us not take Him as reconstructed for ourselves in a way after our own choosing, but let us receive the Lord Jesus Christ "as He is offered to us in the Gospel." When we so receive Him, we have a wonderful confirmation of the documentary evidence. Possibly you may have a certain feeling of dissatisfaction with what I have been saying tonight; possibly you may feel that while we may argue about these intricacies of historical criticism, somehow what we want is immediacy of conviction with regard to Jesus. Well, you may have such immediacy of conviction, because by accepting this Gospel message you may come into living communion with Christ. But right there is where modern men go wrong. They say: "We have our communion with the living Christ, and so we do not care whether the Bible is true or not. We care nothing for the element of history in the Bible. The Bible is infallible only in the sphere of the inner life." That is very sad. It looks as though you had climbed up to the heights of Christian experience by means of the Bible, and when you are there you kick your ladder down, thus preventing others from coming up by it. But as a matter of fact the Bible is not a ladder but a foundation. Here is what Christian experience does: it does not give you Christ whether the Bible is true or not, but it is confirmatory evidence to show you that as a matter of fact the Bible *is* true. What I think we ought to be opposed to is a partial view of the evidences of Christianity. Let us not appeal to experience as over against the Bible; let us take along with the documentary evidence in the Gospels the great wealth of evidence that comes to us in other spheres, the evidence provided by the consciousness of sin, of the need of salvation, the need of a Saviour. Then we can come to the wonderful message of the gospel. It has then evidencing value enough. Accept it, and come to the feet of Jesus, and hear Him say to you, as you contemplate Him upon the Cross: "Thy faith hath saved thee. Go in peace."

# V

## The Virgin Birth of Christ

A CCORDING to the belief of all the historic branches of the
Christian Church, Jesus of Nazareth was born without
human father, being conceived by the Holy Ghost and born of
the virgin Mary. In the present lecture we shall consider very
briefly the origin of this belief. The belief of the Christian Church
in the virgin birth of Christ is a fact of history which requires an
explanation. And two kinds of explanation are possible. In the
first place the belief may be explained as being based upon fact.
It may be held that the Church came to believe in the virgin birth
because as a matter of fact Jesus was born of a virgin. Or in the
second place it may be held that the belief arose in some other
way. The task of the historian is to balance these two kinds of
explanation against each other. Is it easier to explain the belief
of the Church in the virgin birth on the hypothesis that it originated in fact or on the hypothesis that it arose in some other
way?

We shall first examine the former hypothesis—that the belief
in the virgin birth is based upon fact. Of course, the most obvious thing to say is that this belief appears in the New Testament
in the clearest possible terms. And most of our time will be taken
up in examining the New Testament evidence. But before we
come to examine the New Testament evidence it may be well to
glance at the later Christian literature.

At the close of the second century, when the Christian literature outside of the New Testament becomes abundant, when we
have full information about the belief of the Church at Alexandria,

in Asia Minor, at Rome and in the West, we find that everywhere the virgin birth was accepted as a matter of course as one of the essential things in the Christian view of Christ. But this same kind of belief appears also at an earlier time; for example, in the old Roman baptismal confession which was the basis of our Apostles' Creed, in Justin Martyr at the middle of the second century, and in Ignatius, bishop of Antioch, at the beginning of the century. There were, it is true, denials of the virgin birth not only by opponents of Christianity but also by some who professed a kind of Christian faith. But all of these denials look far more as though they were due to philosophical prepossession than to any genuine historical tradition. The plain fact is that the virgin birth appears just as firmly fixed at the beginning of the second century as at the end of it; it is quite impossible to detect any gradual establishment of the doctrine as though it had to make its way against opposition. Particularly the testimony of Ignatius and of the Apostles' Creed shows not only that the virgin birth was accepted at a very early time, but that it was accepted as a matter of course and as one of the facts singled out for inclusion even in the briefest summaries of the most important things which the Christian needed to know about Christ. Even this evidence from outside the New Testament would suffice to show that a firm belief in the virgin birth existed in the Christian Church well before the close of the first century.

But still more important is the New Testament evidence, and to that evidence we now turn.

The virgin birth is attested in two of the New Testament books, the Gospel according to Matthew and the Gospel according to Luke. The value which will be attributed to this testimony depends of course to a considerable extent upon the view which one holds of each of these two gospels as a whole. Obviously it will not be possible to discuss these questions here; it would carry us too far afield to discuss the evidence for the early date and high historical value of the two Gospels in which the virgin birth

appears.   But one remark at least may be made in passing: it may
at least be observed that the credit of the great double work, Luke-
Acts, has been steadily rising in recent years even in circles which
were formerly most hostile.   The extraordinary strength of the
literary evidence has led even men like Professor Harnack of Berlin, Professor C. C. Torrey of Yale, and the distinguished historian Professor Eduard Meyer, despite their rejection of the
whole supernatural content of the book, to accept the traditional
view that Luke-Acts was actually written by Luke the physician,
a companion of Paul.   It will not be possible here to review that
literary evidence in detail; but surely the evidence must be very
strong if it has been able to convince even those whose presuppositions render hypothesis of Lucan authorship so extremely
uncomfortable.

But if the Third Gospel was really written by Luke, its testimony as to events in Palestine must surely be received with the
greatest possible respect.   According to the information derived
from the use of the first person plural in the Book of Acts, Luke
had been in contact with James, the Lord's own brother, and with
many other members of the primitive Jerusalem Church.   Moreover he was in Palestine in A. D. 58 and appears there again two
years later; so that presumably he was in the country during the
interval.   Obviously such a man had the fullest possible opportunity for acquainting himself, not only with events concerning the
Gentile version of Paul but also with events in the life of our
Lord in Palestine.   It is therefore a matter of no small importance
that the virgin birth is narrated in the Third Gospel.

But the virgin birth is not merely narrated in the Third Gospel;
it is narrated in a very peculiar part of that Gospel.   The first
two chapters of the Gospel are possessed of very remarkable
literary characteristics.   The hand of the author of the whole book
has indeed been at work in these chapters, as the elaborate researches of Harnack and others have clearly shown; but the
author's hand has not been allowed to destroy the underlying

literary character of the narrative. And that underlying character is very strongly marked. The truth is that the first two chapters of Luke, with the exception of the typical Greek sentence in Luke 1:1-4, are in spirit and style nothing in the world but a bit of the Old Testament embedded in the midst of the New Testament. Nowhere is there a narrative more transparently Jewish and Palestinian than this. It is another question how the Palestinian character of the narrative is to be explained. Some have supposed that Luke used a written Palestinian source, which had already been translated into Greek or which he himself translated; others have supposed that without written sources he has simply caught the truly Semitic flavor of the oral information that came to him in Palestine. At any rate, however the Palestinian character of the narrative is to be explained, that Palestinian character itself is perfectly plain; in the first two chapters of Luke we are evidently dealing with a narrative that came from Palestinian soil.

That fact is of great importance for the question of the virgin birth. It shows that the virgin birth was narrated not merely in Gentile Christian documents but also in the country which was the scene of the narrated event. But there is still another reason why the Palestinian character of the narrative is important. We shall observe in the latter part of the lecture that the great majority of these modern scholars who reject the fact of the virgin birth suppose that the *idea* of the virgin birth was derived from pagan sources. But if that hypothesis be accepted, the question arises how a pagan idea came to be attested just by the most transparently Jewish and Palestinian portion of the whole New Testament. The Palestinian Judaism of the first century was passionately opposed to pagan influences, especially that loyal type of Palestinian Judaism which appears with such beautiful clearness in Luke 1 and 2. How could a pagan idea possibly find a place in such a narrative?

The question is really unanswerable; and in order to attempt to answer it, many modern scholars have had recourse to a truly

desperate expedient — they have maintained that the virgin birth
was not originally contained in the Palestinian narrative found in
the first two chapters of Luke but has been later inserted into
that narrative by interpolation. This interpolation theory has
been held in two forms. According to the more radical form the virgin birth has been interpolated into the completed Gospel. This
hypothesis is opposed by the great weight of manuscript attestation, there being not the slightest evidence among the many hundreds of manuscripts containing the Gospel of Luke that there
ever was a form of that Gospel without the verses narrating the
virgin birth. A more cautious form of the interpolation theory
has therefore sometimes been preferred. According to that more
cautious form, although the words attesting the virgin birth formed
an original part of the Third Gospel they did not form an original
part of the Palestinian source which the author of the Gospel was
using in the first two chapters, but were interpolated by the author
himself into the source which elsewhere he was closely following.

What shall be said of this interpolation theory? Very often
the best and only refutation of an interpolation theory is the refutation which Dr. Francis L. Patton is once said to have applied to
theosophy. A lady is reported to have asked Dr. Patton after
one of his lectures to give her the strongest argument against
theosophy. "Madam," said Dr. Patton, "the strongest argument
against theosophy is that there is no argument in its favor."
Similarly it may be said that the burden of proof is clearly against
those who advance an interpolation hypothesis; if no clear evidence can be adduced in its favor the hypothesis must be rejected,
and the narrative must be taken as it stands. Even such a consideration would be decisive against the interpolation theory
regarding the virgin birth in the infancy narrative of the Third
Gospel. The advocates of the theory have signally failed to prove
their point. The virgin birth is not merely narrated with great
clearness in Luke 1:34, 35, but is implied in several other verses;
and no reason at all adequate for supposing that these portions of

the narrative have been tampered with has yet been adduced. But as a matter of fact we are in the present case by no means limited to such a merely negative method of defense. The truth is that in the present case we can do far more than disprove the arguments for the interpolation hypothesis; we can also actually prove positively that that hypothesis is false. A careful examination shows clearly that the virgin birth, far from being an addition to the narrative in the first chapter of Luke is the thing for which the whole narrative exists. There is a clear parallelism between the account of the birth of John and that of the birth of Jesus. Even the birth of John was wonderful, since his parents were old. But the birth of Jesus was more wonderful still, and clearly it is the intention of the narrator to show that it was more wonderful. Are we to suppose that while narrating the wonderful birth of John the narrator simply mentioned an ordinary, non-miraculous birth of Jesus? The supposition is quite contrary to the entire manner in which the narrative is constructed. The truth is that if the virgin birth be removed from the first chapter of Luke the whole point is removed, and the narrative becomes quite meaningless. Never was an interpolation hypothesis more clearly false.

But personally I am very glad that the interpolation hypothesis has been proposed, because it indicates the desperate expedients to which those who deny the virgin birth are reduced. The great majority of these who reject the virgin birth of Christ suppose that the idea arose on pagan ground, and admit that other derivations of the idea are inadequate. But in order to hold this view they are simply forced to hold the interpolation theory regarding the first chapter of Luke; for only so can they explain how a pagan idea came to find a place in so transparently Jewish a narrative. But the interpolation theory being demonstrably false, the whole modern way of explaining the idea of the virgin birth of Christ results in signal failure. The naturalistic historians in other words are forced by their theory to hold the interpolation hypothesis; they stake their all upon that hypothesis. But that hypothesis is clearly false; hence the entire construction falls to the ground. So much then for the account of the virgin birth in Luke. Let us now turn to the Gospel according to Matthew. Here the virgin birth is narrated with a plainness which leaves nothing to be desired. Some men used to say that the first two chapters of the Gospel are a later addition, but this hypothesis has now been almost universally abandoned.

The value of this testimony depends of course upon the view that is held of the Gospel as a whole. But it is generally admitted by scholars of the most diverse points of view that the Gospel was written especially for Jews, and the Jewish character of the infancy narrative in the first two chapters is particularly plain.

If this lecture were being delivered under the conditions that prevailed some years ago it might be thought necessary for us to enter at length into the question of Matthew 1:16. Some time ago the textual question regarding this verse was discussed even in the newspapers and created a good deal of excitement. It was maintained by some persons that an ancient manuscript of the Gospels which was discovered in the monastery of St. Catherine on Mount Sinai provided a testimony against the virgin birth. The manuscript referred to is the so-called Sinaitic Syriac, a manuscript of an ancient translation of the Gospels into the Syriac language. This manuscript is not, as has sometimes been falsely asserted, the most ancient New Testament manuscript; since it is later than the two greatest manuscripts, the Codex Vaticanus and the Codex Sinaiticus, which also have the inestimable advantage of being manuscripts of the original Greek, not of a mere Syriac translation. But the Sinaitic Syriac is a very ancient manuscript, having been produced at about 400 A. D., and despite the fact that the extravagant claims made for it have now for the most part been abandoned, a few words about it may still be in place.

The Sinaitic Syriac has a curious reading at Matthew 1:16. But the importance of this witness must not be exaggerated. In order to accept the witness of the Sinaitic Syriac against all other documents one must suppose (1) that this manuscript has correctly reproduced at the point in question the ancient Syriac translation from which it is descended by a process of transmission, (2) that this ancient Syriac translation (which was probably produced in the latter part of the second century) correctly represents at this point the Greek manuscript from which the translation was made, and (3) that that Greek manuscript correctly represented at this point the autograph of the Gospel from which it was descended by a process of transmission. All of this is exceedingly uncertain in view of the overwhelming mass of evidence on the other side. To accept one witness against all the other witnesses is a very precarious kind of textual criticism where the evidence is so exceedingly abundant as it is in the case of the New Testament.

But as a matter of fact the Sinaitic Syriac does not deny the virgin birth at all. It attests the virgin birth in Matthew 1:18-25 just as clearly as do the other manuscripts, and it implies it even in Matthew 1:16. The reading of the Sinaitic Syriac which has given rise to the discussion is as follows: "Jacob begat Joseph; Joseph, to whom was betrothed Mary the virgin, begat Jesus that is called the Messiah." That would be self-contradictory if the word "begat" meant what it means in English. But as a matter of fact the scribe of the Sinaitic Syriac, if he thought of what he was doing and was not simply making a careless mistake, clearly used the word "begat" in the sense, "had as a legal descendant." It is interesting to note that Professor F. C. Burkitt, the greatest British authority on the Syriac manuscripts, who certainly is far from being prejudiced in favor of the virgin birth, holds that even if the original text were simply "Joseph begat Jesus" (which as a matter of fact appears in no manuscript) it would be absolutely without significance as a testimony against the virgin birth; for it would only mean that Joseph had Jesus as his legal heir. The author of the First Gospel is interested in two things, in one of them just as much as in the other. He is interested in showing (1) that Jesus was the heir of David through Joseph and (2) that He was a gift of God to the house of David in a more wonderful way than would have been the case if He had been descended from David by ordinary generation.

Thus even if the Sinaitic Syriac did represent the original text, it would not deny the virgin birth. But as a matter of fact it does not represent the original text at all. The original text of Matthew 1:16 is exactly the text that we are familiar with in our Bibles.

Accordingly we have an unequivocal double witness to the virgin birth of Christ in the Gospel according to Matthew and in the Gospel according to Luke. These two witnesses are clearly independent. If one thing is clear to modern scholars—and to every common-sense reader—it is that Matthew has not used Luke and Luke has not used Matthew. The very difficulties of fitting the two infancy narratives together is, to the believer in the virgin birth, a blessing in disguise; for it demonstrates at least the complete independence of the two accounts. The unanimity of these two independent witnesses constitutes the very strongest possible testimony to the central fact about which they are perfectly and obviously agreed.

But at this point an objection is often made. The rest of the New Testament, we are told, says nothing about the virgin birth; Paul says nothing about it, neither does Mark. Hence the testimony in favor of it is often said to be weak; men are often impressed with this argument from silence.

And the argument from silence needs to be used with a great deal of caution. The silence of a writer about any detail is without significance unless it had been shown that if the writer in question had known and accepted that detail he would have been obliged to mention it.

The Virgin Birth of Christ 75

But that is just exactly what cannot be shown in the case of the silence about the virgin birth. Paul, for example, does not mention the virgin birth, and much has been made of his silence. "What is good enough for Paul," we are told in effect, "is good enough for us; if he got along without the virgin birth we can get along without it too." It is rather surprising, indeed, to find the Modernists of today advancing that particular argument; it is rather surprising to find them laying down the principle that what is good enough for Paul is good enough for them, and that things which are not found in Paul cannot be essential to Christianity. For the center of their religion is found in the ethical teaching of Jesus, especially in the Golden Rule. But where does Paul say anything about the Golden Rule, and where does he quote at any length the ethical teachings of Jesus? We do not mean at all that the silence about such things in the Epistles shows that Paul did not know or care about the words and example of our Lord in the days of His flesh. On the contrary there are clear intimations that the reason why the Apostle does not tell more about what Jesus did and said in Palestine is not that these things were to him unimportant but that they were so important that instruction about them had been given at the very beginning in the churches and so did not need to be repeated in the Epistles, which are addressed to special needs. And where Paul does give details about Jesus, the incidental way in which he does so shows clearly that there is a great deal else which he would have told if he had found occasion. The all-important passage in I Corinthians 15:3-8 provides a striking example. In that passage Paul gives a list of appearances of the risen Christ. He would not have done so if it had not been for the chance (humanly speaking) of certain misunderstandings that had arisen in Corinth. Yet if he had not done so, it is appalling to think of the inferences which would have been drawn from his silence by modern scholars. And yet, even if the occasion for mentioning the list of appearances had not happened to arise in the Epistles it would still have remained

true that that list of appearances was one of the absolutely fundamental elements of teaching which Paul gave to the churches at
the very beginning.

That example should make us extremely cautious about drawing inferences from the silence of Paul. In the Epistles Paul
mentions very few things about the earthly life of Jesus; yet
clearly he knew far more than he has found occasion to tell in
the Epistles. It does not at all follow therefore that because he
does not mention a thing in the Epistles he did not know about
it. Hence the fact that he does not mention the virgin birth
does not prove that the virgin birth was to him unknown.

Moreover, although Paul does not mention the virgin birth the
entire account which he gives of Jesus as an entirely new beginning in humanity, as the second Adam, is profoundly congruous
with the virgin birth and profoundly incongruous with the view
that makes Jesus the son, by ordinary generation, of Joseph and
Mary. The entire Christology of Paul is a powerful witness to
the same event that is narrated in Matthew and Luke; the religion of Paul presupposes a Jesus who was conceived by the Holy
Ghost and born of the Virgin Mary.

The silence of Mark is of just as little importance as the silence
of Paul. The Gospel according to Mark was preeminently the
missionary gospel; it was not intended to give all the facts about
Jesus, but simply those which needed to be given first to those
who had not already been won to Christ. Reading the Second
Gospel, you stand in astonishment like those who were in the
synagogue at Capernaum in the scene described in the first chapter. You see the wonderful works of Jesus; you stand afar off
looking at Him; you are not introduced to Him with the intimacy of detail which one finds in Matthew and Luke. The fact
that Mark does not narrate the virgin birth does not prove that
he does not believe in the virgin birth or that it is to him less important than other facts; but shows merely that the narration of
the birth of Jesus in any form is quite contrary to the plan of his

Gospel, which begins with the public ministry. The most important things that need to be said are not always the first things; and Mark is concerned with the first things that would make an impression even upon those who had not already been won to Christ.

The New Testament does indeed imply that the contemporaries of Jesus in Palestine were unaware of the story of the virgin birth, and perhaps it also makes probable that the virgin birth formed no part of the earliest missionary preaching of the Apostles in Jerusalem. But all that is just what could be expected even if the virgin birth were a fact. The virgin birth was a holy mystery which was capable of the grossest misunderstanding; certainly it would not be spoken of by a person like Mary whose meditative character is so delicately and so vividly depicted in the first two chapters of Luke. It would not be spoken of to the hostile multitude, and least of all would it be spoken of to the brothers of Jesus. Also it would certainly not be mentioned in the earliest public missionary preaching before the crowds in Jerusalem. Only at some time after the resurrection, when the miracle of the virgin birth had at last been vindicated by the resurrection and exaltation of Jesus would Mary breathe the mystery of Jesus' birth to sympathetic ears. Hence it found its way into the wonderful narrative preserved by Luke and from there into the hearts of Christians of all the ages.

Such is the course of events which would be expected if the virgin birth were a fact. And the attestation of the event in the New Testament is just exactly what is suited to these antecedent probabilities. The attestation in the very nature of the case could not be equal to that of an event like the resurrection, of which there were many eye-witnesses; but it is just what it would naturally be if the event really occurred in the manner in which it is said to have occurred in Matthew and Luke.

But the full force of the New Testament evidence can be appreciated only if the accounts are allowed to speak for themselves.

These narratives are wonderfully self-evidencing; they certainly
do not read as though they were based on fiction; and they are
profoundly congruous with that entire account of Jesus without
which the origin of the Christian religion is an insoluble puzzle.

If this testimony is to be rejected, what is to be put in its place?
If the belief of the Christian Church in the virgin birth was not
founded upon fact, how did it actually originate? The consideration of this question constitutes the second main division of our
subject. If the virgin birth is not a fact, how did the idea find a
place in the New Testament and at the center of the Church's
belief? If Jesus was really born of Joseph and Mary, how shall
we explain the fact that in the New Testament we have this
strange false account of His birth?

The first explanation which has been proposed is that the false
idea arose in Jewish-Christian ground. We have observed that
the New Testament narratives of the virgin birth are strikingly
Jewish in character; it is natural then to find the origin of the idea
among the Jews. Some scholars therefore have supposed that
the virgin birth was attributed to Jesus because devout Jewish
Christians desired to find a fulfillment for the prophecy of Isaiah
7:14, "Behold the virgin shall conceive." But this method of
explaining the origin of New Testament narratives has come into
general disfavor in recent years; and such disfavor is particularly
well-deserved with regard to Isaiah 7:14. There is not the
slightest evidence for supposing that verse was ever interpreted
by the pre-Christian Jews as indicating a virgin birth of the
Messiah. We do not mean that Isaiah 7:14 is not a true prophecy;
on the contrary we regard it as a very precious prophecy of the
virgin birth of the Lord. But it is one thing to understand such
a prophecy after the event and quite a different thing to understand the prophecy before the event. In general, adherents of the
mythical theory about the New Testament have become much less
confident than they formerly were about supposing that the myths
arose in order to show fulfillment of Old Testament prophecies.

Usually it is admitted to be clearly the other way around; only after certain things came to be believed about Jesus on independent grounds, were the Old Testament prophecies interpreted as referring to him.

But the advocates of the Jewish derivation of the idea of the virgin birth also point to the wonderful birth of heroes like Isaac. Isaac, it is said, was born by a kind of miracle after his parents were old; it was therefore only a slight step to suppose that there was an even greater miracle in the case of one who was greater than Isaac; and thus in the case of Jesus the human father was excluded altogether. This explanation ignores the characteristic Jewish attitude toward marriage and the begetting of children. There was among the Jews not the slightest tendency toward asceticism; and far from being only a slight step in advance, the exclusion of the human father makes the birth of Jesus totally different from that of Isaac. The very point of the narrative about Isaac is that Abraham actually was in a physical sense his father; it is just the paternity of Abraham which the narrative stresses. There is nothing in the story of Isaac therefore which could have caused the development of the story of the virgin birth among the Jews. It is no wonder then that most modern scholars are inclined to agree with Adalbert Merx in saying that the idea of the virgin birth is "as un-Jewish as possible."

If then the Jewish derivation of the supposed myth of the virgin birth is impossible, recourse is often had to pagan influences. Sometimes, it is true, attention has been called to the philosophic Judaism of Philo of Alexandria, who combined a strange allegorical interpretation of the Old Testament with acceptance of the doctrines of Greek philosophy. But there is not to be found in the works of Philo any real parallel to the virgin birth of Christ, the apparent parallels being due to the fact that in his treatment of Old Testament characters such as Abraham and Isaac Philo has often lost sight of the literal significance of the history and is thinking only of the allegorical interpretation in accordance with which these characters represent only spiritual qualities or the like.  Moreover the whole atmosphere of Philo is as remote as anything could possibly be from the Palestinian atmosphere that appears with such wonderful clearness in the infancy narratives of Matthew and Luke.  It is no wonder then, in view of the obvious insufficiency of the Jewish derivation of the idea of the virgin birth, that the majority of modern scholars who have denied the fact have had recourse, for the explanation of the origin of the idea, to purely pagan sources.

But at this point a double protest must be raised.  How could a pagan idea find a place in primitive Christianity?  Against the entrance of such an idea there was a two-fold barrier.  In the first place there was the barrier that separated all of primitive Christianity from the pagan world.  Christianity at its inception involved a tremendous protest against paganism, and nothing would have been more abhorrent to the early Christians than the introduction into their thought about Jesus of the crassly pagan idea of the begetting of men by the gods, an idea which belonged not merely to paganism but to paganism in its most revolting and immoral aspects.  That was the first barrier that needed to be surmounted before a pagan idea could find a place in the infancy narratives of Matthew and Luke.  This barrier has been rightly and very ably insisted upon by Professor Harnack, though in the interests not of a defense of the virgin birth but of a derivation of the idea from Jewish sources.

But even if this barrier were surmounted another question would still remain.  Even if the supposed pagan idea could have attained a place in the belief of the early Church, how could it ever have entered, not into Gentile Christian documents, but into the most clearly Jewish and Palestinian narratives in the whole New Testament, particularly into the infancy narrative of Luke?  This question constitutes an insuperable objection, at the start, to the whole hypothesis of pagan influence, unless the interpolation theory regarding Luke 1 and 2 be correct.  The hypothesis of pagan influence is absolutely bound up with the interpolation theory. But that interpolation theory, as we have already observed, is clearly false. The virgin birth is an integral part of the narrative in Luke, to say nothing of its place in Matthew. But in reading the infancy narrative in Luke we are simply breathing the atmosphere of Palestine, and are separated by whole worlds from the life of the Gentiles. Every word breathes the spirit of the Jewish expectation of the Messiah, and of Jewish life, and thought. And yet it is supposed that a crassly pagan idea has found a place in such a narrative!

Thus the double barrier remains against the entrance of a pagan idea into the infancy narratives: first, the barrier that separated the whole of primitive Christianity, whether Jewish or Gentile from pagan ideas; and, second, the barrier that separated Palestinian Judaism from the Gentile world. In view of these initial objections, it is only for the sake of the argument that we examine the alleged pagan parallels at all. And as a matter of fact the parallels upon examination all break down.

The Modernist preachers of the day, in their attack upon the New Testament account of our Lord, sometimes speak of "virgin births" in pagan mythology as though they were the commonest things in the world. But as a matter of fact, in Greek mythology at least, there is no such thing as a virgin birth at all. Certain heroes were regarded as having been born without human father, but that means not that they were born of virgin mothers, but that the Greek gods were conceived of in a thoroughly anthropomorphic way as possessing human passions and as falling into very human sins. The children begotten of certain women by Zeus, in the course of his numerous amours, were certainly not virgin-born. The same notion was transferred to certain historical characters such as Plato and Alexander the Great and the emperor Augustus. Whether seriously or not, these characters by a form of flattery were sometimes said to have been begotten, like the demigods of old, by some god, who took the place of the human father. But such a conception was possible only because of the grossly anthropomorphic way in which the Greek gods were conceived.

But in the infancy narratives in Matthew and Luke we find ourselves in an entirely different circle of ideas. In these narratives Jesus is represented as conceived by the Holy Ghost. But certainly the divine Spirit is not regarded in any anthropomorphic way. Indeed, as has often been observed, the word for "Spirit" in Hebrew is not of masculine but of feminine gender. And what is more important still is the character of the narrative as a whole. In these chapters the lofty spiritual monotheism of the Old Testament prophets is preserved to the very full; and the conception of our Lord in the womb of the virgin Mary is regarded not in any anthropomorphic way but as a creative act of the same divine Spirit who was active in the first creation in accordance with the majestic narrative of Genesis. It is inconceivable that such a narrative should be the product of invention; but it is still more inconceivable that it should have been derived from the most degraded and immoral parts of Greek mythology.

But one more explanation for the origin of the idea of our Lord's virgin birth has been proposed in recent years. Certain scholars belonging to the most "advanced" school of comparative religion, having detected the impossibility of the hypotheses which we have just considered, have advanced a new hypothesis of their own. They have recognized the fact that the idea of the virgin birth is "as un-Jewish as possible," and so have rejected the derivation of the supposed virgin-birth myth on Jewish ground. On the other hand they have recognized the integrity of the narrative in Luke 1 and have rejected the interpolation hypothesis which makes the virgin birth a later insertion. A pagan idea—that of the virgin birth—does stand, therefore, they hold, in a Jewish narrative. But, they suppose, this curious fact was possible because even before the time of Christ the Jews had, under the influence of oriental paganism, already come to believe in a virgin birth of the coming Messiah. Thus in the New Testament the virgin birth appears in a Jewish narrative; but that means, it is supposed, not that the idea was originally Jewish, but only that a pagan idea had become so well naturalized among the pre-Christian Jews that in the first century its pagan origin had been forgotten.

This hypothesis is an interesting testimony to the defects of the alternative theories. But in itself it is improbable in the extreme. What evidence is there that late pre-Christian Judaism had come to expect a virgin birth for the Messiah? There is really no evidence whatever. We do know something of the late pre-Christian Jewish doctrine of the Messiah, and what we know not only contains no mention of a virgin birth but is rather contrary to any such idea. Surely it is quite inadmissable to posit such an idea without any positive evidence and simply in the interests of a theory regarding the Christian doctrine of the virgin birth of Jesus.

Thus all of the modern theories regarding the origin of the idea of the virgin birth supposing it not to have been founded on fact have been tried and found wanting. And it is interesting to observe how the advocates of one theory are often the best critics of the others. Thus Harnack, in the interests of his Jewish derivation of the idea, does excellent service in showing the impossibility of the entrance of such an idea from pagan sources; advocates of the pagan derivation have well demonstrated the insufficiency of the Jewish derivation; and finally the most recent school of comparative religion has triumphantly and quite correctly insisted upon the falsity of the interpolation theory regarding Luke 1 upon which the ordinary hypothesis of pagan derivation is based. The truth is that if the belief in the virgin birth of Christ be not founded upon fact no other satisfactory way of explaining the origin of the belief and its inclusion in Matthew and Luke has yet been proposed.

Shall we then simply accept the attestation of the virgin birth, which we have seen is very strong and very early? We should probably not be able to do so, despite all that has been said, if the virgin birth stood absolutely alone, if it were a question simply of a virgin birth of a man of the first century about whom we knew nothing. For the virgin birth is a stupendous miracle, and if it stood alone there would be a tremendous burden of proof against it. But as a matter of fact it does not stand alone, but is supported by a great mass of other facts; it is not a question simply of a virgin birth of some man of the first century about whom we know nothing, but it is a question of the virgin birth of one about whom we know a great deal, namely, Jesus of Nazareth. If the New Testament picture of Jesus is false as a whole, then of course we shall not accept the virgin birth; but if Jesus was really in general what the New Testament represents Him as being, then we shall believe with the utmost firmness, on the basis of abundant evidence, that He was conceived by the Holy Ghost and born of the virgin Mary.

But what is the importance of the matter? That question has loomed large in recent discussion, and some have held that although they accept the virgin birth of Christ themselves they can make common cause in Christian service with those who do not accept it. But this indifferentist position is really almost worse from the Christian point of view than any doctrinaire denial could be. As a matter of fact the virgin birth is of central importance for Christian faith.

In the first place, it is important because of its bearing upon the question of the authority of the Bible. No one denies that the attestation of the virgin birth forms an integral part of the Bible; it is not a question whether the Bible teaches the virgin birth but whether, teaching the virgin birth as it admittedly does, the Bible is true or false. We must therefore face the question frankly. If the Bible has allowed myth to enter at this point into the representation not of something on the periphery but of Christ himself, then Scripture authority is gone, and some different basis must be sought for Christian doctrine and Christian life. Deny the virgin birth of Christ, and you must relinquish the authority of the Bible; accept the virgin birth and you may continue to regard the Bible as the very Word of God.

In the second place, the virgin birth is a test as to the view which a man holds in general, about Christ. Two opposite views of Jesus of Nazareth are struggling for the ascendancy in the Church today. According to one view He was a teacher who initiated a new type of religious life, who founded Christianity by being the first Christian; according to the other view He was the eternal Son of God who came voluntarily into this world from outside the world and who founded Christianity by redeeming men from the guilt and power of sin. The conflict between these two views is the conflict between naturalism and supernaturalism; and that is a conflict not between two varieties of Christianity, but between two mutually exclusive religions. But how can we tell which view any individual holds? Conceivably one might ask him whether he believes in the deity of Christ. But unfortunately the word "deity" or the word "god" has been degraded so low in Modernist parlance that when the Modernist says that "Jesus is God" he means something even far more remote from Christian belief than the Unitarian meant when he said that "Jesus is not God." Or it may conceivably be asked whether the individual in question believes in the resurrection. But here again the answer may mean nothing; since the word resurrection is often interpreted (quite absurdly, it is true) to mean simply the continued existence of Jesus or His continued influence, and not to involve the miracle of the emergence of His body from the tomb. But, over against all such ambiguities, when a man says that he believes Jesus to have had no human father, one can tell pretty clearly where he stands.

The impression is indeed often produced that many men who reject the virgin birth maintain in general the New Testament account of our Lord. But that impression is entirely false. There have been, it is true, a few men in the history of the modern Church who have rejected the virgin birth and yet have accepted the supernatural Christ and have believed in His true resurrection from the dead. But these men have been few and far between; and it would probably be impossible to name a single one of any prominence who is living today. Particularly false is the notion that many men who deny the virgin birth yet accept the incarnation; for the men who deny the virgin birth usually mean by "incarnation" almost the exact opposite of what Christians mean by that term. The truth is that the conflict about the virgin birth is only one phase of the great religious conflict of the day. And that conflict is a conflict between the Christian religion and a naturalistic or agnostic Modernism which is anti-Christian to the core.

In the third place, the virgin birth is important in itself—even aside from its importance as being connected with the question of the authority of Scripture and as being a test for the differentiating of naturalism from supernaturalism. The Christian world, in other words, has a clearer and better conception of Christ than it would have had if God had never told us of the virgin birth and had allowed us to think that Jesus was the son, by ordinary generation, of Joseph and Mary. Conceivably indeed we might have been Christians even if God had never told us of the virgin birth. Certainly never to have heard of the virgin birth would have been a much less serious thing than it is to reject it now that we have heard of it. But it is easy to see the errors which might then have arisen, or which would have attained additional momentum, if God had never told us of the virgin birth of our Lord. What the knowledge of the virgin birth does is to fix with inescapable clearness the supernaturalism of the life of Jesus from the very beginning; the virgin birth for example intensifies the impossibility of holding that our Lord only grew up gradually into His divinity, or of holding in gnostic fashion that the Son of God descended upon a man Jesus at the baptism. All such errors are excluded by many things in the New Testament. But they are excluded with special clearness in the precious narrative of the virgin birth. That narrative represents our Lord clearly as no product of sinful humanity but as one who came into the world by a mighty creative act of God. And that representation is at the very center and core of the Christian faith.

No doubt the virgin birth is not the point at which one should begin in trying to convince a man who has not yet come to Christian faith. No doubt one should begin rather with the resurrection, in which the direct testimony is, and must be in the very nature of the case, vastly more abundant. But when a man has once been convinced that Jesus is truly the risen and ascended Lord and when he has once accepted Him as Saviour, then his faith will be unstable and incomplete unless he goes forward to accept the precious testimony of Matthew and Luke as to our Lord's entrance into the world.

The truth is that the New Testament account of Christ is a wonderfully unitary thing, and an integral part of it is the virgin birth. Believe that Jesus is simply the fairest flower of humanity, and the infancy narrative of the gospels, despite its marvelous beauty, will be to you abhorrent; but accept the dear Lord and Saviour presented to you in the Word of God, and you will believe and confess, with a heart full of gratitude and love and joy, that He was "conceived by the Holy Ghost, born of the Virgin Mary."

# VI

# The Resurrection of Christ

SOME nineteen hundred years ago, in an obscure corner of the Roman Empire, there lived one who, to a casual observer, might have seemed to be a remarkable man.  Up to the age of about thirty years, He lived an obscure life in the midst of an humble family.  Then He began a remarkable course of ethical and religious teaching, accompanied by a ministry of healing.  At first He was very popular.  Great crowds followed Him gladly, and the intellectual men of His people were interested in what He had to say.  But His teaching presented revolutionary features, and He did not satisfy the political expectations of the populace.  And so, before long, after some three years, He fell a victim to the jealousy of the leaders of His people and the cowardice of the Roman governor.  He died the death of the criminals of those days, on the cross.  At His death, the disciples whom He had gathered about Him were utterly discouraged.  In Him had centered all their loftiest hopes.  And now that He was taken from them by a shameful death, their hopes were shattered.  They fled from Him in cowardly fear in the hour of His need, and an observer would have said that never was a movement more hopelessly dead.  These followers of Jesus had evidently been far inferior to Him in spiritual discernment and in courage.  They had not been able, even when He was with them, to understand the lofty teachings of their leader.  How, then, could they understand Him when He was gone?  The movement depended, one

might have said, too much on one extraordinary man, and when
He was taken away, then surely the movement was dead.

But then the astonishing thing happened. The plain fact, which
no one doubts, is that those same weak, discouraged men who had
just fled in the hour of their Master's need, and who were altogether hopeless on account of His death, suddenly began in Jerusalem, a very few days or weeks after their Master's death, what
is certainly the most remarkable spiritual movement that the world
has ever seen. At first, the movement thus begun remained
within the limits of the Jewish people. But soon it broke the
bands of Judaism, and began to be planted in all the great cities
of the Roman world. Within three hundred years, the Empire
itself had been conquered by the Christian faith.

But this movement was begun in those few decisive days after
the death of Jesus. What was it which caused the striking change
in those weak, discouraged disciples, which made them the spiritual conquerors of the world?

Historians of today are perfectly agreed that something must
have happened, something decisive, after the death of Jesus, in
order to begin this new movement. It was not just an ordinary
continuation of the influence of Jesus' teaching. The modern
historians are at least agreed that some striking change took
place after the death of Jesus, and before the beginning of the
Christian missionary movement. They are agreed, moreover, to
some extent even about the question what the change was; they
are agreed in holding that this new Christian movement was begun
by the belief of the disciples in the resurrection of Jesus; they are
agreed in holding that in the minds and hearts of the diciples there
was formed the conviction that Jesus had risen from the dead. Of
course, that was not formerly admitted by every one. It used to
be maintained, in the early days of modern skepticism, that the disciples of Jesus only pretended that He had risen from the dead.
Such hypotheses have long ago been placed in the limbo of discarded theories. The disciples of Jesus, the intimate friends of

Jesus, it is now admitted, in a short time after His death came to believe honestly that He had risen from the dead. The only difference of opinion comes when we ask what in turn produced this belief. The New Testament answer to this question is perfectly plain. According to the New Testament, the disciples believed in the resurrection of Jesus because Jesus really, after His death, came out of the tomb, appeared to them, and held extended intercourse with them, so that their belief in the resurrection was simply based on fact.

Of course, this explanation is rejected by those modern men who are unwilling to recognize in the origin of Christianity an entrance of the creative power of God, in distinction from the laws which operate in nature. And so another explanation has been proposed. It is that the belief of the disciples in the resurrection was produced by certain hallucinations in which they thought they saw Jesus, their teacher, and heard perhaps words of His ringing in their ears. A hallucination is a phenomenon well known to students of pathology. In an hallucination, the optic nerve is affected, and the patient therefore does actually in one sense "see" someone or something. But this effect is produced, not by an external object, but by the pathological condition of the subject himself. That is the view of the "appearances" of the risen Christ which is held today by those who reject the miraculous in connection with the origin of Christianity.

It is also held, it is true, that what was decisive in the resurrection faith of the early disciples was the impression which they had received of Jesus' person. Without that impression, it is supposed, they could never have had those pathological experiences which they called appearances of the risen Christ; so that those pathological experiences were merely the necessary form in which the continued impression of Jesus' person made itself felt in the life of the first disciples. But after all, on this hypothesis, the resurrection faith of the disciples, upon which the Christian church is founded, was really based upon a pathological experience in which these men thought they saw Jesus, and heard perhaps a word or two of His ringing in their ears, when there was nothing in the external world to make them think that they were in His presence.

Formerly, it is true, there were other explanations. It used to be held sometimes that the disciples came to believe in the resurrection because Jesus was not really dead. When He was placed in the cool air of the tomb, He revived and came out, and the disciples thought that He had arisen. A noteworthy scholar of today is said to have revived this theory, because he is dissatisfied with the prevailing idea. But the great majority of scholars today believe that this faith of the disciples was caused by hallucinations, which are called "appearances" of the risen Lord.

But let us examine the New Testament account of the resurrection of Jesus, and of the related events. This account is contained particularly in six of the New Testament books. Of course, all the New Testament books presuppose the resurrection, and witness is borne to it in all of them. But there are six of these books, above all others, which provide the details of the Resurrection. These are the four Gospels, the Book of Acts, and the First Epistle of Paul to the Corinthians.

According to these six books, if their witness be put together, Jesus died on a Friday. His body was not allowed to remain and decompose on the cross, but was buried that same evening. He was placed in a grave chosen by a leader of the people, a member of the Sanhedrin. His burial was witnessed by certain women. He remained in the grave during the Sabbath. But on the morning of the first day of the week, He arose. Certain women who came to the grave found it empty, and saw angels who told them He had risen from the dead. He appeared to these women. The grave was visited that same morning by Peter and the beloved disciple. In the course of the day Jesus appeared to Peter. In the evening He appeared to two unnamed disciples who were walking to Emmaus; and apparently later on the same evening, He appeared to all the apostles save Thomas. Then a week later He appeared again to the apostles, Thomas being present. Then He appeared in Galilee, as we learn from Matthew 28. Paul is probably mentioning this same appearance when he says that "He appeared to above five hundred brethren at once," I Corinthians 15:6. It was probably then, also, that He appeared to the seven disciples on the sea of Galilee, John 21. Then He appeared in Jerusalem, and ascended from the Mount of Olives. Some time in the course of the appearances there was one to James, His own brother, I Corinthians 15:7. Later on He appeared to Paul. Such is the New Testament account of the resurrection appearances of our Lord.

There are two features of this account to which great prominence has been given in recent discussions. These are, (1) the place, and (2) the character, of the appearances of Jesus.

According to the New Testament, the place was first Jerusalem, then Galilee, and then Jerusalem again. The appearances took place, not only in Galilee and in Jerusalem, but both in Jerusalem and in Galilee; and the first appearances took place in Jerusalem.

So much for the place of the appearances. As for the character of the appearances, they were, according to the New Testament, of a plain, physical kind. In the New Testament Jesus is represented even as holding table companionship with His disciples after His resurrection, and as engaging in rather extended intercourse with them. There is, it is true, something mysterious about this intercourse; it is not just a continuation of the old Galilean relationship. Jesus' body is independent of conditions of time and space in a way that appeared only rarely in His previous ministry. There was a change. But there is also continuity. The body of Jesus came out of the tomb and appeared to the disciples in such a way that a man could put his finger in the mark of the nails in His hands.

In two particulars, this account is contradicted by modern scholars. In the first place, the character of the appearances, is supposed to have been different. The disciples of Jesus, it is supposed, saw Him just for a moment in glory, and perhaps heard a word or two ringing in their ears. Of course this was not, according to the modern naturalistic historians, a real seeing and hearing, but an hallucination. But the point is, that those who regard these appearances as hallucinations are not able to take the New Testament account and prove from it that these appearances were hallucinations and were not founded upon the real presence of the body of Jesus; but are obliged first to reduce the New Testament account to manageable proportions. The reason is that there are limits to an hallucination. No sane men could think that they had had extended companionship with one who was not really present, or could believe that they had walked with Him and talked with Him after His death. You cannot enter upon the modern explanation of these happenings as genuine experiences but at the same time mere visions, until you modify the account that is given of the appearances themselves. And if this modified account be true, there must be a great deal in the New Testament account that is legendary. You must admit this, if you are going to explain these appearances as hallucinations. So there is a difference concerning the *nature* of the appearances, according to modern reconstruction, as over against the New Testament.

And there is a difference also concerning the *place* of the appearances. According to the customary modern view of naturalistic historians, the first appearances took place in Galilee, and not in Jerusalem. But what is the importance of that difference of opinion? It looks at first sight as though it were a mere matter of detail. But in reality it is profoundly important for the whole modern reconstruction. If you are going to explain these experiences as hallucinations, the necessary psychological conditions must have prevailed in order for the disciples to have had the ex-

periences. Therefore modern historians are careful to allow time
for the profound discouragement of the disciples to be gotten rid
of — for the disciples to return to Galilee, and to live again in
the scenes where they had lived with Jesus; to muse upon Him,
and be ready to have these visions of Him. Time must be permitted, and the place must be favorable. And then there is another
important element.

We come here to one of the most important things of all —
the empty tomb. If the first appearances were in Jerusalem,
why did not the disciples or the enemies investigate the tomb,
and refute this belief by finding the body of Jesus still there?
This argument is thought to be refuted by the Galilean hypothesis
regarding the first appearances. If the first appearances took
place not till weeks afterward and in Galilee, this mystery is
thought to be explained. There would be no opportunity to investigate the tomb until it was too late; and so the matter could
have been allowed to pass, and the resurrection faith could have
arisen. Of course, this explanation is not quite satisfactory, because one cannot see how the disciples would not have been stimu-
lated to investigate the tomb, whenever and wherever the appearances took place. We have not quite explained the empty tomb,
even by this Galilean hypothesis. But you can understand the
insistence of the modern writers that the first appearances took
place in Galilee.

So there is a difference between the modern historian and the
New Testament account in the matters of the *manner* and of the
*place* of these experiences. Were they of a kind such that they
could be explained as hallucinations or were they such that they
could only be regarded as real appearances? Was the first appearance three days after Jesus' death, and near the tomb, or later
on in Galilee?

Let us come now to the New Testament account.

The first source that we should consider is the first Epistle of
Paul to the Corinthians. It is probably the earliest of the sources.

But what is still more important — the authorship and date of
this particular source of information have been agreed upon even
by the opponents of Christianity. So this is not only a source
of first-rate historical importance but it is a source of *admitted*
importance. We have here a fixed starting-point in all controversy.

We must examine, then, this document with some care. It
was probably written, roughly speaking, about 55 A. D., about
twenty-five years after the death of Jesus, about as long after
the death of Jesus as 1924 is after the Spanish-American War.
That is not such a very long period of time. And of course,
there is one vital element in the testimony here, which does not
prevail in the case of the Spanish War. Most people have forgotten many details of the Spanish-American War, because they
have not had them continuously in mind. But it would not be so
in the case now under consideration. The resurrection of Jesus
was the thing which formed the basis of all the thought of the
early Christians, and so the memory of it when it was twenty-five
years past was very much fresher than the memory of an event
like the Spanish-American War of twenty-five years ago, which
has passed out of our consciousness.

Let us turn, then, to I Corinthians 15, and read the first verses.
"Moreover, brethren, I declare unto you the gospel which I
preached unto you, which also ye have received, and wherein
ye stand; by which also ye are saved, if ye keep in memory what
I preached unto you, unless ye have believed in vain. For I
delivered unto you first of all that which I also received." "First
of all," or "among the first things," may mean first in point of
time, or first in point of importance. At any rate, this was a part
of Paul's fundamental preaching in Corinth, in about the year
51 or 52. So we get back a little farther than the time when the
Epistle was written. But these things were evidently also first
and fundamental in Paul's preaching in other places, so that you
are taken back an indefinite period in the ministry of Paul for this

evidence. But then you are taken back by the next words farther still — "that which I also received." There is a common
agreement as to the source from which Paul "received" this information; it is pretty generally agreed that he received it from
the Jerusalem church. According to the Epistle to the Galatians,
he had been in conference with Peter and James only three years
after his conversion. That was the time for Paul to receive this
tradition. Historians are usually willing to admit that this information is nothing less than the account which the primitive
Church, including Peter and James, gave of the events which
lay at the foundation of the Church. So you have here, even in
the admission of modern men, a piece of historical information
of priceless value.

"For I delivered unto you first of all that which I also received,
how that Christ died for our sins according to the Scriptures;
and that he was buried, and that he rose again the third day according to the Scriptures." Why does Paul mention the burial
of Jesus? The impression which the mention of the burial pro-
duces upon every reader who comes to it as for the first time is
that Paul means to say that the body of Jesus was laid in the
tomb. The burial, in other words, implies the empty tomb. And
yet a great many modern historians say that Paul "knows nothing" about the empty tomb! Surely such an assertion is quite
false. Paul does not indeed mention the empty tomb in so many
words; he does not give a detailed description of it here. But that
does not mean that he knew nothing about it. Those to whom he
was writing believed in it already, and he is simply reviewing a
previous argument in order to draw inferences from it with regard
to the resurrection of Christians. To say that Paul knows nothing
about the empty tomb ignores the fact that the mention of the
burial is quite meaningless unless Paul had in mind the empty
tomb. I do not see how any one can get any other impression.
Moreover is not that what resurrection means, after all? Modern
historians say that Paul was interested simply in the continued

life of Jesus in a new body which had nothing to do with the body which lay in the tomb. That is rather strange in this connection. Paul is arguing, in this passage, not against men who denied the immortality of the soul, but against men who held the Greek view of the immortality of the soul without the body. The view that they were holding, would logically make of the resurrection of Jesus just the simple continuance of His personal life. There is no point at all, then, in what Paul says against them unless he is referring to the resurrection from the tomb. Unless he is referring to this, he is playing into the hands of his opponents. But many men nowadays have such a strangely unhistorical notion of what "resurrection" meant to the early disciples. They talk as though the resurrection faith meant that those disciples simply believed that Jesus continued to exist after His crucifixion. This is absurd. Those men believed in the continued existence after death of every man. There is not the slightest doubt about that. They were thoroughly imbued with this belief. They were not Sadducees. Even in those first three days after Jesus' crucifixion, they still believed that He was alive. If that is all that resurrection meant, there was nothing in it to cause joy. Conviction of the continued life of Jesus would not make Him any different from other men. But what changed sadness into joy and brought about the founding of the Church was the substitution, for a belief in the continued existence of Jesus, of a belief in the emergence of His body from the tomb. And Paul's words imply that as clear as day.

"And that he rose again *the third day.*" Of all the important things that Paul says, this is perhaps the most important, from the point of view of modern discussion. There are few words in the New Testament that are more disconcerting to modern naturalistic historians than the words, "on the third day." We have just observed what the modern reconstruction is. The disciples went back to Galilee, it is supposed, and there, some time after the crucifixion, they came to believe that Jesus was alive. But if the first appearance took place on the third day, this explanation is not possible. The modern reconstruction disappears altogether if you believe that the first appearances were on the third day. If Paul's words are to be taken at their face value, the whole elaborate psychological reconstruction of the conditions in the disciples' minds, leading up to the hallucinations in Galilee, disappears.

Many men, it is true, have an answer ready. "Let us not," they say in effect, "go beyond what Paul actually says! Paul does not say that the first appearance occurred on the third day, but only that Christ rose on that day. He might have risen some time before He first appeared to them; the resurrection might have occurred on the third day and yet the first appearance might have occurred some weeks after, in Galilee."

But why, if nothing in particular happened on the third day, and if the first appearance occurred some weeks after, did the disciples hit upon just the third day as the day of the supposed resurrection? Surely it was very strange for them to suppose that Jesus had really risen a considerable time before He appeared to them and had left them all that time in their despair. So strange a supposition on the part of the disciples surely requires an explanation. Why was it, if nothing happened on the third day, that the disciples ever came to suppose that the resurrection occurred on that day and not on some other day?

One proposed explanation is that the third day was hit upon as the day of the supposed resurrection because Scripture was thought to require it. Paul says, it will be remembered, that Jesus rose the third day *according to the Scriptures.* But where will you find in the Old Testament Scriptures any clear reference to the third day, as the day of the resurrection of Christ. No doubt there is the "sign of Jonah," and there is also Hosea 6:2 We are certainly not denying that these passages (at least the former) are true prophecies of the resurrection on the third day. But could they ever have been understood before the fulfilment had come?

That is more than doubtful. Indeed it is not even quite clear whether Paul means the words "according to the Scriptures" to refer to the third day at all, and not merely to the central fact of the resurrection itself. At any rate the Scripture passages never could have suggested the third day to the disciples unless something had actually happened on that day to indicate that Christ had then risen.

But had not Jesus Himself predicted that He would rise on the third day, and might not this prediction have caused the disciples to suppose that He had risen on that day even if the first appearance did not occur till long afterwards? This is an obvious way out of the difficulty, but it is effectually closed to the modern naturalistic historian. For it would require us to suppose that Jesus' predictions of His resurrection, recorded in the Gospels, are historical. But the naturalistic historians are usually concerned with few things more than with the denial of the authenticity of these predictions. According to the ordinary "liberal" view, Jesus certainly could not have predicted that He would rise from the dead in the manner recorded in the Gospels. So for the "liberal" historians this explanation of "the third day" becomes impossible. The explanation would perhaps explain "the third day" in the belief of the disciples, but it would also destroy the whole account of the "liberal Jesus".

Accordingly it becomes necessary to seek explanations farther afield. Some have appealed to a supposed belief in antiquity to the effect that the soul of a dead person hovered around the body for three days and then departed. This belief, it is said, might have seemed to the disciples to make it necessary to put the supposed resurrection not later than the third day. But how far did this belief prevail in Palestine in the first century? The question is perhaps not capable of satisfactory answer. Moreover, it is highly dangerous from the point of view of the modern naturalistic historians to appeal to this belief, since it would show that some interest was taken in the body of Jesus; and yet that is what these modern historians are most concerned to deny. For if interest was taken in the body, the old question arises again why the tomb was not investigated. And the whole vision hypothesis breaks down.

Since these explanations have proved unsatisfactory, some modern scholars have had recourse to a fourth explanation. There was in ancient times, they say, a pagan belief about a god who died and rose again. On the first day the worshippers of the god were to mourn, but on the third day they were to rejoice, because of the resurrection of the god. So it is thought that the disciples may have been influenced by this pagan belief. But surely this is a desperate expedient. It is only a very few students of the history of religions who would be quite so bold as to believe that in Palestine, in the time of Christ, there was any prevalence of this pagan belief with its dying and rising god. Indeed the importance and clearness of this belief have been enormously exaggerated in recent works — particularly as regards the rising of the god on the third day.

The truth is that the third day in the primitive account of the resurrection of Christ remains, and that there is no satisfactory means of explaining it away. Indeed some naturalistic historians are actually coming back to the view that perhaps we cannot explain this third day away, and that perhaps something did happen on the third day to produce the faith of the disciples. But if this conclusion be reached, then the whole psychological reconstruction disappears, and particularly the modern hypothesis about the place of the appearances. Something must have happened to produce the disciples' belief in the resurrection not far off in Galilee but near to the tomb in Jerusalem. But if so, there would be no time for the elaborate psychological process which is supposed to have produced the visions, and there would be ample opportunity for the investigation of the tomb.

It is therefore a fact of enormous importance that it is just Paul, in a passage where he is admittedly reproducing the tradition of the primitive Jerusalem Church, who mentions the third day.

Then, after mentioning the third day, Paul gives a detailed account which is not quite complete, of the resurrection appearances. He leaves out the account of the appearances to the women, because he is merely giving the official list of the appearances to the leaders in the Jerusalem church.

So much for the testimony of Paul. This testimony is sufficient of itself to refute the modern naturalistic reconstruction. But it is time to glance briefly at the testimony in the Gospels.

If you take the shortest Gospel, the Gospel according to Mark, you will find, first, that Mark gives an account of the burial, which is of great importance. Modern historians cannot deny that Jesus was buried, because that is attested by the universally accepted source of information, I Corinthians 15. Mark is here confirmed by the Jerusalem tradition as preserved by Paul. But the account of the burial in Mark is followed by the account of the empty tomb, and the two things are indissolubly connected. If one is historical, it is difficult to reject the other. Modern naturalistic historians are in a divided condition about this matter of the empty tomb. Some admit that the tomb was empty. Others deny that it ever was. Some say what we have just outlined — that the tomb was never investigated at all until it was too late, and that then the account of the empty tomb grew up as a legend in the Church. But other historians are clear-sighted enough to see that you cannot get rid of the empty tomb in any such fashion.

But if the tomb was empty, why was it empty? The New Testament says that it was empty because the body of Jesus had been raised out of it. But if this be not the case, then why was the tomb empty? Some say that the enemies of Jesus took the body away. If so, they have done the greatest possible service to the resurrection faith which they so much hated. Others have said that the disciples stole the body away to make the people believe that Jesus was risen. But no one holds that view now.

Others have said that Joseph of Arimathea changed the place of burial. That is difficult to understand, because if such were the case, why should Joseph of Arimathea have kept silence when the resurrection faith arose? Other explanations, no doubt, have been proposed. But it cannot be said that these hypotheses have altogether satisfied even those historians who have proposed them. The empty tomb has never been successfully explained away.

We might go on to consider the other accounts. But I think we have pointed out some of the most important parts of the evidence. The resurrection was of a bodily kind, and appears in connection with the empty tomb. It is quite a misrepresentation of the state of affairs when people talk about "interpreting" the New Testament in accordance with the modern view of natural law as operating in connection with the origin of Christianity. What is really being engaged in is not an interpretation of the New Testament but a complete contradiction of the New Testament at its central point. In order to explain the resurrection faith of the disciples as caused by hallucinations, you must first pick and choose in the sources of information, and reconstruct a statement of the case for which you have no historical information. You must first reconstruct this account, different from that which is given in the only sources of information, before you can even begin to explain the appearances as hallucinations. And even then you are really no better off. It is after all quite preposterous to explain the origin of the Christian Church as being due to pathological experiences of weak-minded men. So mighty a building was not founded upon so small a pin-point.

So the witness of the whole New Testament has not been put out of the way. It alone explains the origin of the Church, and the change of the disciples from weak men into the spiritual conquerors of the world.

Why is it, then, if the evidence be so strong, that so many modern men refuse to accept the New Testament testimony to the resurrection of Christ? The answer is perfectly plain. The resurrection, if it be a fact, is a stupendous miracle and against the miraculous or the supernatural there is a tremendous opposition in the modern mind.

But is the opposition well-grounded? It would perhaps be well-grounded if the direct evidence for the resurrection stood absolutely alone — if it were simply a question whether a man of the first century, otherwise unknown, really rose from the dead. There would in that case be a strong burden of proof against the belief in the resurrection. But as a matter of fact the question is not whether any ordinary man rose from the dead, but whether *Jesus* rose from the dead. We know something of Jesus from the Gospels, and as thus made known He is certainly different from all other men. A man who comes into contact with His tremendous personality will say to himself, "It is impossible that *Jesus* could ever have been holden of death." Thus when the extraordinary testimony to the resurrection faith which has been outlined above comes to us, we add to this our tremendous impression of Jesus' Person, gained from the reading of the Gospels, and we accept this strange belief which comes to us and fills us with joy, that the Redeemer really triumphed over death and the grave and sin.

And if He be living, we come to Him today. And thus finally we add to the direct historical evidence our own Christian experience. If He be a living Saviour, we come to Him for salvation today, and we add to the evidence from the New Testament documents an immediacy of conviction which delivers us from fear. The Christian man should indeed never say, as men often say, "Because of my experience of Christ in my soul I am independent of the basic facts of Christianity; I am independent of the question whether Jesus rose from the grave or not." But Christian experience, though it cannot make us Christians whether Jesus rose or not, still can add to the direct historical evidence a confirming witness that, as a matter of fact, Christ did really rise from the dead on the third day, according to the Scriptures. The "witness of the Spirit" is not, as it is often quite falsely represented today, independent of the Bible; on the contrary it is a witness by the Holy Spirit, who is the author of the Bible, to the fact that the Bible is true.

# VII

# Relations Between Jews and Christians

THE present gathering, as I understand it, is intended to promote a better relationship between Jews and Christians in America and particularly in New York. I have been asked to consider the problem from the point of view of orthodox Christianity, and I regard it as a very high privilege, and also as a very great pleasure, to accede as best I can to the request.

In doing so I might choose either one of two possible methods of approach. In the first place, I might put my best foot forward; I might present first the positive side — I might tell you what I think can actually be done toward the solution of the problem. That method would seem at first sight to be desirable. But as a matter of fact it would be fraught with considerable danger. The concessions which it might seem to involve would almost certainly be misinterpreted and exaggerated, and when in the latter part of my remarks those misinterpretations would be corrected my hearers might have the feeling that they had been unfairly treated, that pleasant words had been used to cloak a really fundamental divergence of opinion.

The danger of misunderstanding always presents itself in discussions like that in which we are engaged tonight; the *suaviter in modo* sometimes obscures the *fortiter in re*. If you will pardon a personal example, I may say that last year I was invited to engage in a discussion at the Rutgers Presbyterian Church of this city with a leader of the Modernist point of view in the Protestant Episcopal Church. A correspondent in one of our Presbyterian Church papers drew rather far-reaching conclusions from

the meeting.    He was delighted with it, he said in effect; these
two gentlemen did not call each other names; and thus it became
evident that conservatives and Modernists in the Church could
stand on common ground after all.    Now is that not absurd?    The
meeting between this man and myself was, I trust, a courteous
one; but its courtesy did not at all obscure the fact that in my opinion he is a vigorous opponent of the Christian religion and that
there is in the religious sphere absolutely no common ground between us.    We are fellow-citizens, and I trust that when we discuss serious questions we can be courteous to each other, but
"brethren" in the religious sense we certainly are not.

The fact is that in discussing matters about which there are differences of opinion it is really more courteous to be frank — more
courteous with that deeper courtesy which is based upon the
Golden Rule.    For my part, I am bound to say that the kind of
discussion which is irritating to me is the discussion which begins
by begging the question and then pretends to be in the interests
of peace.    I should be guilty of such a method if I should say to
a Roman Catholic, for example, that we can come together with
him because forms and ceremonies like the mass and membership in a certain definite organization are of course matters of
secondary importance — if I should say to him that he can go
on being a good Catholic and I can go on geing a good Protestant and yet we can unite on a common Christian basis. If I
should talk in that way I should show myself guilty of the crassest narrowness of mind, for I should be showing that I had never
taken the slightest trouble to understand the Roman Catholic point
of view.    If I had taken that trouble I should have come to see
plainly that what I should be doing is not to seek common ground
between the Roman Catholic and myself but simply to ask the
Roman Catholic to become a Protestant and give up everything
that he holds most dear.

It is a similar begging of the question when the Modernist
preachers represent themselves as speaking in the interests of

peace. "Let us," they say in effect, "recognize the right both of conservatives and of Liberals in the Church; let us not allow doctrinal differences to separate us, for doctrine after all is simply the necessarily changing expression of Christian experience and various doctrines will find their unity if they only be translated back into the experience from which they came." The man who speaks in that way is, it seems to me, guilty of a really astonishing narrowness of mind. For he has simply begged the whole question, and has shown that he has never given himself any trouble to understand the other man's point of view. Of course if doctrine is merely the necessarily changing expression of experience, then the whole debate is ended; but it is ended not by a compromise but a complete victory for the Modernist and a complete relinquishment by us of everything that we hold most dear.

The very center and core of our faith is the conviction that instead of doctrine springing from life, life springs from doctrine; that doctrine is not the necessarily changing expression of experience — that seems to us to be simply the most abysmal skepticism — but, on the contrary, the setting forth of those facts upon which experience is based — facts which are facts now, which are facts not only for us but for whatever demons there may be in hell, and which will remain facts beyond the end of time. It is not necessarily narrow-minded to combat that view of ours. It is, I think, wrong; but it is not necessarily narrow-minded. But what is narrow-minded is to combat that view and then represent oneself as speaking, not in defense of one's own opposing view, but in the interest of peace. For that simply shows that one has not given oneself the trouble to understand one's opponent's point of view.

So to my mind the most inauspicious beginning for any discussion is found when the speaker utters the familiar words: "I think, brethren, that we are all agreed about this. . ." and then proceeds to trample ruthlessly upon the things that are dearest to my heart. Far more kindly is it if the speaker says at the start that he sees a miserable narrow-minded conservative in the audience whose views he intends to ridicule and refute. After such a speaker gets through perhaps I may be allowed to say that I regard him as just as narrow-minded as he regards me, and then having both spoken our full mind we may part, certainly not as brothers (it is ridiculous to degrade that word) but at least as friends.

Accordingly I am going to put what may seem to be my *worst* foot forward, and speak first of those things about which agreement with a part of you at least cannot possibly be attained. It is better to speak of those things first in order that the conditions of the problem may be known at the start.

In the first place, then, let me say that Christianity as we hold it begins with the most thoroughgoing pessimism that could possibly be imagined. I was almost amused a short time ago in reading in the *Atlantic Monthly* an article by Dr. Gordon of the Old South Church in Boston which held that, although many things formerly connected with Christianity have been given up, we are still Christians because we hold an optimistic view of the future of the human race. As a matter of fact not optimism but the deepest pessimism is the starting point of Christianity. It is paganism which finds hope in the development of the resources of man; whereas Christianity is the religion of the broken heart. Paganism finds popular expression in sermons like a recent one of Dr. Fosdick the burden of which was that a central article of our creed should be the clause, "I believe in man." In one sense indeed Christians "believe in man." They believe in the reality of man's soul, as over against the materialistic psychology of our day. But that belief in the reality of the soul leads of itself not to hope but to the greater despair; it is a terrible belief; it means that the soul of man is capable of falling into depths which otherwise could not be conceived. A stick or stone cannot be "lost" in the Christian sense, but the soul of man, just because it exists, can be lost and is lost indeed. How terrible a thing is the true Christian belief in the soul of man! How totally different at any rate from the pagan optimism which masquerades under the name of Christianity today! "I believe in man" — that is paganism. "Strait is the gate and narrow the way that leadeth unto life, and few there be that find it," "There is none righteous, no not one," "All sinned and came short of the glory of God" — that is Christianity.

There are some phenomena of the present day which seem to support this Christian doctrine of sin and guilt. There was a time a few years ago when to the superficial observer all might have seemed to be going well. But now our complacency has been destroyed and we are facing elemental depths. I am not referring merely to the war or to the orgy of vindictive cruelty which has followed upon the alleged "peace" of Versailles. But I am referring rather to the appalling intellectual as well as moral decadence which was going on before the war began and which is enormously hastened today. When one contemplates the decadence of our age, the lamentable growth of ignorance, the breakdown of education, the absence of great men, the silence of true poetry, one ceases to be much impressed with the corresponding advance in the material realm. We have improved the means of communication but in doing so we have ceased to have anything to say. We have the radio, but what is broadcasted through it is rather pitiable stuff. Strange indeed is the complaceny of such an age.

But the true grounds for holding the Christian doctrine of sin are far deeper than all that — they lie in the terrible law revealed in the Bible and most terribly of all in Jesus, and they lie in the confirmation of that law in the depths of our own souls. A man who has never been under the conviction of sin — not the sins of other people but his own sin — can never even begin to understand what the Christian man feels. At the very basis of Christianity is the cry "Woe is me" and woe to a lost and sinful world.

But that is not the end of Christianity but its beginning. For the darkness has been lightened by a radiance of divine light. It has been lightened by the coming of our Lord. Nineteen hundred years ago, the Christian holds, a strong Saviour came from the outside into this sinful world and led mankind out from Egyptian bondage into a land of freedom and hope. It was done not by a discovery but by an act; not by an influence brought to bear upon man, but by a change in the relationship between man and God. We were under God's just wrath and curse: the Lord Jesus took upon Himself the curse and set us free. But how pitiful are my words! I despair of letting you see how we Christians *feel,* how we hang with all our hearts upon just the thing that other men despise, how we abhor any subjectivizing of the work of Christ, how we depend above all just upon the fact that Christ has done not merely something *in* us but something *for* us when he died for us upon the Cross and made all well between us and the holy God. What a mystery it is — and how simple to the man who believes!

It is that sheer objectivity of our salvation, that sheer factual basis of our religion, which the Modernist preachers cannot understand, and because they cannot understand wound us yet more and more by every reference that they make to the cross of Christ. Christianity, we hold, is rooted not in something that was discovered, but in something that *happened* when the Lord Jesus died for our sins and rose again for our justification.

The narration of that happening constitutes the "gospel," the good news, which puts a new face on life. Without it the world is dark, and particularly dark is the awful God whom Jesus bade men to fear. But when the gospel comes into a man's heart, then for him, despite the blackness of his former despair, there is naught but light — light and yet more glorious light. Can you not put yourselves for a moment into our place? Can you not understand how inexpressibly grieved and hurt we are when a preacher not outside but within our Church pours out the vials of his scorn upon this thing to which we cling with all the energy of our souls?

But however the sheer factual basis of our religion may be misunderstood now, it was not misunderstood in the first days. At the center of early Christianity were the words "Christ died for our sins according to the Scriptures, he was buried, he rose again the third day according to the Scriptures." That was the gospel, "the good news." And when it was heard, and was accepted and received in faith, then there was life. Without it, all was lost in the blackness of sin; with it, when it was received by faith and used by the regenerating power of the Spirit, all was shouting and joy for time and for eternity.

Such was Christianity then and such is Christianity, we hold, now. But then as now it was offensive to the world. The offense was found not at all in the fact that a new Saviour was offered to the attention of men. Then as now the world was looking for new saviours and welcomed them when they came. But the offense came because this Saviour was offered as the one and only Saviour. Without Him every single man, no matter what his relative goodness, and no matter what his achievements and what his pride, was represented as lost forever under the wrath of God. With Him alone, the early Christians held, there was life. The offense of Christianity was found in the universality and exclusiveness of its appeal. Without that exclusiveness, the Christians would have been honored by the Roman world; because of it, and because of it alone, they suffered and died.

Similar is the case today. The offense of Christianity is still found in the universality and exclusiveness of its appeal. Christians would be welcomed no doubt as the benefactors of the race if they would only acquiesce in the proposal of "Nathan der Weise" — if they would only allow Judaism, Mohammedanism, and Christianity to live peacefully side by side, each contributing its necessary quota to the welfare of humanity. But be perfectly clear about one thing — Christianity, if it ever accedes to such a program, has ceased to be Christian at all.

Here no doubt, you will say, is the chief obstacle which orthodox Christianity (or as we would say all Christianity that is really Christian) opposes to the purposes aimed at by your group. And we do not think that the obstacle can be dodged. The plain fact is that we Christians regard all of you who are not Christians as lost under the guilt of sin. And since we regard you thus, what do you expect us to do? Do you expect us to promise that we will avoid proselytizing? Do you not see that such a promise would involve, from our point of view, the most awful bloodguiltiness of which a man could ever possibly be guilty? Do you not see that holding the view that we hold — a view that is at the very root of the Christian religion — we cannot possibly avoid proselytizing, but must say, "Woe is me, no matter in whose presence I am, if I preach not the gospel"? Do you not see that, holding the view which we hold, we should, if we ceased to proselytize among you, be not kind and considerate but guilty of the most heartless neglect that could possibly be conceived?

No, it is perfectly clear, I think, that "Nathan der Weise" cannot help us at all tonight. Our religion makes an absolutely universal appeal and it refuses to stop short at the bounds of the people that we regard as the chosen people of God, from whom all our joy and all our salvation came. We look for real unity only when you as well as we have been saved by the one Saviour of all.

But meanwhile what can be done? Can we respect each other even without such a consummation which you indeed expect never to come? Can we help each other in certain of the affairs of life? I think that we can.

First we can help each other in the promotion of tolerance. But what do we mean by tolerance, and what do we mean by intolerance? We mean almost exactly the reverse of what often seems to be meant by these terms today. Thus it is often held that the Presbyterian Church is guilty of intolerance if it excludes a heretical minister. To me on the other hand the real intolerance seems to be found in those who would deny the right of the Church to exclude him. Let us look at the thing in its simplest terms. Here is a group of people who believe that the greatest thing in the world is to proclaim a way of salvation, a system of "doctrine," if you will, that is summarized in the Westminster Confession. For mutual help they come together in a body called the Presbyterian Church. The real question is whether they are to be allowed to do so. No doubt the purpose of their organization, which is set forth as plain as day in their constitution, seems to be very foolish to many. It seems so very foolish, that they can hardly grant such a foolish organization the right to exist. So to prevent its existence they regard themselves as justified in doing what they would never do in any other sphere of life: they regard themselves as justified in making the necessary subscription with a mental reservation which completely reverses its meaning, in order that the character of the organization may then, when they have entered into it, be changed. Is that tolerance? Surely not. Surely it is on the contrary intolerance of the crassest kind. It is intolerance because it is based upon the denial of that right of voluntary association which is at the very basis of liberty. A creedal church seems foolish to the Modernist preachers, but if they are really tolerant they will recognize its right in a free country to exist and to maintain its existence by insisting that its accredited representatives shall not combat its fundamental purpose from within. We who insist upon honesty in creed-subscription are really insisting not merely upon honesty but also upon the central principles of freedom.

But such right of voluntary association — voluntary association even for purposes which to other persons seem foolish and absurd — is possible only where there is tolerance on the part of the State. There is a fundamental distinction between an involuntary organization like the State, an organization to which a man must belong

114 What Is Christianity?

whether he will or no, and a purely voluntary organization like the Church. It is absolutely no interference with liberty for the Church to insist upon one type of teaching on the part of its accredited representatives who are speaking not merely with their own authority but with the authority of the Church. For if a man does not agree with that type of teaching he can seek another platform in which he can really speak his full mind. How absurd it is, then, to say that the Presbyterian Church, for example, is trying to "silence" certain men! Surely it is doing nothing of the kind. Surely it is merely seeking to avoid the dishonesty of allowing a creedal Church to carry on a propaganda which is the very opposite of that for which the Church exists. I suppose I have an old-fashioned view of the moral law; but I am bound to say that I do not think that plain honesty of speech ought to stop at the Church door.

But entirely different is an involuntary association like the State. For the State to force any one type of teaching upon its citizens, or upon the children of its citizens, is the crassest tyranny. Within the State there should be tolerance, or liberty is at an end.

Tolerance, moreover, means not merely tolerance for that with which we are agreed but also tolerance for that to which we are most thoroughly opposed. A few years ago there was passed in New York the abominable Lusk Law requiring private teachers in any subjects whatever to obtain a state license. It was aimed, I believe, at the Socialists, and primarily at the Rand School in New York City. Now certainly I have no sympathy with Socialism. Because of its hostility to freedom it seems to me to be just about the darkest thought that has ever entered the mind of man. But certainly such opposition to Socialism did not temper in the slightest degree my opposition to that preposterous law. Tolerance, to me, does not mean merely tolerance for what I hold to be good, but also tolerance for what I hold to be abominably bad.

The attack upon tolerance in America is appearing most clearly in the sphere of education. The Oregon school law, it is true, with its provision that children should be taken by brute force from their parents and delivered over to the tender mercies of whatever superintendent of education happens to be in power in the district where they reside, will probably be declared unconstitutional by the Supreme Court. And the Nebraska language law, which made literary education a crime was thrown out by the same tribunal. But the same ends may well be accomplished by indirect means, and if the Sterling-Reed Bill is passed by Congress we shall have sooner or later that uniformity of education under the control of the state which is the worst calamity into which any nation can fall.

Against such tyranny, I do cherish some hope that Jews and Christians, Roman Catholics and Protestants, if they be lovers of liberty, may present a united front. I am for my part an inveterate propagandist; but the same right of propaganda which I desire for myself I want to see also in the possession of others. What absurdities are uttered in the name of a pseudo-Americanism today! People object to the Roman Catholics, for example, because they engage in "propaganda." But why should they not engage in propaganda? And how could we have any respect for them, if holding the view which they do hold, that outside of the Roman Church there is no salvation, they did not engage in propaganda first, last and all the time. Clearly they have a right to do so, and clearly we have a right to do the same.

But in insisting upon the right of unlimited proselytizing, we hope that we shall not throw all discretion to the winds. Certainly in trying to convert other people we do not mean that we are ourselves setting up to be better than they. On the contrary we are doing exactly the opposite. It is just because we are so conscious of our own unworthiness that we are unable to satisfy ourselves with the skeptical view that Christianity is a life and not a doctrine. It is just because we are not able to stand upon the basis of our lives before God, or, to use a figure proper to the present moment, upon our "record," that we cling to the gospel of Christ and try to bring to others the joy that that has brought to us.

Does that mean then that we must eternally bite and devour one another, that acrimonious debate must never for a moment be allowed to cease? We do not think that it does. But how can it help doing so? We Christians think that you — as we should be ourselves — are lost and hopeless without Christ. How then shall we live with you in peace and avoid making ourselves insufferable by constant arguments and appeals?

There is a common solution of the problem which we think ought to be taken to heart. It is the solution provided by family life. In countless families, there is a Christian parent who with untold agony of soul has seen the barrier of religious difference set up between himself or herself and a beloved child. Salvation, it is believed with all the heart, comes only through Christ, and the child, it is believed, unless it has really trusted in Christ is lost. These, I tell you, are the real tragedies of life. And how trifling, in comparison, is the experience of bereavement or the like! But what do these sorrowing parents do? Do they make themselves uselessly a nuisance to their child? In countless cases they do not; in countless such cases there is hardly a mention of the subject of religion; in countless cases there is nothing but prayer, and an agony of soul bravely covered by helpfulness and cheer.

There is the solution of the problem presented by the inveterately proselytizing tendency of Christianity. It is a solution which I admit in the larger sphere about which we are talking tonight, is only very, very imperfectly tried. But if it were tried it would work. The problem is very difficult. But love would find a way.

VIII

# Christian Scholarship and Evangelism

I T SEEMS to me, as I stand here before you to-day, that there is
one blessing in these days of defection and unbelief which we
have come to value as we never valued it before. That is the blessing of Christian fellowship in the presence of a hostile world, and
in the presence of a visible Church which too often has departed
from the Word of God. To-day, during the three meetings of this
League, in the portion of the meetings which has been allotted to
me, I am to have the privilege of delivering three addresses on
the subject, "The Importance of Christian Scholarship."

It is no doubt unfortunate that the person who speaks about
this subject should have so limited an experimental acquaintance
with the subject about which he is endeavouring to speak; but in
these days of anti-intellectualism you may be willing to hear a
word in defence of the intellect, even from one whose qualifications for speaking on that subject are so limited as mine.

There was a time when the raising of the question as to the
importance of Christian scholarship might have seemed to be
ridiculous; there was a time when a man who does so much talking as a minister or a Sunday School teacher does, and as no
doubt every Christian ought to do, in the propagation of the Faith
to which he adheres, would have regarded it as a matter of course
that he ought to know something about the subject of which he
undertakes to talk.

But in recent years we have got far beyond all such elementary
considerations as that; modern pedagogy has emancipated us,
whether we be in the pulpit or in the professor's chair or in the

117

pew, from anything so irksome as earnest labour in the acquisition of knowledge.   It never seems to occur to many modern teachers that the primary business of the teacher is to study the subject that he is going to teach.  Instead of studying the subject that he is going to teach, he studies "education"; a knowledge of the methodology of teaching takes the place of a knowledge of the particular branch of literature, history or science to which a man has devoted his life.

This substitution of methodology for content in the preparation of the teacher is based upon a particular view of what education is.  It is based upon the view that education consists primarily, not in the imparting of information, but in a training of the faculties of the child; that the business of the teacher is not to teach, but to develop in the child a faculty which will enable the child to learn.

This child-centered notion of education seems to involve emancipation from a vast amount of drudgery.  It used to be thought necessary to do some hard work at school.  When a textbook was given to a class, it was expected that the contents of the textbook should be mastered.  But now all that has been changed.  Storing up facts in the mind was a long and painful process, and it is indeed comforting to know that we can now do without it.  Away with all drudgery and all hard work!  Self-expression has taken their place.  A great pedagogic discovery has been made—the discovery that it is possible to think with a completely empty mind.

It cannot be said that the results of the discovery are impressive. This child-centered notion of education has resulted, particularly in America, where it has been most ruthlessly applied, in a boundless superficiality of which we Americans certainly have little reason to be proud; but it has probably not been confined to America by any means.  I wonder when the reaction will come. I wonder when we shall have that revival of learning which we so much need, and which I verily believe might be, in the providence of God, as was the Renaissance of the fifteenth century, the precursor of a Reformation in the Church. When that revival of learning comes, we may be sure that it will sweep away the present absurd over-emphasis upon methodology in teaching at the expense of content. We shall never have a true revival of learning until teachers turn their attention away from the mere mental processes of the child, out into the marvelous richness and variety of the universe and of human life. Not teachers who have studied the methodology of teaching, but teachers who are on fire with a love of the subjects that they are going to teach are the real torch-bearers of intellectual advance.

Certainly the present view of education is, when it is applied to the work of the preacher and of the teacher in the Church, sceptical to the core. It is summed up in what is called "religious education." I wonder sometimes at the readiness with which Christian people — I do not mean Church-members, but real Bible-believing Christians — use that term; for the ordinary implications of the term are quite opposed to the Christian religion. The fundamental notion underlying the ordinary use of the term "religious education" is that the business of the teacher in the Church is not to impart knowledge of a fixed body of truth which God has revealed, but to train the religious faculty of the child. The religious faculty of the child, it is supposed, may be trained by the use of the most widely diverse doctrinal content; it may be trained in this generation, perhaps, by the thought of a personal God; but in another generation it may be trained equally well by the thought of an ideal humanity as the only God there is. Thus the search for objective and permanent truth is given up, and instead we have turned our attention to the religious faculties of man. In other words men have become interested to-day in religion because they have ceased to believe in God.

As over against such scepticism, the Bible, from Genesis to Revelation, presents a body of truth which God has revealed; and if we hold the Biblical view, we shall regard it as our supreme function, as teachers and as preachers and as Christian parents and as simple Christians, to impart a knowledge of that body of truth. The Christian preacher, we shall hold, needs above all to know the thing that he is endeavouring to preach.

But if knowledge is necessary to preaching, it does seem probable that the fuller the knowledge is, the better the preacher will be able to do his work. Underlying preaching, in other words, is Christian scholarship; and it is in defence of Christian scholarship that I have thought it might be fitting to say a few words to you to-day.

Christian scholarship is necessary to the preacher, and to the man who in whatever way, in public or in private, endeavours to proclaim the gospel to his fellow-men, in at least three ways.

In the first place, it is necessary for evangelism. In saying so, I am perfectly well aware of the fact that I am putting myself squarely in conflict with a method of religious work which is widely prevalent at the present time. Knowledge, the advocates of that method seem to think, is quite unnecessary to faith; at the beginning a man may be a Fundamentalist or a Modernist, he may hold a Christian or an anti-Christian view of Christ. Never mind; he is to be received, quite apart from his opinions, on the basis of simple faith. Afterwards, indeed, he will, if he has really been converted, read his Bible and come to a more and more correct view of Christ and of the meaning of Christ's death. If he does not come to a more and more correct view, one may perhaps suspect that his conversion was not a real one after all. But at the beginning all that is thought to be unnecessary. All that a man has to believe in at the beginning is conversion: he is saved on the basis of simple faith; correct opinions about God and Christ come later.

With regard to this method, it may of course be said at once that the "simple faith" thus spoken of is not faith at all; or, rather, it is not faith in Christ. A man cannot trust a person whom he holds to be untrustworthy. Faith always contains an intellectual element. A very little knowledge is often sufficient if a man is to believe, but some knowledge there must be. So if a man is to trust Christ he must know something about Christ; he may know only a very little, but without some knowledge he could not believe at all.

What these advocates of a "simple faith" which involves no knowledge of Christ really mean by "simple faith" is faith, perhaps; but it is not faith in Christ. It is faith in the practitioners of the method; but it is not faith in Christ. To have faith in Christ one must have knowledge of Christ, however slight; and it is not a matter of indifference whether the opinions held about Christ are true or false.

But is this modern anti-intellectualistic view of faith in accordance with the New Testament? Does the New Testament offer a man salvation first, on the basis of a psychological process of conversion or surrender — falsely called faith — and then preach the gospel to him afterwards; or does the New Testament preach the gospel to him first, set forth to him first the facts about Christ and the meaning of His death, and then ask him to accept the One thus presented in order that his soul may be saved?

That question can be answered very simply by an examination of the examples of conversion which the New Testament contains.

Three thousand were converted on the day of Pentecost. They were converted by Peter's sermon. What did Peter's sermon contain? Did it contain merely an account of Peter's own experience of salvation; did it consist solely in exhortation to the people to confess their sins? Not at all. What Peter did on the day of Pentecost was to set forth the facts about Jesus Christ — His life, His miracles, His death, His resurrection. It was on the basis of that setting forth of the facts about Christ that the three thousand believed, confessed their sins, and were saved.

Paul and Silas were in prison one night at Philippi. There was a miracle: the prisoners were released. The gaoler was impressed and said, "What must I do to be saved?" Paul and Silas said;

"Believe on the Lord Jesus Christ, and thou shalt be saved." Did the gaoler believe then and there; was he saved without further delay? I think not. We are expressly told that Paul and Silas, after that, "spake unto him the word of the Lord." Then and not till then was he baptized, and I think we are plainly to understand that then and not till then was he saved.

Our Saviour sat one day by the well. He talked with a sinful woman, and laid his finger upon the sore spot in her life. "Thou hast had five husbands," he said; "and he whom thou now hast is not thy husband." The woman then apparently sought to evade the consideration of the sin in her own life by asking a theological question regarding the right place in which to worship God. What did Jesus do with her theological question? Did he brush it aside after the manner of modern religious workers? Did he say to the woman: "You are evading the real question; do not trouble yourself about theological matters, but let us return to the consideration of the sin in your life." Not at all. He answered that theological question with the utmost fulness as though the salvation of the woman's soul depended on her obtaining the right answer. In reply to that sinful woman, and to what modern religious workers would have regarded as an evasive question, Jesus engaged in some of the profoundest theological teaching in the whole New Testament. A right view of God, according to Jesus, is not something that comes merely after salvation, but it is something important for salvation.

The Apostle Paul in the First Epistle to the Thessalonians gives a precious summary of his missionary preaching. He does so by telling what it was to which the Thessalonians turned when they were saved. Was it a mere programme of life to which they turned? Was it a "simple faith," in the modern sense which divorces faith from knowledge and supposes that a man can have "simple faith" in a person of whom he knows nothing or about whom he holds opinions that make faith in him absurd? Not at all. In turning to Christ those Thessalonian Christians turned to a whole system of theology. "Ye turned to God from idols," says Paul, "to serve the living and true God; and to wait for His Son from heaven, whom He raised from the dead, even Jesus, which delivereth us from the wrath to come." "Ye turned to God from idols" — there is theology proper. "And to wait for His Son from heaven" — there is Christology. "Whom He raised from the dead" — there is the supernatural act of God in history. "Even Jesus" — there is the humanity of our Lord. "Which delivereth us from the wrath to come" — there is the Christian doctrine of sin and the Christian doctrine of the Cross of Christ. So it is in the New Testament from beginning to end. The examples might be multiplied indefinitely. The New Testament gives not one bit of comfort to those who separate faith from knowledge, to those who hold the absurd view that a man can trust a person about whom he knows nothing. What many men despise to-day as "doctrine" the New Testament calls the gospel; and the New Testament treats it as the message upon which salvation depends.

But if that be so, if salvation depends upon the message in which Christ is offered as Saviour, it is obviously important that we should get the message straight. That is where Christian scholarship comes in. Christian scholarship is important in order that we may tell the story of Jesus and His love straight and full and plain.

At this point, indeed, an objection may arise. Is not the gospel a very simple thing, it may be asked; and will not its simplicity be obscured by too much scholarly research? The objection springs from a false view of what scholarship is; it springs from the notion that scholarship leads a man to be obscure. Exactly the reverse is the case. Ignorance is obscure; but scholarship brings order out of confusion, places things in their logical relations, and makes the message shine forth clearly.

There are, indeed, evangelists who are not scholars, but scholarship is necessary to evangelism all the same. In the first place,

124 What Is Christianity?

though there are evangelists who are not scholars, the greatest
evangelists, like the Apostle Paul and like Martin Luther, have
been scholars. In the second place, the evangelists who are not
scholars are dependent upon scholars to help them get their message straight; it is out of a great underlying fund of Christian
learning that true evangelism springs.

That is something that the Church of our day needs to take to
heart. Life, according to the New Testament, is founded upon
truth; and the attempt to reverse the order results only in despair
and in spiritual death. Let us not deceive ourselves, my friends.
Christian experience is necessary to evangelism; but evangelism
does not consist merely in the rehearsal of what has happened in
the evangelist's own soul. We shall, indeed, be but poor witnesses
for Christ if we can tell only what Christ has done for the world
or for the Church and cannot tell what He has done personally
for us. But we shall also be poor witnesses if we recount only
the experiences of our own lives. Christian evangelism does not
consist merely in a man's going about the world saying: "Look at
me, what a wonderful experience I have, how happy I am, what
wonderful Christian virtues I exhibit; you can all be as good and
as happy as I am if you will just make a complete surrender of
your wills in obedience to what I say." That is what many religious workers seem to think that evangelism is. We can preach
the gospel, they tell us, by our lives, and do not need to preach it
by our words. But they are wrong. Men are not saved by the
exhibition of our glorious Christian virtues; they are not saved
by the contagion of our experiences. We cannot be the instruments of God in saving them if we preach to them thus only ourselves. Nay, we must preach to them the Lord Jesus Christ; for
it is only through the gospel which sets Him forth that they can
be saved.

If you want health for your souls, and if you want to be the
instruments of bringing health to others, do not turn your gaze
forever within, as though you could find Christ there. Nay, turn

your gaze away from your own miserable experiences, away from your own sin, to the Lord Jesus Christ as He is offered to us in the gospel. "As Moses lifted up the serpent in the wilderness, even so must the Son of Man be lifted up." Only when we turn away from ourselves to that uplifted Saviour shall we have healing for our deadly hurt.

It is the same old story, my friends — the same old story of the natural man. Men are trying to-day, as they have always been trying, to save themselves — to save themselves by their own act of surrender, by the excellence of their own faith, by mystic experiences of their own lives. But it is all in vain. Not that way is peace with God to be obtained. It is to be obtained only in the old, old way — by attention to something that was done once for all long ago, and by acceptance of the living Saviour who there, once for all, brought redemption for our sin. Oh, that men would turn for salvation from their own experience to the Cross of Christ; oh, that they would turn from the phenomena of religion to the living God!

That that may be done, there is but one way. It is not found in a study of the psychology of religion; it is not found in "religious education"; it is not found in an analysis of one's own spiritual status. Oh, no. It is found only in the blessed written Word. There are the words of life. There God speaks. Let us attend to His voice. Let us above all things know the Word. Let us study it with all our minds, let us cherish it with all our hearts. Then let us try, very humbly, to bring it to the unsaved. Let us pray that God may honour not the messengers but the message, that despite our unworthiness He may make His Word upon our unworthy lips to be a message of life.

# IX

# Christian Scholarship and the Defence of the Faith

I N SPEAKING of Christian scholarship before the Bible League, I am somewhat in the position of bringing coals to Newcastle, but perhaps you will take what I am saying as being an expression of hearty agreement with that scholarly work which your League has been carrying on so successfully for many years. This morning we considered the importance of Christian scholarship for evangelism. The gospel message, we observed, is not brought to a man after salvation has already been received, but it is brought to him in order that salvation may be received; and the fuller and plainer the message is, so much the more effective is it for the saving of souls.

But Christian scholarship is also necessary, in the second place, for the defence of the faith, and to this aspect of the subject I invite your attention this afternoon. There are, indeed, those who tell us that no defence of the faith is necessary. "The Bible needs no defence," they say; "let us not be forever defending Christianity, but instead let us go forth joyously to propagate Christianity." But I have observed one curious fact — when men talk thus about propagating Christianity without defending it, the thing that they are propagating is pretty sure not to be Christianity at all. They are propagating an anti-intellectualistic, non-doctrinal Modernism; and the reason why it requires no defence is simply that it is so completely in accord with the current of the age. It causes no more disturbance than does a chip that floats downward with a stream. In order to be an adherent of it, a man does not need to resist anything at all; he needs only to drift, and automatically his Modernism will be of the most approved and popular kind. One thing need always be remembered in the Christian Church — true Christianity, now as always, is radically contrary to the natural man, and it cannot possibly be maintained without a constant struggle. A chip that floats downwards with the current is always at peace; but around every rock the waters foam and rage. Show me a professing Christian of whom all men speak well, and I will show you a man who is probably unfaithful to His Lord.

Certainly a Christianity that avoids argument is not the Christianity of the New Testament. The New Testament is full of argument in defence of the faith. The Epistles of Paul are full of argument — no one can doubt that. But even the words of Jesus are full of argument in defence of the truth of what Jesus was saying. "If ye then, being evil, know how to give good gifts unto your children, how much more shall your Father which is in heaven give good things to them that ask him?" Is not that a well-known form of reasoning, which the logicians would put in its proper category? Many of the parables of Jesus are argumentative in character. Even our Lord, who spoke in the plenitude of divine authority, did condescend to reason with men. Everywhere the New Testament meets objections fairly, and presents the gospel as a thoroughly reasonable thing.

Some years ago I was in a company of students who were discussing methods of Christian work. An older man, who had had much experience in working among students, arose and said that according to his experience you never win a man to Christ until you stop arguing with him. When he said that, I was not impressed.

It is perfectly true, of course, that argument alone is quite insufficient to make a man a Christian. You may argue with him from now until the end of the world; you may bring forth the most magnificent arguments: but all will be in vain unless there be one other thing — the mysterious, creative power of the Holy

Spirit in the new birth. But because argument is insufficient, it does not follow that it is unnecessary. Sometimes it is used directly by the Holy Spirit to bring a man to Christ. But more frequently it is used indirectly. A man hears an answer to objections raised against the truth of the Christian religion; and at the time when he hears it he is not impressed. But afterwards, perhaps many years afterwards, his heart at last is touched: he is convicted of sin; he desires to be saved. Yet without that half-forgotten argument he could not believe; the gospel would not seem to him to be true, and he would remain in his sin. As it is, however, the thought of what he has heard long ago comes into his mind; Christian apologetics at last has its day; the way is open, and when he will believe he can believe because he has been made to see that believing is not an offence against truth.

Sometimes, when I have tried — very imperfectly, I confess — to present arguments in defence of the resurrection of our Lord or of the truth, at this point or that, of God's Word, someone has come up to me after the lecture and has said to me very kindly: "We liked it, and we are impressed with the considerations that you have adduced in defence of the faith; but, the trouble is, we all believed in the Bible already, and the persons that really needed the lecture are not here." When someone tells me that, I am not very greatly disturbed. True, I should have liked to have just as many sceptics as possible at my lecture; but if they are not there I do not necessarily think that my efforts are all in vain. What I am trying to do by my apologetic lecture is not merely — perhaps not even primarily — to convince people who are opposed to the Christian religion. Rather am I trying to give to Christian people — Christian parents or Sunday School teachers — materials that they can use, not in dealing with avowed sceptics, whose backs are up against Christianity, but in dealing with their own children or with the pupils in their classes, who love them, and long to be Christians as they are, but are troubled by the hostile voices on every side.

It is but a narrow view of Christian apologetics that regards the defence of the faith as being useful only in the immediate winning of those who are arguing vigorously on the other side. Rather is it useful most of all in producing an intellectual atmosphere in which the acceptance of the gospel will seem to be something other than an offence against truth. Charles Spurgeon and D. L. Moody, in the latter years of the nineteenth century, were facing a situation entirely different from that which faces the evangelists of today. They were facing a world in which many people in their youth had been imbued with Christian convictions, and in which public opinion, to a very considerable extent, was in favour of the Christian faith. To-day, on the other hand, public opinion even in England and America, is predominantly opposed to the Christian faith, and the people from their youth are imbued with the notion that Christian convictions are antiquated and absurd. Never was there a stronger call of God than there is to-day for a vigorous and scholarly defence of the faith.

I believe that the more thoughtful of the evangelists are coming to recognize that fact. There was a time, twenty-five or thirty years ago, when the evangelists regarded the work of Christian apologists as either impious or a waste of time. Here are souls to be saved, they said; and professors in theological seminaries insist on confusing their students' minds with a lot of German names, instead of preaching the simple gospel of Christ. But to-day a different temper often prevails. Evangelists, if they be real evangelists, real proclaimers of the unpopular message that the Bible contains, are coming more and more to see that they cannot do without those despised theological professors after all. It is useless to proclaim a gospel that people cannot hold to be true: no amount of emotional appeal can do anything against the truth. The question of fact cannot permanently be evaded. Did Christ or did He not rise from the dead; is the Bible trustworthy or is it false? In other words, the twelfth chapter of I Corinthians is coming again to its rights. We are coming to understand how

many-sided is the work of Christ; the eye is ceasing to "say to the
hand, 'I have no need of thee.' " Certainly one thing is clear —
if Christian apologetics suffers, injury will come to every member
of the body of Christ.

But if we are to have Christian apologetics, if we are to have
a defence of the faith, what kind of defence of the faith should it
be?

In the first place, it should be directed not only against the opponents outside the Church but also against the opponents within.
The opponents of Holy Scripture do not become less dangerous,
but they become far more dangerous, when they are within ecclesiastical walls.

At that point, I am well aware that widespread objection arises
at the present time. Let us above all, men say, have no controversy in the Church; let us forget our small theological differences
and all repeat together Paul's hymn to Christian love. As I listen to such pleas, my Christian friends, I think I can detect in
them rather plainly the voice of Satan. That voice is heard, sometimes, on the lips of good and truly Christian men, as at Caesarea
Philippi it was heard on the lips of the greatest of the Twelve.
But Satan's voice it is, all the same.

Sometimes it comes to us in rather deceptive ways.

I remember, for example, what was said in my hearing on one
occasion, by a man who is generally regarded as one of the leaders
of the evangelical Christian Church. It was said at the climax of
a day of devotional services. "If you go heresy-hunting for the
sin in your own wicked hearts," said the speaker, as nearly as I
can remember his words, "you will have no time for heresy-
hunting for the heretics outside."

Thus did temptation come through the mouth of a well-meaning
man. The "heretics," to use the term that was used by that
speaker, are, with their helpers, the indifferentists, in control of
the church within the bounds of which that utterance was made,
the Presbyterian Church in the United States of America, as they

are in control of nearly all the larger Protestant churches in the world. A man hardly needs to "hunt" them very long if he is to oppose them. All that he needs to do is to be faithful to the Lord Jesus Christ, and his opposition to those men will follow soon enough.

But is it true, as this speaker seemed to imply, that there is a conflict between faithfulness to Christ in the ecclesiastical world and the cultivation of holiness in one's own inner life? My friends, it is not true, but false, A man cannot successfully go heresy-hunting against the sin in his own life if he is willing to deny His Lord in the presence of the enemies outside. The two battles are intimately connected. A man cannot fight successfully in one unless he fights also in the other.

Again, we are told that our theological differences will disappear if we will just get down on our knees together in prayer. Well, I can only say about that kind of prayer, which is indifferent to the question whether the gospel is true or false, that it is not Christian prayer; it is bowing down in the house of Rimmon. God save us from it! Instead, may God lead us to the kind of prayer in which, recognizing the dreadful condition of the visible Church, recognizing the unbelief and the sin which dominate it today, we who are opposed to the current of the age both in the world and in the Church, facing the facts as they are, lay those facts before God, as Hezekiah laid before Him the threatening letter of the Assyrian enemy, and humbly ask Him to give the answer.

Again, men say that instead of engaging in controversy in the Church, we ought to pray to God for a revival; instead of polemics, we ought to have evangelism. Well, what kind of revival do you think that will be? What sort of evangelism is it that is indifferent to the question what evangel is it that is to be preached? Not a revival in the New Testament sense, not the evangelism that Paul meant when he said, "Woe is unto me, if I preach not the gospel." No, my friends, there can be no true evangelism which makes common cause with the enemies of the Cross of Christ. Souls will hardly be saved unless the evangelists can say with Paul: "If we or an angel from heaven preach any other gospel than that which we preached unto you, let him be accursed!" Every true revival is born in controversy, and leads to more controversy. That has been true ever since our Lord said that He came not to bring peace upon the earth but a sword. And do you know what I think will happen when God sends a new Reformation upon the Church? We cannot tell when that blessed day will come. But when the blessed day does come, I think we can say at least one result that it will bring. We shall hear nothing on that day about the evils of controversy in the Church. All that will be swept away as with a mighty flood. A man who is on fire with a message never talks in that wretched, feeble way, but proclaims the truth joyously and fearlessly, in the presence of every high thing that is lifted up against the gospel of Christ.

But men tell us that instead of engaging in controversy about doctrine we ought to seek the power of the living Holy Spirit. A few years ago we had in America, as I suppose you had here, a celebration of the anniversary of Pentecost. At that time, our Presbyterian Church was engaged in a conflict, the gist of which concerned the question of the truth of the Bible. Was the Church going to insist, or was it not going to insist, that its ministers should believe that the Bible is true? At that time of decision, and almost, it seemed, as though to evade the issue, many sermons were preached on the subject of the Holy Spirit. Do you think that those sermons, if they really were preached in that way, were approved by Him with whom they dealt. I fear not, my friends. A man can hardly receive the power of the Holy Spirit if he seeks to evade the question whether the blessed Book that the Spirit has given us is true or false.

Again, men tell us that our preaching should be positive and not negative, that we can preach the truth without attacking error. But if we follow that advice we shall have to close our Bible and desert its teachings. The New Testament is a polemic book almost from beginning to end. Some years ago I was in a company of teachers of the Bible in the colleges and other educational institutions of America. One of the most eminent theological professors in the country made an address. In it he admitted that there are unfortunate controversies about doctrine in the Epistles of Paul; but, said he in effect, the real essence of Paul's teaching is found in the hymn to Christian love in the thirteenth chapter of I Corinthians; and we can avoid controversy today, if we will only devote the chief attention to that inspiring hymn. In reply, I am bound to say that the example was singularly ill-chosen. That hymn to Christian love is in the midst of a great polemic passage; it would never have been written if Paul had been opposed to controversy with error in the Church. It was because his soul was stirred within him by a wrong use of the spiritual gifts that he was able to write that glorious hymn. So it is always in the Church. Every really great Christian utterance, it may almost be said, is born in controversy. It is when men have felt compelled to take a stand against error that they have risen to the really great heights in the celebration of truth.

But in defending the faith against the attack upon it that is being made both without and within the Church, what method of defence should be used?

In answer to that question, I have time only to say two things. In the first place, the defence, with the polemic that it involves, should be perfectly open and above board. I have just stated, that I believe in controversy. But in controversy I do try to observe the Golden Rule; I do try to do unto others as I would have others do unto me. And the kind of controversy that pleases me in an opponent is a controversy that is altogether frank.

Sometimes I go into a company of modern men. A man gets up upon the platform, looks out benignly upon the audience, and says: "I think, brethren, that we are all agreed about this" — and then proceeds to trample ruthlessly upon everything that is dearest to my heart. When he does that, I feel aggrieved. I do not feel aggrieved because he gives free expression to opinions that are different from mine. But I feel aggrieved because he calls me his "brother" and assumes, prior to investigation, that I agree with what he is going to say. A kind of controversy that pleases me better than that is a kind of controversy in which a man gets up upon the platform, looks out upon the audience, and says: "What is this? I see that one of those absurd Fundamentalists has somehow strayed into this company of educated men" — and then proceeds to call me by every opprobrious term that is to be found in one of the most unsavoury paragraphs of Roget's *Thesaurus*. When he does that, I do not feel too much distressed. I can even endure the application to me of the term "Fundmentalist," though for the life of me I cannot see why adherents of the Christian religion, which has been in the world for some nineteen hundred years, should suddenly be made an "-ism," and be called by some strange new name. The point is that that speaker at least does me the honour of recognizing that a profound difference separates my view from his. We understand each other perfectly, and it is quite possible that we may be, if not brothers (I object to the degradation of that word), yet at least good friends.

In the second place, the defence of the faith should be of a scholarly kind. Mere denunciation does not constitute an argument; and before a man can refute successfully an argument of an opponent, he must understand the argument that he is endeavouring to refute. Personalities, in such debate, should be kept in the background; and analysis of the motives of one's opponents has little place.

That principle, certainly in America, has been violated constantly by the advocates of the Modernist or indifferentist position in the Church. It has been violated by them far more than by the defenders of God's Word. Yet the latter, strangely enough, have received the blame. The representatives of the dominant Modern-indifferentist forces have engaged in the most violent adjectival abuse of their opponents; yet they have been called sweet and beautiful and tolerant: the defenders of the Bible, and of the historic position of the Church have spoken courteously, though plainly, in opposition, and have been called "bitter" and "extreme." I am reminded of the way in which an intelligent American Indian is reported (I saw it in the American magazine *The Saturday Evening Post,* a few months ago) to have characterised the terminology used in histories of the wars between the white men and the men of his race. "When you won," said the Indian, "it was, according to your histories, a 'battle'; when we won, it was a 'massacre.' "

Such, I suppose, is the treatment of the unpopular side in every conflict. Certainly it is the treatment which we receive today. Men have found it to be an effective way of making themselves popular, to abuse the representatives of so unpopular a cause as that which we Bible-believing Christians represent.

Yet I do not think we ought to be dismayed. If in these days of unbelief and defection in the Church we are called upon to bear just a little bit of the reproach of Christ, we ought to count ourselves honoured, and certainly we ought not mitigate in the slightest measure the plainness either of our defence of the truth or of our warnings against error. Men's favour is worth very little after all, in comparison with the favour of Christ.

But certainly we should strive to keep ourselves free from that with which we are charged. Because our opponents are guilty, that is no reason why we should make ourselves guilty too.

It is no easy thing to defend the Christian faith against the mighty attack that is being brought against it at the present day. Knowledge of the truth is necessary, and also clear acquaintance with the forces hostile to the truth in modern thought.

At that point, a final objection may arise. Does it not involve a terrible peril to men's souls to ask them — for example, in their preparation for the ministry — to acquaint themselves with things that are being said against the gospel of the Lord Jesus Christ?

Would it not be safer to learn only of the truth, without acquainting ourselves with error? We answer, "Of course it would be *safer.*" It would be far safer, no doubt, to live in a fool's paradise and close one's eyes to what is going on in the world today, just as it is safer to remain in secure dugouts rather than to go over the top in some great attack. We save our souls, perhaps, by such tactics, but the Lord's enemies remain in possession of the field. It is a great battle indeed, this intellectual battle of today; deadly perils await every man who engages in that conflict; but it is the Lord's battle, and He is a great Captain in the fight.

There are, indeed, some perils that should be avoided — particularly the peril of acquainting ourselves with what is said against the Christian religion without ever obtaining any really orderly acquaintance with what can be said for it. That is the peril to which a candidate for the ministry, for example, subjects himself when he attends only one of the theological colleges where the professors are adherents of the dominant naturalistic view. What does such a course of study mean? It means simply this, that a man does not think the historic Christian faith, which has given him his spiritual nurture, to be worthy of a fair hearing. That is my only argument in advising a man to study, for example, at an institution like Westminster Theological Seminary, which I have the honour to serve. I am not asking him to close his eyes to what can be said against the historic faith. But, I am telling him that the logical order is to learn what a thing is before one attends exclusively to what can be said against it; and I am telling him further, that the way to learn what a thing is is not to listen first to its opponents, but to grant a full hearing to those who believe in it with all their minds and hearts. After that has been done, after our students, by pursuing the complete course of study, have obtained something like an orderly acquaintance with the marvelous system of truth that the Bible contains, then the more they listen to what can be said against it, the better defenders of it they will probably be.

Let us, therefore, pray that God will raise up for us today true defenders of the Christian faith. We are living in the midst of a mighty conflict against the Christian religion. The conflict is carried on with intellectual weapons. Whether we like it or not, there are millions upon millions of our fellowmen who reject Christianity for the simple reason that they do not believe Christianity to be true. What is to be done in such a situation?

We can learn, at this point, a lesson from the past history of the Church. This is not the first time during the past nineteen hundred years when intellectual objections have been raised against the gospel of Christ. How have those objections been treated? Have they been evaded, or have they been faced? The answer is writ large in the history of the Church. The objections have been faced. God has raised up in time of need, not only evangelists to appeal to the multitudes, but also Christian scholars to meet the intellectual attack. So it will be in our day, my friends. The Christian religion flourishes not in the darkness but in the light. Intellectual slothfulness is but a quack remedy for unbelief; the true remedy is consecration of intellectual powers to the service of the Lord Jesus Christ.

Let us not fear for the result. Many times, in the course of the past nineteen hundred years, men have predicted that in a generation or so the old gospel would be forever forgotten. Yet the gospel has burst forth again, and set the world aflame. So it may be in our age, in God's good time and in His way. Sad indeed are the substitutes for the gospel of Christ. The Church has been beguiled into By-path Meadow, and is now groaning in the dungeon of Giant Despair. Happy is the man who can point out to such a Church the straight, high road that leads over hill and valley to the City of God.

# X

# Christian Scholarship and the Building Up of the Church

W E HAVE been discussing today the uses of Christian scholarship. It is important, we showed this morning, for evangelism; it is important, in the second place, as we showed this afternoon, for the defence of the faith. But it has still another use. It is important, in the third place, for the building up of the Church.

At this point, as at the first two points, we have the New Testament on our side. At the beginning of the Church's life, as we are told in the Book of Acts, the Apostolic Church continued steadfastly, not only in fellowship and in breaking of bread and prayers, but also in the apostles' teaching. There is no encouragement whatever, in the New Testament, for the notion that when a man has been converted all has been done for him that needs to be done. Read the Epistles of Paul, in particular, from that point of view. Paul was the greatest of evangelists, and he gloried particularly in preaching the gospel just in places where it had never been heard; yet his Epistles are full of the edification or building up of those who have already been won; and the whole New Testament clearly discourages the exclusive nourishment of Christians with milk instead of with solid food.

In the modern Church, this important work of edification has been sadly neglected; it has been neglected even by some of those who believe that the Bible is the Word of God. Too often doctrinal preaching has been pushed from the primary place, in which it rightly belongs, to a secondary place; exhortation has taken the place of systematic instruction; and the people have not been built up. Is it any wonder that a Church thus nurtured is carried away with every wind of doctrine and is helpless in the presence of unbelief? A return to solid instruction in the pulpit, at the desk of the Sunday School teacher, and particularly in the home, is one of the crying needs of the hour.

I do not mean that a sermon should be a lecture; I do not mean that a preacher should address his congregation as a teacher addresses his class. No doubt some young preachers do err in that way. Impressed with the truth that we are trying to present tonight, they have endeavoured to instruct the people in Christian doctrine; but in their efforts to be instructive they have put entirely too many points into one sermon and the congregation has been confused. That error, unquestionably, should be avoided. But it should be avoided not by the abandonment of doctrinal preaching, but by our making doctrinal preaching real *preaching*. The preacher should present to his congregation the doctrine that the Holy Scripture contains; but he should fire the presentation of that doctrine with the devotion of the heart, and he should show how it can be made fruitful for Christian life.

One thing that impresses me about preaching today is the neglect of true edification even by evangelical preachers. What the preacher says is often good, and by it genuine Christian emotion is aroused. But a man could sit under the preaching for a year or ten years and at the end of the time he would be just about where he was at the beginning. Such a lamentably small part of Scripture truth is used; the congregation is never made acquainted with the wonderful variety of what the Bible contains. I trust that God may raise up for us preachers of a different type; I trust that those preachers may not only build upon the one foundation which is Jesus Christ, but may build upon that foundation not wood, hay, stubble, but gold, silver, precious stones. Do you, if you are preachers or teachers in the Church, want to be saved merely so as through fire, or do you want your work to endure in the day of Jesus Christ? There is one work at least which I think we may hold, in all humility, to be sure to stand the test of judgment fire; it is the humble impartation, Sunday by Sunday, or day by day, of a solid knowledge not of what you say or what any man has said, but of what God has told us in His Word.

Is that work too lowly; is it too restricted to fire the ambition of our souls? Nay, my friends, a hundred lifetimes would not begin to explore the riches of what the Scriptures contain.

Some years ago, when I was still at Princeton Theological Seminary, before the reorganisation of that institution, we received one of the countless questionnaires which in America have become, with one's neighbour's radio, one of the nuisances of modern life. The man who sent out the questionnaire was threatening, I believe, to write a book on theological education: and afterwards he carried out his threat. The questionnaire begged the question as many questionnaires do; it was not, if I remember rightly, in the slightest interested in the question whether a high scholarly standard was maintained in the study of the Bible; it did not seem to be much interested in discovering whether the students were or were not required to know the languages in which the Bible is written: but there were all sorts of questions about courses in hygiene and the like. In short, one prominent purpose of sending us the questionnaire seemed to be that of discovering whether Princeton Theological Seminary was or was not a medical school.

I am no longer connected wth Princeton Theological Seminary, since its reorganisation in 1929, and so cannot speak for that institution. But I may say that Westminster Theological Seminary, which I now have the honour to serve, is not pretending to be a medical school at all. We are not striving to train experts in hygiene or in first-aid; we are not trying to make specialists in sociology or even specialists in religion. But what we are trying to do is to make specialists in the Bible, and we think that that is a large enough specialty for any man to give to it his life.

What a world in itself the Bible is, my friends! Happy are those who in the providence of God can make the study of it very specifically the business of their lives; but happy also is every Christian who has it open before him and seeks by daily study to penetrate somewhat into the wonderful richness of what it contains.

A man does not need to read very long in the Bible before that richness begins to appear. It appears in the very first verse of the Bible; for the very first verse sets forth the being of God: "In the beginning God created the heaven and the earth."

We are told today, indeed, that that is metaphysics, and that it is a matter of indifference to the Christian man.* To be a Christian, it is said, a man does not need at all to settle the question how the universe came into being. The doctrine of "fiat creation," we are told, belongs to philosophy, not to religion; and we can be worshippers of goodness even though goodness is not clothed with the vulgar trappings of power.

But to talk thus is to talk nonsense, for the simple reason that goodness divorced from power is a mere abstraction which can never call forth the devotion of a man's heart. Goodness inheres only in persons; goodness implies the power to act. Make God good only and not powerful, and you have done away not only with God, but with goodness as well.

Very different from such a pale abstraction, which identifies God with one aspect of the universe, is the God whom the first verse of Genesis presents. That God is the living God; it is He by whom the worlds were made and by whom they are upheld.

No, my friends, it is altogether wrong to say that the Christian religion can do perfectly well with many different types of philosophy, and that metaphysical questions are a matter of indifference

---

* With what follows compare the treatment by the lecturer in *What is Faith,* 1925, pp. 46-66.

to the Christian man. Nothing could be farther from the truth. As a matter of fact, everything else that the Bible contains is based upon the stupendous metaphysic that the first verse of Genesis contains. That was the metaphysic of our Lord Jesus Christ, and without it everything that He said and everything that He did would be in vain. Underlying all His teaching and all His example is the stupendous recognition that God is the Maker and Ruler of the world; and the Bible from beginning to end depends upon that same "philosophy" of a personal God.

That philosophy ought to have been clear from an examination of the universe as it is; the Maker is revealed by the things that He has made. "The Heavens declare the glory of God, and the firmament sheweth His handy-work." "The invisible things of Him from the creation of the world are clearly seen, being understood by the things that are made, even His eternal power and Godhead." Natural religion has, therefore, the full sanction of the Bible; and at the foundation of every theological course should be philosophical apologetics, including the proof of the existence of a personal God, Creator and Ruler of the world.

I know there are those who tell us today that no such study is necessary; there are those who tell us that we should begin with Jesus, and that all we need to know is that God is like Jesus. They talk to us in that sense, about the "Christlike God." But do you not see that if you relinquish the thought of a personal God, Creator and Ruler of the world, you are dishonouring the teaching of Jesus from beginning to end. Jesus saw in the lilies of the field the weaving of God; and the man who wipes out of his consciousness the whole wonderful revelation of God in nature, and then says that all that he needs to know is that God is like Jesus, is dishonouring at the very root of His teaching and of His example that same Jesus whom he is purporting to honour and serve.

The existence of a personal God should have been clear to us from the world as it is, but that revelation of God in nature has been obscured by sin, and to recover it and confirm it we need the blessed supernatural revelation that the Scriptures contain. How graciously that revelation is given! When we rise from the reading of the Bible, if we have read with understanding and with faith, what a wonderful knowledge we have of the living God!

In His presence, indeed, we can never lose the sense of wonder. Infinitesimal are the things that we know compared with things that we do not know; a dreadful curtain veils the being of God from the eyes of man. Yet that curtain, in the infinite goodness of God, has been pulled gently aside, and we have been granted just a look beyond. Never can we cease to wonder in the presence of God; but enough knowledge has been granted to us that we may adore.

The second great mystery that the Bible presents is the mystery of man. And we are not allowed to wait long for that mystery. It is presented to us, as is the mystery of God, in the early part of the first book of the Bible. Man is there presented in his utter distinctness from the rest of the creation; and then he is presented to us in the awful mystery of his sin.

At that point, it is interesting to observe how the Bible, unlike modern religious literature, always defines its terms; and at the beginning, when the Bible speaks of sin, it makes clear exactly what sin is. According to the Westminster Shorter Catechism, if you will pardon an allusion to that upon which your speaker was brought up, "sin is any want of conformity unto, or transgression of, the law of God." I do not remember, at the moment, what proof-texts the authors of the Westminster Standards used to support that definition. But they need hardly have looked farther for such proof-texts than to the early part of Genesis. "Ye shall not eat of the tree," said God; man ate of the tree and died. Sin is there presented with the utmost clearness as the transgression of law. So it is presented in the whole of the Bible. Sin and law belong together. When we say "sin," we have said "law";

when we have said "law," then, man being what he now is, we have said "sin."

At the present time, the existence of law is being denied. Men no longer believe that there is such a thing as a law of God; and naturally they do not believe that there is such a thing as sin. Thoughtful men, who are not Christians, are aware of the problem that this stupendous change in human thinking presents to the modern world. Now that men no longer believe that there is a law of God, now that men no longer believe in obligatory morality, now that the moral law has been abandoned, what is to be put in its place, in order that an ordinarily decent human life may be preserved upon the earth? It cannot be said that the answers proposed for that question are as satisfactory as the way in which the question itself is put. It is impossible to keep back the raging seas of human passion with the flimsy mud embankments of an appeal either to self-interest, or to what Walter Lippmann calls "disinterestedness." Those raging seas can only be checked by the solid masonry of the law of God.

Men are wondering today what is wrong with the world. They are conscious of the fact that they are standing over some terrible abyss. Awful ebullitions rise from that abyss. We have lost altogether the sense of the security of our Western civilization. Men are wondering what is wrong.

It is perfectly clear what is wrong. The law of God has been torn up, as though it were a scrap of paper, and the inevitable result is appearing with ever greater clearness. When will the law be rediscovered? When it is re-discovered, that will be a day of terror for mankind: but it will also be a day of joy; for the law will be a schoolmaster unto Christ. Its terrors will drive men back to the little wicket gate, and to the way that leads to that place somewhat ascending where they will see the Cross.

Those are the two great presuppositions of everything else that the Bible contains; the two great presuppositions are the majesty of the transcendent God and the guilt and misery of man in his sin.

But we are not left to wait long for the third of the great mysteries — the mystery of salvation. That too is presented at the beginning of Genesis, in the promise of a redemption to come.

The rest of the Bible is the unfolding of that promise. And when I think of that unfolding, when I try to take the Bible, not in part, but as a whole, when I contemplate not this doctrine or that, but the marvelous *system* of doctrine that the Bible contains. I am amazed that in the presence of such riches men can be content with that other gospel which now dominates the preaching in the Church.

When I think again of the wonderful metaphysic in the first verse of Genesis — "In the beginning God created the heaven and the earth" — when I think of the way in which throughout the Old Testament the majesty of that Creator God is presented with wonderful clearness, until the presentation culminates in the matchless fortieth chapter of Isaiah — "It is he that sitteth upon the circle of the earth, and the inhabitants thereof are as grasshoppers, that stretcheth out the heavens as a curtain, and spreadeth them out as a tent to dwell in" — when I think of the way in which in that same chapter the tenderness and the gentleness of that same awful God are presented. in a manner far beyond all human imagining — "He shall feed his flock like a shepherd: he shall gather the lambs with his arm, and carry them in his bosom, and shall gently lead those that are with young" — when I think of the wonderful gallery of portraits in the Old Testament, and compare it with the best efforts of men who have sought to penetrate into the secrets of human life and of the human heart; when I think of the gracious dealings of God with His people in Old Testament times, until the fulness of the time was come, and the Saviour was born into the world; when I think of the way in which His coming was accomplished, by a stupendous miracle indeed, but in wonderful quietness and lowliness; when I think of the songs of the heaven-

ly host, and the way in which the infant Saviour was greeted in
the Temple by those who had waited for the redemption of Jerusalem; when I stand in awe before that strange answer of the
youthful Jesus, "Wist ye not that I must be about my Father's
business?"; when I try to keep my imagination at rest, as Scripture bids me do, regarding those long, silent years at Nazareth;
when I think of the day of His showing to Israel; when I think
of the sternness of His teaching, the way in which He pulled the
cloak from human sin, the way in which, by revealing through
His words and His example the real demands of God, He took
from mankind its last hope of any salvation to be obtained through
its own goodness; when I think, again, of the wonderful kindness
of the Saviour; when I read how He forgave where none other
would forgive, and helped where all other helpers had failed;
when I think, above all, of that blessed thing which He did not
only for men of long ago, who saw Him with their bodily eyes,
but for every one of us if we be united with Him through faith,
when He died in our stead upon the cross, and said in triumph,
at the moment when His redeeming work was done, "It is finish-
ed"; when I enter into both the fear and the joy of those who
found the tomb empty and saw the vision of angels which also
said, "He is not here: for He is risen"; when I think of the way
in which He was known to His disciples in the breaking of bread;
when I think of Pentecost and the pouring out of His Spirit upon
the Church; when I attend to the wonderful way in which the
Bible tells us how this Saviour may be our Saviour today, how
you and I, sitting in this house tonight, can come into His presence, in even far more intimate fashion than that which was en-
joyed by those who pushed their way unto Him as He sat amidst
Scribes and Pharisees when He was on earth; when I think of the
application of His redeeming work by the Holy Spirit:

> *Be of sin the double cure,*
> *Cleanse me from its guilt and power;*

when I think of the glories of the Christian life, opened to us, not on the basis of human striving, but of that mighty act of God; when I read the last book of the Bible, and think of the unfolding of the glorious hope of that time when the once lowly Jesus, now seated on the throne of all being, shall come again with power — when I think of these things, I am impressed with the fact that the other gospel, which is dominant in the Church today, preached though it is by brilliant men, and admirable though it might have seemed if we had not compared it with something infinitely greater, is naught but "weak and beggarly elements," and that the humblest man who believes that the Bible is the Word of God is possessed of riches greater by far than all the learning of all the world and all the eloquence of all the preachers who now have the ear of an unfaithful Church.

## XI

# The Christian View of Missions

SOME nineteen hundred years ago a remarkable movement emerged from the obscurity of Palestine into the cosmopolitan life of the Roman Empire. That movement was the Christian Church.

What were its characteristics in those first glorious days?

This question is important for at least two reasons. In the first place, the Church in those first days had everything that it so signally lacks today. It had joy, it had power, it had life. Perhaps that life and that power may be regained if we return to what the Church was then. In the second place, by considering what the Church was then we can answer the question what can rightly bear the name "Christian" today. If we have a new thing, let us use a new name; but if we claim to be Christian, we must show some conformity to that to which the name "Christian" was first applied.

But what was it to which the name was first applied; what was the Christian movement when it first appeared?

With regard to that question, there may be a certain amount of agreement even between historians who are themselves Christians and historians who are not Christians, even between historians of widely diverse views. Difference of opinion prevails about the question whether Christianity is true; but about the question what Christianity is and what it was in those first days a certain amount of agreement may be attained.

One thing, at least, is clear, on the basis of all our sources of historical information. The earliest Christian Church was a mis-

sionary Church. If Christianity ever settles down to be the religion merely of one nation or of one group of nations, it will have
become entirely untrue to the tradition which was established for
it at the beginning. There was evidently a tremendous urge
among those early Christians to carry their message to the ends
of the earth.

What, then, was the mission of that missionary Church? What
was the Christianity that it propagated in that ancient Roman
world?

In the first place, the Christianity that it propagated did *not*
present itself as a new religion. On the contrary, it appealed to
an ancient revelation; and it claimed to stand in the full continuity of an age-long plan of God. It should never be forgotten —
though it often is forgotten — that the Christian Church at the
very beginning had a Bible. Its Bible was the Old Testament;
and it regarded that Bible as the Word of God, just as Bible-
believing Christians regard the Scriptures of the Old and New
Testaments today.

In so regarding the Old Testament, it was in exact accord with
the Person Whom it presented as the foundation of its life —
namely, Jesus Christ. One thing is clear to the historian. Jesus
of Nazareth, whether we like it or not, did hold the view of the
Old Testament which was generally accepted in the Israel of His
day; He did hold the Old Testament to be true throughout; He
did hold it to be authoritative and divine. When He said that
some of its commands were temporary, and were to be superseded
or modified in the new era which His sovereign coming ushered
in, He did not at all mean that those commands were not commands of God, absolutely valid in the sphere and in the time in
which they were intended by God to prevail. It is a fact of history that Jesus as well as His first disciples held the loftiest view
of the divine authority and full truthfulness of the Old Testament
Scriptures. From the beginning Christianity was a religion
founded upon a Book,

That Book proclaimed, and the early Church proclaimed on the
basis of it, in the first place, the one living and true God, Maker
of Heaven and earth; and that proclamation was the basis of
everything else that the Church proclaimed. "Ye turned to God,"
says Paul, in describing his missionary preaching, his preaching
to unconverted people at Thessalonica, "ye turned to God from
idols to serve the living and true God."

I know that some men have represented that as though it were
a mere piece of metaphysics that the Church could and can do
without. The doctrine of "fiat creation," they tell us, has nothing
to do with vital religion; and even in those early days, they tell
us, Jesus could be accepted as Saviour-god without any settlement
of the question regarding His connection with the Creator and
Ruler of the world. But men who tell us that are entirely wrong.
Certainly Jesus was God; but calling Jesus God has no meaning
unless one first tells what one means by "God"; and calling Jesus
God while one is indifferent to the existence of a God Who is
Creator and Ruler of the world runs directly counter to the teaching of Jesus Himself. No, both Jesus and His earliest disciples
were first of all monotheists; they believed that before the world
was God was, that this universe came into being by the fiat of
His will, and that He is eternally free as over against the things
that He has made. That is what the Bible means by the living
and holy God; and it was that living and holy God Whom those
first Christian missionaries proclaimed.

In the second place, again on the basis of the Old Testament
Scriptures, the early Church proclaimed the universal sinfulness
of mankind — a mankind lost under the guilt and power of sin,
and subject to the wrath of God.

Men do not like that doctrine of the wrath of God today.
But it is not the historian's business, when he deals with past
ages, to find what he likes; it is his business to find what was;
and every historian must admit that the doctrine of the wrath
of God was at the very foundation of the message of the

earliest Christian Church. Every historian must also admit, what is more, that that same doctrine was at the very heart of the teaching of Jesus. If you want the really terrible descriptions of the wrath of God and of the divine retribution for sin in the other world, do not turn to the theologians of the Church or even to the Apostle Paul. But turn to the teaching of Jesus of Nazareth — His teaching not only as it is recorded in the New Testament, but even as it has been reconstructed and reduced by modern negative criticism.

I know that people tell us it is an unworthy thing to appeal to the motive of fear. In missionary endeavor, particularly, they tell us, that motive is out of date. But it is strange that those who tell us that, should appeal to Jesus as their authority in religion. For if there ever was a religious teacher who appealed to the motive of fear, it was Jesus. "Be not afraid of them that kill the body," He said, "and after that have no more that they can do. But I will forewarn you whom ye shall fear: Fear him, which after he hath killed hath power to cast into Hell; yea, I say unto you, Fear him." These words are no mere excrescence in the teaching of Jesus. No, they are at the very heart of it; they give to the ethical teaching of Jesus its stupendous earnestness. And they are also at the very heart of the missionary message of the earliest Christian Church.

One thing is perfectly clear — no missionary work that consists merely in presenting to the people in foreign lands a thing that has proved to be mildly valuable in the experience of the missionary himself, which he thinks may perhaps prove helpful in foreign lands in building up a better life upon this earth, can possibly be regarded as real Christian missions. At the very heart of the real Christian missionary message is the conviction that every individual hearer to whom the missionary goes is in deadly peril, and that unless the message is heeded he is without hope in this world and in the dreadful world that is to come.

Then, on the basis of those two great presuppositions — the aw-

ful holiness of God, and a mankind lost under the guilt and power
of sin — the first Christian missionaries preached Jesus Christ.

But how did they preach Him? Did they preach Him as a
great Teacher and Example, as a great Inspirer of a new religious
life? Did they go about the world saying: "We have come under
the spell of a great Person, Jesus of Nazareth; contact with that
Person has changed our lives; we proclaim Him to you as He
lives in our lives; and we beg you to let Him change your lives,
too"?

Well, that is what modern men might have expected those first
Christian missionaries to say; but every historian must admit
that as a matter of fact they said nothing of the kind. Every historian must admit that as a matter of fact they proclaimed Jesus
not primarily as an Example or as an Inspirer, but as a Saviour
from divine wrath and from the awful bondage of sin.

In so proclaiming Him they appealed to their holy Book. The
case is not as though they appealed to the Old Testament merely
for the presuppositions of the Gospel and then turned away from
it when they preached the Gospel itself. No, even in preaching
Jesus they turned to God's written Word. They did not preach
Jesus as One Whose coming was a sort of after-thought of God;
One Who had no connection with what God had done before. No,
they preached Him as the fulfilment of a glorious divine Promise,
as the culmination of a mighty divine Plan.

But then they proclaimed Him in the great wealth of fresh information handed on by those who had seen and heard Him when
He was on earth. In particular, they proclaimed His death and
His resurrection from the dead. "You are justly subject to God's
wrath and curse," they said, "but Christ took that curse upon Himself, He died there on the Cross in your stead. That just and holy
God, Creator and Ruler of the world, is also God of an infinite
love; He sent His eternal Son to die for you. That One Who
died is risen from the dead. He lives, and He is waiting for you
to trust Him and have life."

At the basis of the Christian message, in other words, was not an exhortation, but a gospel; not a program, but a piece of news. So much must be admitted by modern historians of all shades of opinion. The early Christian Church was radically doctrinal. It proclaimed facts: the facts about God the Father, the facts about mankind lost in sin, the facts about Jesus Christ. That is true not merely of Paul but of the very earliest Church in Jerusalem, whose message Paul reproduces for us when he tells us at the beginning of the fifteenth chapter of I Corinthians what he had "received."

So much, at least, must be admitted. The early Church, even the very earliest Church in Jerusalem, did more than proclaim Jesus as an example; it proclaimed Him as a Saviour. It made Him not merely the author, but also the substance, of the Gospel. It did more than proclaim what He proclaimed about God; no, it proclaimed Him.

But, men tell us, although that is what the early Church preached, that is not what Jesus preached, and we can now return from the early Church to Jesus Himself. The early Church proclaimed Him as Saviour by His atoning death; but He Himself, we are told, kept Himself out of His Gospel and preached a simple and universal gospel of the fatherhood of God and the brotherhood of man; and we ought now, rejecting all doctrinal accretions, to return to that simple gospel which Jesus preached.

But is it not a strange thing that those first disciples of Jesus should so completely have misunderstood their Teacher's words and work? And is it not strange that that misunderstanding of the teaching of Jesus should have been so much more powerful in the world than the teaching which it misunderstood? Is it not a strange thing that this supposed gospel of Jesus Himself should have been so powerless, and that only when it was perverted into becoming a gospel about Jesus, a gospel which set Jesus forth, it conquered the world? Yes, it is strange; and not only is it strange but it is untrue. Even the most radical criticism is enabling us to see that. All our sources of information — including not only the Gospels, but the earliest sources supposed, rightly or wrongly, to underlie the Gospels — are dominated by the view that Jesus was no mere proclaimer of a supposed universal fatherhood of God and brotherhood of man, but a divine Redeemer. What is the conclusion? Why, says radical criticism, the conclusion is that we cannot tell what sort of person Jesus was; because all of our sources of information are vitiated by this false Christian notion that He was the Saviour of mankind.

A strange conclusion that is, and a conclusion that is contradicted by the self-evidencing quality of the wonderful picture of Jesus which the Gospels contain. Our conclusion is different from that of these radical critics. It is that the picture is from the life — that God did walk upon this earth, that the whole Bible that sets forth that divine Christ is true, and that we are in His holy Presence today.

I have set forth what Christian missions were in those first glorious days. I have tried to make you understand and sympathize with the joy of those slaves and humble tradesmen in Corinth and in other places who faced the awful wrath of God and then found Jesus to be their Saviour from that wrath.

But is that all? Must we be historians merely? Must we look wistfully at the joys of those first glorious days of the Church without ever having them for ourselves?

No, my friends, those same joys may be ours, and in exactly the same way.

That is known full well by some of you who are my hearers at this hour. You are listening to my voice that you may receive comfort from one — be he never so humble and never so unworthy — who has resisted the current of the times and has a faith like unto yours. Others of you, I suppose, have listened in out of curiosity — that you may hear for yourselves one of those strange persons, not often heard, whom their opponents call "Fundamentalists." But for whatever reason you have listened, there is one thing that I desire to say to you. I desire to say to you that your hour may come when you expect it least. God may speak to your soul. He may use even my poor words to touch some forgotten chord in your heart and to bring again to your mind the great and precious promises of the holy Book. There may even now be one of you who will say: "All my wisdom, all my goodness, all my striving are vain; oh, Lord Jesus, be my Saviour now!"

# XII

## Christianity and Culture

ONE OF the greatest of the problems that have agitated the Church is the problem of the relation between knowledge and piety, between culture and Christianity. This problem has appeared first of all in the presence of two tendencies in the Church — the scientific or academic tendency, and what may be called the practical tendency. Some men have devoted themselves chiefly to the task of forming right conceptions as to Christianity and its foundations. To them no fact, however trivial, has appeared worthy of neglect; by them truth has been cherished for its own sake, without immediate reference to practical consequences. Some, on the other hand, have emphasized the essential simplicity of the gospel. The world is lying in misery, we ourselves are sinners, men are perishing in sin every day. The gospel is the sole means of escape; let us preach it to the world while yet we may. So desperate is the need that we have no time to engage in vain babblings or old wives' fables. While we are discussing the exact location of the churches of Galatia, men are perishing under the curse of the law; while we are settling the date of Jesus' birth, the world is doing without its Christmas message.

The representatives of both of these tendencies regard themselves as Christians, but too often there is little brotherly feeling between them. The Christian of academic tastes accuses his brother of undue emotionalism, of shallow argumentation, of cheap methods of work. On the other hand, your practical man is ever loud in his denunciation of academic indifference to the dire needs of humanity. The scholar is represented either as a dangerous disseminator of doubt, or else as a man whose faith is a faith without works. A man who investigates human sin and the grace of God by the aid solely of dusty volumes, carefully secluded in a warm and comfortable study, without a thought of the men who are perishing in misery every day!

But if the problem appears thus in the presence of different tendencies in the Church, it becomes yet far more insistent within the consciousness of the individual. If we are thoughtful, we must see that the desire to know and the desire to be saved are widely different. The scholar must apparently assume the attitude of an impartial observer — an attitude which seems absolutely impossible to the pious Christian laying hold upon Jesus as the only Saviour from the load of sin. If these two activities — on the one hand the acquisition of knowledge, and on the other the exercise and inculcation of simple faith — are both to be given a place in our lives, the question of their proper relationship cannot be ignored.

The problem is made for us the more difficult of solution because we are unprepared for it. Our whole system of school and college education is so constituted as to keep religion and culture as far apart as possible and ignore the question of the relationship between them. On five or six days in the week, we were engaged in the acquisition of knowledge. From this activity the study of religion was banished. We studied natural science without considering its bearing or lack of bearing upon natural theology or upon revelation. We studied Greek without opening the New Testament. We studied history with careful avoidance of that greatest of historical movements which was ushered in by the preaching of Jesus. In philosophy, the vital importance of the study for religion could not entirely be concealed, but it was kept as far as possible in the background. On Sundays, on the other hand, we had religious instruction that called for little exercise of the intellect. Careful preparation for Sunday-school lessons as for lessons in mathematics or Latin was unknown. Religion seemed to be something that had to do only with the emotions and the will, leaving the intellect to secular studies. What wonder that after such training we came to regard religion and culture as belonging to two entirely separate compartments of the soul, and their union as involving the destruction of both?

Upon entering the Seminary, we are suddenly introduced to an entirely different procedure. Religion is suddenly removed from its seclusion; the same methods of study are applied to it as were formerly reserved for natural science and for history. We study the Bible no longer solely with the desire of moral and spiritual improvement, but also in order to know. Perhaps the first impression is one of infinite loss. The scientific spirit seems to be replacing simple faith, the mere apprehension of dead facts to be replacing the practice of principles. The difficulty is perhaps not so much that we are brought face to face with new doubts as to the truth of Christianity. Rather is it the conflict of method, of spirit that troubles us. The scientific spirit seems to be incompatible with the old spirit of simple faith. In short, almost entirely unprepared, we are brought face to face with the problem of the relationship between knowledge and piety, or, otherwise expressed, between culture and Christianity.

This problem may be settled in one of three ways. In the first place, Christianity may be subordinated to culture. That solution really, though to some extent unconsciously, is being favored by a very large and influential portion of the Church today. For the elimination of the supernatural in Christianity — so tremendously common today — really makes Christianity merely natural. Christianity becomes a human product, a mere part of human culture. But as such it is something entirely different from the old Christianity that was based upon a direct revelation from God. Deprived thus of its note of authority, the gospel is no gospel any longer; it is a check for untold millions — but without the signature at the bottom. So in subordinating Christianity to culture we have really destroyed Christianity, and what continues to bear the old name is a counterfeit. The second solution goes to the opposite extreme. In its effort to give religion a clear field, it seeks to destroy culture. This solution is better than the first. Instead of indulging in a shallow optimisim or deification of humanity, it recognizes the profound evil of the world, and does not shrink from the most heroic remedy. The world is so evil that it cannot possibly produce the means for its own salvation. Salvation must be the gift of an entirely new life, coming directly from God. Therefore, it is argued, the culture of this world must be a matter at least of indifference to the Christian. Now in its extreme form this solution hardly requires refutation. If Christianity is really found to contradict that reason which is our only means of apprehending truth, then of course we must either modify or abandon Christianity. We cannot therefore be entirely independent of the achievements of the intellect. Furthermore, we cannot without inconsistency employ the printing-press, the railroad, the telegraph in the propagation of our gospel, and at the same time denounce as evil those activities of the human mind that produced these things. And in the production of these things not merely practical inventive genius had a part, but also, back of that, the investigations of pure science animated simply by the desire to know. In its extreme form, therefore, involving the abandonment of all intellectual activity, this second solution would be adopted by none of us. But very many pious men in the Church today are adopting this solution in essence and in spirit. They admit that the Christian must have a part in human culture. But they regard such activity as a necessary evil — a dangerous and unworthy task necessary to be gone through with under a stern sense of duty in order that thereby the higher ends of the gospel may be attained. Such men can never engage in the arts and sciences with anything like enthusiasm — such enthusiasm they would regard as disloyalty to the gospel. Such a position is really both illogical and unbiblical.

God has given us certain powers of mind, and has implanted within us the ineradicable conviction that these powers were intended to be exercised. The Bible, too, contains poetry that exhibits no lack of enthusiasm, no lack of a keen appreciation of beauty. With this second solution of the problem we cannot rest content. Despite all we can do, the desire to know and the love of beauty cannot be entirely stifled, and we cannot permanently regard these desires as evil.

Are then Christianity and culture in a conflict that is to be settled only by the destruction of one or the other of the contending forces? A third solution, fortunately, is possible — namely consecration. Instead of destroying the arts and sciences or being indifferent to them, let us cultivate them with all the enthusiasm of the veriest humanist, but at the same time consecrate them to the service of our God. Instead of stifling the pleasures afforded by the acquisition of knowledge or by the appreciation of what is beautiful, let us accept these pleasures as the gifts of a heavenly Father. Instead of obliterating the distinction between the Kingdom and the world, or on the other hand withdrawing from the world into a sort of modernized intellectual monasticism, let us go forth joyfully, enthusiastically to make the world subject to God.

Certain obvious advantages are connected with such a solution of the problem. In the first place, a logical advantage. A man can believe only what he holds to be true. We are Christians because we hold Christianity to be true. But other men hold Christianity to be false. Who is right? That question can be settled only by an examination and comparison of the reasons adduced on both sides. It is true, one of the grounds for our belief is an inward experience that we cannot share — the great experience begun by conviction of sin and conversion and continued by communion with God — an experience which other men do not possess, and upon which, therefore, we cannot directly base an argument. But if our position is correct, we ought at least to be able to show the other man that *his* reasons *may* be inconclusive. And that involves careful study of both sides of the question. Furthermore, the field of Christianity is the world. The Christian cannot be satisfied so long as any human activity is either opposed to Christianity or out of all connection with Christianity. Christianity must pervade not merely all nations, but also all of human thought. The Christian, therefore, cannot be indifferent to any branch of earnest human endeavor. It must all be brought into *some* relation to the gospel. It must be studied either in order to be demonstrated as false, or else in order to be made useful in advancing the Kingdom of God. The Kingdom must be advanced not merely extensively, but also intensively. The Church must seek to conquer not merely every man for Christ, but also the whole of man. We are accustomed to encourage ourselves in our discouragements by the thought of the time when every knee shall bow and every tongue confess that Jesus is Lord. No less inspiring is the other aspect of that same great consummation. That will also be a time when doubts have disappeared, when every contradiction has been removed, when all of science converges to one great conviction, when all of art is devoted to qne great end, when all of human thinking is permeated by the refining, ennobling influence of Jesus, when every thought has been brought into subjection to the obedience of Christ.

If to some of our practical men, these advantages of our solution of the problem seem to be intangible, we can point to the merely numerical advantage of intellectual and artistic activity within the Church. We are all agreed that at least one great function of the Church is the conversion of individual men. The missionary movement is the great religious movement of our day. Now it is perfectly true that men must be brought to Christ one by one. There are no labor-saving devices in evangelism. It is all handwork. And yet it would be a great mistake to suppose that all men are equally well prepared to receive the gospel. It is true that the decisive thing is the regenerative power of God. That can overcome all lack of preparation, and the absence of that makes even the best preparation useless. But as a matter of fact God usually exerts that power in connection with certain prior conditions of the human mind, and it should be ours to create, so far as we can, with the help of God, those favorable conditions for the reception of the gospel. False ideas are the greatest obstacles to the reception of the gospel. We may preach with all the fervor of a reformer and yet succeed only in winning a straggler here and there, if we permit the whole collective thought of the nation or of the world to be controlled by ideas which, by the resistless force of logic, prevent Christianity from being regarded as anything more than a harmless delusion. Under such circumstances, what God desires us to do is to destroy the obstacle at its root. Many would have the seminaries combat error by attacking it as it is taught by its popular exponents. Instead of that they confuse their students with a lot of German names unknown outside the walls of the universities. That method of procedure is based simply upon a profound belief in the pervasiveness of ideas. What is today matter of academic speculation begins tomorrow to move armies and pull down empires. In that second stage, it has gone too far to be combatted; the time to stop it was when it was still a matter of impassionate debate. So as Christians we should try to mould the thought of the world in such a way as to make the acceptance of Christianity something more than a logical absurdity. Thoughtful men are wondering why the students of our great Eastern universities no longer enter the ministry or display any very vital interest in Christianity. Various totally inadequate explanations are proposed, such as the increasing attractiveness of other professions — an absurd explanation, by the way, since other professions are becoming so over-crowded that a man can barely make a living in them. The real difficulty amounts to this — that the thought of the day, as it makes itself most strongly felt in the universities, but from them spreads inevitably to the masses of the people, is profoundly opposed to

Christianity, or at least — what is nearly as bad — it is out of all connection with Christianity. The Church is unable either to combat it or to assimilate it, because the Church simply does not understand it. Under such circumstances, what more pressing duty than for those who have received the mighty experience of regeneration, who, therefore, do not, like the world, neglect that whole series of vitally relevant facts which is embraced in Christian experience — what more pressing duty than for these men to make themselves masters of the thought of the world in order to make it an instrument of truth instead of error? The Church has no right to be so absorbed in helping the individual that she forgets the world.

There are two objections to our solution of the problem. If you bring culture and Christianity thus into close union — in the first place, will not Christianity destroy culture? Must not art and science be independent in order to flourish? We answer that it all depends upon the nature of their dependence. Subjection to any external authority or even to any human authority would be fatal to art and science. But subjection to God is entirely different. Dedication of human powers to God is found, as a matter of fact, not to destroy but to heighten them. God gave those powers. He understands them well enough not bunglingly to destroy His own gifts. In the second place, will not culture destroy Christianity? Is it not far easier to be an earnest Christian if you confine your attention to the Bible and do not risk being led astray by the thought of the world? We answer, of course it is *easier*. Shut yourself up in an intellectual monastery, do not disturb yourself with the thoughts of unregenerate men, and of course you will find it *easier* to be a Christian, just as it is easier to be a good soldier in comfortable winter quarters than it is on the field of battle. You save your own soul — but the Lord's enemies remain in possession of the field.

But by whom is this task of transforming the unwieldy, resisting mass of human thought until it becomes subservient to the gospel — by whom is this task to be accomplished? To some extent, no doubt, by professors in theological seminaries and universities. But the ordinary minister of the gospel cannot shirk his responsibility. It is a great mistake to suppose that investigation can successfully be carried on by a few specialists whose work is of interest to nobody but themselves. Many men of many minds are needed. What we need first of all, especially in our American churches, is a more general interest in the problems of theological science. Without that, the specialist is without the stimulating atmosphere which nerves him to do his work.

But no matter what his station in life, the scholar must be a regenerated man — he must yield to no one in the intensity and depth of his religious experience. We are well supplied in the world with excellent scholars who are without that qualification. They are doing useful work in detail, in Biblical philology, in exegesis, in Biblical theology, and in other branches of study. But they are not accomplishing the great task, they are not assimilating modern thought to Christianity, because they are without that experience of God's power in the soul which is of the essence of Christianity. They have only one side for the comparison. Modern thought they know, but Christianity is really foreign to them. It is just that great inward experience which it is the function of the true Christian scholar to bring into some sort of connection with the thought of the world.

During the last thirty years there has been a tremendous defection from the Christian Church. It is evidenced even by things that lie on the surface. For example, by the decline in church attendance and in Sabbath observance and in the number of candidates for the ministry. Special explanations, it is true, are sometimes given for these discouraging tendencies. But why should we deceive ourselves, why comfort ourselves by palliative explanations? Let us face the facts. The falling off in church attendance, the neglect of Sabbath observance — these things are simply surface indications of a decline in the power of Christianity. Christianity is exerting a far less powerful direct influence in the civilized world today than it was exerting thirty years ago. What is the cause of this tremendous defection? For my part, I have little hesitation in saying that it lies chiefly in the intellectual sphere. Men do not accept Christianity because they can no longer be convinced that Christianity is true. It may be useful, but is it true? Other explanations, of course, are given. The modern defection from the Church is explained by the practical materialism of the age. Men are so much engrossed in making money that they have no time for spiritual things. That explanation has a certain range of validity. But its range is limited. It applies perhaps to the boom towns of the West, where men are intoxicated by sudden possibilities of boundless wealth. But the defection from Christianity is far broader than that. It is felt in the settled countries of Europe even more strongly than in America. It is felt among the poor just as strongly as among the rich. Finally it is felt most strongly of all in the universities, and that is only one indication more that the true cause of the defection is intellectual. To a very large extent, the students of our great Eastern universities — and still more the universities of Europe — are not Christians. And they are not Christians often just because they are students. The thought of the day, as it makes itself most strongly felt in the universities, is profoundly opposed to Christianity, or at least it is out of connection with Christianity. The chief obstacle to the Christian religion today lies in the sphere of the intellect.

That assertion must be guarded against two misconceptions. In the first place, I do not mean that most men reject Christianity consciously on account of intellectual difficulties. On the contrary, rejection of Christianity is due in the vast majority of cases simply to indifference. Only a few men have given the subject real attention. The vast majority of those who reject the gospel do so simply because they know nothing about it. But whence comes this indifference? It is due to the intellectual atmosphere in which men are living.  The modern world is dominated by ideas which ignore the gospel.  Modern culture is not altogether opposed to the gospel.  But it is out of all connection with it.  It not only prevents the acceptance of Christianity.  It prevents Christianity even from getting a hearing.

In the second place, I do not mean that the removal of intellectual objections will make a man a Christian.  No conversion was ever wrought simply by argument.  A change of heart is also necessary.  And that can be wrought only by the immediate exercise of the power of God.  But because intellectual labor is insufficient it does not follow, as is so often assumed, that it is unnecessary.  God may, it is true, overcome all intellectual obstacles by an immediate exercise of His regenerative power.  Sometimes He does. But He does so very seldom.  Usually He exerts His power in connection with certain conditions of the human mind.  Usually He does not bring into the Kingdom, entirely without preparation, those whose mind and fancy are completely dominated by ideas which make the acceptance of the gospel logically impossible.

Modern culture is a tremendous force.  It affects all classes of society. It affects the ignorant as well as the learned. What is to be done about it?  In the first place the Church may simply withdraw from the conflict. She may simply allow the mighty stream of modern thought to flow by unheeded and do her work merely in the back-eddies of the current.  There are still some men in the world who have been unaffected by modern culture.  They may still be won for Christ without intellectual labor.  And they must be won. It is useful, it is necessary work. If the Church is satisfied with that alone, let her give up the scientific education of her ministry. Let her assume the truth of her message and learn simply how it may be applied in detail to modern industrial and social conditions. Let her give up the laborious study of Greek and Hebrew. Let her abandon the scientific study of history to the men of the world. In a day of increased scientific interest, let the

Church go on becoming less scientific. In a day of increased specialization, of renewed interest in philology and in history, of more rigorous scientific method, let the Church go on abandoning her Bible to her enemies. They will study it scientifically, rest assured, if the Church does not. Let her substitute sociology altogether for Hebrew, practical expertness for the proof of her gospel. Let her shorten the preparation of her ministry, let her permit it to be interrupted yet more and more by premature practical activity. By doing so she will win a straggler here and there. But her winnings will be but temporary. The great current of modern culture will sooner or later engulf her puny eddy. God will save her somehow — out of the depths. But the labor of centuries will have been swept away. God grant that the Church may not resign herself to that. God grant she may face her problem squarely and bravely. That problem is not easy. It involves the very basis of her faith. Christianity is the proclamation of an historical fact — that Jesus Christ rose from the dead. Modern thought has no place for that proclamation. It prevents men even from listening to the message. Yet the culture of to-day cannot simply be rejected as a whole. It is not like the pagan culture of the first century. It is not wholly non-Christian. Much of it has been derived directly from the Bible. There are significant movements in it, going to waste, which might well be used for the defence of the gospel. The situation is complex. Easy wholesale measures are not in place. Discrimination, investigation is necessary. Some of modern thought must be refuted. The rest must be made subservient. But nothing in it can be ignored. He that is not with us is against us. Modern culture is a mighty force. It is either subservient to the gospel or else it is the deadliest enemy of the gospel. For making it subservient, religious emotion is not enough, intellectual labor is also necessary. And that labor is being neglected. The Church has turned to easier tasks. And now she is reaping the fruits of her indolence. Now she must batttle for her life.

The situation is desperate. It might discourage us. But not if
we are truly Christians. Not if we are living in vital communion
with the risen Lord. If we are really convinced of the truth of our
message, then we can proclaim it before a world of enemies, then
the very difficulty of our task, the very scarcity of our allies becomes an inspiration, then we can even rejoice that God did not
place us in an easy age, but in a time of doubt and perplexity and
battle. Then, too, we shall not be afraid to call forth other soldiers
into the conflict. Instead of making our theological seminaries
merely centres of religious emotion, we shall make them battle-
grounds of the faith, where, helped a little by the experience of
Christian teachers, men are taught to fight their own battle,
where they come to appreciate the real strength of the adversary
and in the hard school of intellectual struggle learn to substitute
for the unthinking faith of childhood the profound convictions of
full-grown men. Let us not fear in this a loss of spiritual power.
The Church is perishing to-day through the lack of thinking, not
through an excess of it. She is winning victories in the sphere
of material betterment. Such victories are glorious. God save us
from the heartless crime of disparaging them. They are relieving
the misery of men. But if they stand alone, I fear they are but
temporary. The things which are seen are temporal; the things
which are not seen are eternal. What will become of philanthropy
if God be lost? Beneath the surface of life lies a world of spirit.
Philosophers have attempted to explore it. Christianity has revealed its wonders to the simple soul. There lie the springs of the
Church's power. But that spiritual realm cannot be entered without controversy. And now the Church is shrinking from the conflict. Driven from the spiritual realm by the current of modern
thought, she is consoling herself with things about which there
is no dispute. If she favors better housing for the poor, she need
fear no contradiction. She will need all her courage, she will have
enemies enough, God knows. But they will not fight her with
argument. The twentieth century, in theory, is agreed on social

betterment. But sin, and death, and salvation, and life, and God—about these things there is debate. You can avoid the debate if you choose. You need only drift with the current. Preach every Sunday during your Seminary course, devote the fag ends of your time to study and to thought, study about as you studied in college — and these questions will probably never trouble you. The great questions may easily be avoided. Many preachers are avoiding them. And many preachers are preaching to the air. The Church is waiting for men of another type. Men to fight her battles and solve her problems. The hope of finding them is the one great inspiration of a Seminary's life. They need not all be men of conspicuous attainments. But they must all be men of thought. They must fight hard against spiritual and intellectual indolence. Their thinking may be confined to narrow limits. But it must be their own. To them theology must be something more than a task. It must be a matter of inquiry. It must lead not to successful memorizing, but to genuine convictions.

The Church is puzzled by the world's indifference. She is trying to overcome it by adapting her message to the fashions of the day. But if, instead, before the conflict, she would descend into the secret place of meditation, if by the clear light of the gospel she would seek an answer not merely to the questions of the hour but, first of all, to the eternal problems of the spiritual world then perhaps, by God's grace, through His good Spirit, in His good time, she might issue forth once more with power, and an age of doubt might be followed by the dawn of an era of faith.

# XIII

## History and Faith

THE STUDENT of the New Testament should be primarily an historian. The centre and core of all the Bible is history. Everything else that the Bible contains is fitted into an historical framework and leads up to an historical climax. The Bible is primarily a record of events.

That assertion will not pass unchallenged. The modern Church is impatient of history. History, we are told, is a dead thing. Let us forget the Amalekites, and fight the enemies that are at our doors. The true essence of the Bible is to be found in eternal ideas; history is merely the form in which those ideas are expressed. It makes no difference whether the history is real or fictitious; in either case, the ideas are the same. It makes no difference whether Abraham was an historical personage or a myth; in either case his life is an inspiring example of faith. It makes no difference whether Moses was really a mediator between God and Israel; in any case the record of Sinai embodies the idea of a covenant between God and His people. It makes no difference whether Jesus really lived and died and rose again as He is declared to have done in the Gospels; in any case the Gospel picture, be it ideal or be it history, is an encouragement to filial piety. In this way, religion has been made independent, as is thought, of the uncertainties of historical research. The separation of Christianity from history has been a great concern of modern theology. It has been an inspiring attempt. But it has been a failure.

Give up history, and you can retain some things. You can retain a belief in God. But philosophical theism has never been a powerful force in the world. You can retain a lofty ethical ideal. But be perfectly clear about one point — you can never retain a gospel. For gospel means "good news," tidings, information about something that has happened. In other words, it means history. A gospel independent of history is simple a contradiction in terms.

We are shut up in this world as in a beleaguered camp. Dismayed by the stern facts of life, we are urged by the modern preacher to have courage. Let us treat God as our Father; let us continue bravely in the battle of life. But alas, the facts are too plain—those facts which are always with us. The fact of suffering! How do you know that God is all love and kindness? Nature is full of horrors. Human suffering may be unpleasant, but it is real, and God must have something to do with it. The fact of death! No matter how satisfying the joys of earth, it cannot be denied at least that they will soon depart, and of what use are joys that last but for a day? A span of life—and then, for all of us, blank, unfathomed mystery! The fact of guilt! What if the condemnation of conscience should be but the foretaste of judgment? What if contact with the infinite should be contact with a dreadful infinity of holiness? What if the inscrutable cause of all things should turn out to be a righteous God? The fact of sin! The thraldom of habit! This strange subjection to a mysterious power of evil that is leading resistlessly into some unknown abyss! To these facts the modern preacher responds—with exhortation. Make the best of the situation, he says, look on the bright side of life. Very eloquent, my friend! But alas, you cannot change the facts. The modern preacher offers reflection. The Bible offers more. The Bible offers news — not reflection on the old, but tidings of something new; not something that can be deduced or something that can be discovered, but something that has happened; not philosophy, but history; not exhortation, but a gospel.

something that puts a new face upon life.  What that something
is, is told us in Matthew, Mark, Luke and John.  It is the life and
death and resurrection of Jesus Christ.  The authority of the Bible
should be tested here at the central point.  Is the Bible right about
Jesus?

The Bible account of Jesus contains mysteries, but the essence of
it can be put almost in a word.  Jesus of Nazareth was not a product
of the world, but a Saviour come from outside the world.  His birth
was a mystery.  His life was a life of perfect purity, of awful
righteousness, and of gracious, sovereign power.  His death was
no mere holy martyrdom, but a sacrifice for the sins of the world.
His resurrection was not an aspiration in the hearts of His disciples, but a mighty act of God.  He is alive, and present at this
hour to help us if we will turn to Him.  He is more than one of
the sons of men; He is in mysterious union with the eternal God.

That is the Bible account of Jesus.  It is opposed today by
another account.  That account appears in many forms, but the
essence of it is simple.  Jesus of Nazareth, it maintains was the
fairest flower of humanity.  He lived a life of remarkable purity
and unselfishness.  So deep was His filial piety, so profound His
consciousness of a mission, that He came to regard Himself, not
merely as a prophet, but as the Messiah.  By opposing the hypocrisy of the Jews, or by imprudent obtrusion of His lofty claims,
He suffered martydom.  He died on the cross.  After His death,
His followers were discouraged.  But His cause was not lost; the
memory of Him was too strong; the disciples simply could not
believe that He had perished.  Predisposed psychologically in this
way, they had visionary experiences; they thought they saw Him.
These visions were hallucinations.  But they were the means by
which the personality of Jesus retained its power; they were the
foundation of the Christian Church.

There, in a word, is the issue.  Jesus a product of the world, or
a heavenly being come from without?  A teacher and example,

or a Saviour? The issue is sharp—the Bible against the modern preacher. Here is the real test of Bible authority. If the Bible is right here, at the decisive point, probably it is right elsewhere. If it is wrong here, then its authority is gone. The question must be faced. What shall we think about Jesus of Nazareth?

From the middle of the first century, certain interesting documents have been preserved; they are the epistles of Paul. The genuineness of them — the chief of them at any rate — is not seriously doubted, and they can be dated with approximate accuracy. They form, therefore, a fixed starting-point in controvesy. These epistles were written by a remarkable man. Paul cannot be brushed lightly aside. He was certainly, to say the least, one of the most influential men that ever lived. His influence was a mighty building; probably it was not erected on the sand.

In his letters, Paul has revealed the very depths of a tremendous religious experience. That experience was founded, not upon a profound philosophy or daring speculation, but upon a Palestinian Jew who had lived but a few years before. That Jew was Jesus of Nazareth. Paul had a strange view of Jesus; he separated Him sharply from man and placed Him clearly on the side of God. "Not by man, but by Jesus Christ," he says at the beginning of Galatians, and he implies the same thing on every page of his letters. Jesus Christ, according to Paul, was man, but He was also more.

That is a very strange fact. Only through familiarity have we ceased to wonder at it. Look at the thing a moment as though for the first time. A Jew lives in Palestine, and is executed like a common criminal. Almost immediately after His death He is raised to divine dignity by one of His contemporaries — not by a negligible enthusiast either, but by one of the most commanding figures in the history of the world. So the thing presents itself to the modern historian. There is a problem here. However the problem may be solved, it can be ignored by no one. The man Jesus deified by Paul — that is a very remarkable fact. The late H. J. Holtzmann, who may be regarded as the typical exponent of modern naturalistic criticism of the New Testament, admitted that for the rapid apotheosis of Jesus as it appears in the epistles of Paul he was able to cite no parallel in the religious history of the race.*

The raising of Jesus to superhuman dignity was extraordinarily rapid even if it was due to Paul. But it was most emphatically not due to Paul; it can be traced clearly to the original disciples of Jesus. And that too on the basis of the Pauline Epistles alone. The epistles show that with regard to the person of Christ Paul was in agreement with those who had been apostles before him. Even the Judaizers had no dispute with Paul's conception of Jesus as a heavenly being. About other things there was debate; about this point there is not a trace of a conflict. With regard to the supernatural Christ Paul appears everywhere in perfect harmony with all Palestinian Christians. That is a fact of enormous significance. The heavenly Christ of Paul was also the Christ of those who had walked and talked with Jesus of Nazareth. Think of it! Those men had seen Jesus subject to all the petty limitations of human life. Yet suddenly, almost immediately after His shameful death, they became convinced that He had risen from the tomb and that He was a heavenly being. There is an historical problem here — for modern naturalism, we venture to think, an unsolved problem. A man, Jesus, regarded as a heavenly being, not by later generations who could be deceived by the nimbus of distance and mystery, but actually by His intimate friends! A strange hallucination indeed! And founded upon that hallucination the whole of the modern world!

So much for Paul. A good deal can be learned from him alone — enough to give us pause. But that is not all that we know about Jesus; it is only a beginning. The Gospels enrich our knowledge; they provide an extended picture.

---

* In *Protestantische Monatshefte*, iv (1900), pp. 465 ff., and in *Christliche Welt*, xxiv (1910), column 153.

In their picture of Jesus the Gospels agree with Paul; like Paul, they make of Jesus a supernatural person. Not one of the Gospels, but all of them! The day is past when the divine Christ of John could be confronted with a human Christ of Mark. Historical students of all shades of opinion have now come to see that Mark as well as John (though it is believed in a lesser degree) presents an exalted Christology, Mark as well as John represents Jesus clearly as a supernatural person.

A supernatural person, according to modern historians, never existed. That is the fundamental principle of modern naturalism. The world, it is said, must be explained as an absolutely unbroken development, obeying fixed laws. The supernatural Christ of the Gospels never existed. How then explain the Gospel picture? You might explain it as fiction — the Gospel account of Jesus throughout a myth. That explanation is seriously being proposed today. But it is absurd; it will never convince any body of genuine historians. The matter is at any rate not so simple as that. The Gospels present a supernatural person, but they also present a real person — a very real, a very concrete, a very inimitable person. That is not denied by modern liberalism. Indeed it cannot possibly be denied. If the Jesus who spoke the parables, the Jesus who opposed the Pharisees, the Jesus who ate with publicans and sinners, is not a real person, living under real conditions, at a definite point of time, then there is no way of distinguishing history from sham.

On the one hand, then, the Jesus of the Gospels is a supernatural person; on the other hand, He is a real person. But according to modern naturalism, a supernatural person never existed. He is a supernatural person; He is a real person; and yet a supernatural person is never real! A problem here! What is the solution? Why, obviously, says the modern historian — obviously, there are two elements in the Gospels. In the first place, there is genuine historical tradition. That has preserved the real Jesus. In the second place, there is myth. That has

added the supernatural attributes. The duty of the historian is
to separate the two — to discover the genuine human traits of
the Galilean prophet beneath the gaudy colors which have almost
hopelessly defaced His portrait, to disentangle the human Jesus
from the tawdry ornamentation which has been hung about Him
by naïve and unintelligent admirers.

Separate the natural and the supernatural in the Gospel account of Jesus — that has been the task of modern liberalism.
How shall the work be done? We must admit at least that the
myth-making process began very early; it has affected even the
very earliest literary sources that we know. But let us not be
discouraged. Whenever the mythical elaboration began, it may
now be reversed. Let us simply go through the Gospels and
separate the wheat from the tares. Let us separate the natural
from the supernatural, the human from the divine, the believable
from the unbelievable. When we have thus picked out the work-
able elements, let us combine them into some sort of picture of
the historical Jesus. Such is the method. The result is what is
called "the liberal Jesus." It has been a splendid effort. I know
scarcely any more brilliant chapter in the history of the human
spirit than this "quest of the historical Jesus." The modern world
has put its very life and soul into this task. It has been a splendid
effort. But it has also been — a failure.

In the first place, there is the initial difficulty of separating the
natural from the supernatural in the Gospel narrative. The two
are inextricably intertwined. Some of the incidents, you say, are
evidently historical; they are so full of local color; they could
never have been invented. Yes, but unfortunately the miraculous
incidents possess exactly the same qualities. You help yourself,
then, by admissions. Jesus, you say, was a faith-healer of remarkable power; many of the cures related in the Gospels are
real, though they are not really miraculous. But that does not
carry you far. Faith-healing is often a totally inadequate explanation of the cures. And those supposed faith-cures are not a bit

more vividly, more concretely, more inimitably related than the most uncompromising of the miracles. The attempt to separate divine and human in the Gospels leads naturally to a radical scepticism. The wheat is rooted up with the tares. If the supernatural is untrue, then the whole must go, for the supernatural is inseparable from the rest. This tendency is not merely logical; it is not merely what might naturally be; it is actual. Liberal scholars are rejecting more and more of the Gospels; others are denying that there is any certainly historical element at all. Such scepticism is absurd. Of it you need have no fear; it will always be corrected by common sense. The Gospel narrative is too inimitably concrete, too absolutely incapable of invention. If elimination of the supernatural leads logically to elimination of the whole, that is simply a refutation of the whole critical process. The supernatural Jesus is the only Jesus that we know.

In the second place, suppose this first task has been accomplished. It is really impossible, but suppose it has been done. You have reconstructed the historical Jesus — a teacher of righteousness, an inspired prophet, a pure worshipper of God. You clothe Him with all the art of modern research; you throw upon Him the warm, deceptive, calcium-light of modern sentimentality. But all to no purpose! The liberal Jesus remains an impossible figure of the stage. There is a contradiction at the very centre of His being. That contradiction arises from His Messianic consciousness. This simple prophet of yours, this humble child of God, thought that He was a heavenly being who was to come on the clouds of heaven and be the instrument in judging the earth. There is a tremendous contradiction here. A few extremists rid themselves easily of the difficulty; they simply deny that Jesus ever thought He was the Messiah. An heroic measure, which is generally rejected! The Messianic consciousness is rooted far too deep in the sources ever to be removed by a critical process. That Jesus thought He was the Messiah is nearly as certain as that He lived at all. There is a tremendous problem there. It would be no problem if Jesus were an ordinary fanatic or unbalanced visionary; He might then have deceived Himself as well as others. But as a matter of fact He was no ordinary fanatic, no megalomaniac. On the contrary, His calmness and unselfishness and strength have produced an indelible impression. It was such an one who thought that He was the Son of Man to come on the clouds of heaven. A contradiction! Do not think I am exaggerating. The difficulty is felt by all. After all has been done, after the miraculous has carefully been eliminated, there is still, as a recent liberal writer has said, something puzzling, something almost uncanny, about  Jesus.* He refuses to be forced into the mould of a harmless teacher. A few men draw the logical conclusion. Jesus, they say, was insane. That is consistent. But it is absurd.

Suppose, however, that all these objections have been overcome. Suppose the critical sifting of the Gospel tradition has been accomplished, suppose the resulting picture of Jesus is comprehensible — even then the work is only half done. How did this human Jesus come to be regarded as a superhuman Jesus by His intimate friends, and how, upon the foundation of this strange belief was there reared the edifice of the Christian Church?

In the early part of the first century, in one of the petty principalities subject to Rome, there lived an interesting man. Until the age of thirty years He led an obscure life in a Galilean family, then began a course of religious and ethical teaching accompanied by a remarkable ministry of healing. At first His preaching was crowned with a measure of success, but soon the crowds deserted Him, and after three or four years, He fell victim in Jerusalem to the jealousy of His countrymen and the cowardice of the Roman governor. His few faithful disciples were utterly disheartened; His shameful death was the end of all their high ambitions. After a few days, however, an astonishing thing happened. It is the most astonishing thing in all history. Those same disheartened

---

* Heitmüller, *Jesus*, 1913, p. 71.

men suddenly displayed a surprising activity. They began preaching, with remarkable success, in Jerusalem, the very scene of their disgrace. In a few years, the religion that they preached burst the bands of Judaism, and planted itself in the great centres of the Graeco-Roman world. At first despised, then persecuted, it overcame all obstacles; in less than three hundred years it became the dominant religion of the Empire and it has exerted an incalculable influence upon the modern world.

Jesus, Himself, the Founder, had not succeeded in winning any considerable number of permanent adherents; during His lifetime, the genuine disciples were comparatively few. It is after His death that the origin of Christianity as an influential movement is to be placed. Now it seems exceedingly unnatural that Jesus' disciples could thus accomplish what He had failed to accomplish. They were evidently far inferior to Him in spiritual discernment and in courage; they had not displayed the slightest trace of originality; they had been abjectly dependent upon the Master; they had not even succeeded in understanding Him. Furthermore, what little understanding, what little courage they may have had was dissipated by His death. "Smite the shepherd, and the sheep shall be scattered." How could such men succeed where their Master had failed? How could they institute the mightiest religious movement in the history of the world?

Of course, you can amuse yourself by suggesting impossible hypotheses. You might suggest, for instance, that after the death of Jesus His disciples sat quietly down and reflected on His teaching. "Do unto others as you would have others do unto you." "Love your enemies." These are pretty good principles; they are of permanent value. Are they not as good now, the disciples might have said, as they were when Jesus was alive? "Our Father which art in heaven." Is not that a good way of addressing God? May not God be our Father even though Jesus is now dead? The disciples might conceivably have come to such conclusions. But certainly nothing could be more unlikely. These men had not even understood the teachings of Jesus when He was alive, not even under the immediate impact of that tremendous personality. How much less would they understand after He had died, and died in a way that indicated hopeless failure! What hope could such men have, at such a time, of influencing the world? Furthermore, the hypothesis has not one jot of evidence in its favor. Christianity never was the continuation of the work of a dead teacher.

It is evident, therefore, that in the short interval between the death of Jesus and the first Christian preaching, something had happened. Something must have happened to explain the transformation of those weak, discouraged men into the spiritual conquerors of the world. Whatever that happening was, it is the greatest event in history. An event is measured by its consequences — and that event has transformed the world.

According to modern naturalism, that event, which caused the founding of the Christian Church, was a vision, an hallucination; according to the New Testament, it was the resurrection of Jesus from the dead. The former hypothesis has been held in a variety of forms; it has been buttressed by all the learning and all the ingenuity of modern scholarship. But all to no purpose! The visionary hypothesis may be demanded by a naturalistic philosophy; to the historian it must ever remain unsatisfactory. History is relentlessly plain. The foundation of the Church is either inexplicable, or else it is to be explained by the resurrection of Jesus Christ from the dead. But if the resurrection be accepted, then the lofty claims of Jesus are substantiated; Jesus was then no mere man, but God and man, God come in the flesh.

We have examined the liberal reconstruction of Jesus. It breaks down, we have seen, at least at three points.

It fails, in the first place, in trying to separate divine and human in the Gospel picture. Such separation is impossible; divine and human are too closely interwoven; reject the divine, and you must reject the human too. To-day the conclusion is being drawn. We must reject it all! Jesus never lived! Are you disturbed by such radicalism? I for my part not a bit. It is to me rather the most hopeful sign of the times. The liberal Jesus never existed — that is all it proves. It proves nothing against the divine Saviour. Jesus was divine, or else we have no certain proof that He ever lived. I am glad to accept the alternative.

In the second place, the liberal Jesus, after He has been reconstructed, despite His limitations is a monstrosity. The Messianic consciousness introduces a contradiction into the very centre of His being; the liberal Jesus is not the sort of man who ever could have thought that He was the Messiah. A humble teacher who thought He was the Judge of all the earth! Such an one would have been insane. To-day men are drawing the conclusion; Jesus is being investigated seriously by the alienists. But do not be alarmed at their diagnosis. That Jesus they are investigating is not the Jesus of the Bible. They are investigating a man who thought He was Messiah and was not Messiah; against one who thought He was Messiah and was Messiah they have obviously nothing to say. Their diagnosis may be accepted; perhaps the liberal Jesus, if He ever existed, was insane. But that is not the Jesus whom we love.

In the third place, the liberal Jesus is insufficient to account for the origin of the Christian Church. The mighty edifice of Christendom was not erected upon a pin-point. Radical thinkers are drawing the conclusion. Christianity, they say, was not founded upon Jesus of Nazareth. It arose in some other way. It was a syncretistic religion; Jesus was the name of a heathen god. Or it was a social movement that arose in Rome about the middle of the first century. These constructions need no refutation; they are absurd. Hence comes their value. Because they are absurd, they reduce liberalism to an absurdity. A mild-mannered rabbi will not account for the origin of the Church. Liberalism has left a blank at the beginning of Christian history. History abhors a vacuum. These absurd theories are the necessary consequence; they have simply tried to fill the void.

The modern substitute for the Jesus of the Bible has been tried and found wanting. The liberal Jesus — what a world of lofty thinking, what a wealth of noble sentiment was put into His construction! But now there are some indications that He is about to fall. He is beginning to give place to a radical scepticism. Such scepticism is absurd; Jesus lived, if any history is true. Jesus lived, but what Jesus? Not the Jesus of modern naturalism! But the Jesus of the Bible! In the wonders of the Gospel story, in the character of Jesus, in His mysterious self-consciousness, in the very origin of the Christian Church, we discover a problem, which defies the best efforts of the naturalistic historian, which pushes us relentlessly off the safe ground of the phenomenal world toward the intellectual abyss of supernaturalism, which forces us, despite the resistance of the modern mind, to recognize a very act of God, which substitutes for the silent God of philosophy the God and Father of our Lord Jesus Christ, who, having spoken at sundry times and in divers manners unto the fathers by the prophets, hath in these last days spoken unto us by His Son.

The resurrection of Jesus is a fact of history; it is good news; it is an event that has put a new face upon life. But how can the acceptance of an historical fact satisfy the longing of our souls? Must we stake our salvation upon the intricacies of historical research? Is the trained historian the modern priest without whose gracious intervention no one can see God? Surely some more immediate certitude is required.

The objection would be valid if history stood alone. But history does not stand alone; it is confirmed by experience.

An historical conviction of the resurrection of Jesus is not the end of faith but only the beginning; if faith stops there, it will probably never stand the fires of criticism. We are told that Jesus rose from the dead; the message is supported by a singular weight of evidence. But it is not just a message remote from us; it concerns not merely the past. If Jesus rose from the dead, as He is declared to have done in the Gospels, then He is still alive, and if He is still alive, then He may still be found. He is present with us today to help us if we will but turn to Him. The historical evidence for the resurrection amounted only to probability; probability is the best that history can do. But the probability was at least sufficient for a trial. We accepted the Easter message enough to make trial of it. And making trial of it we found that it is true. Christian experience cannot do without history, but it adds to history that directness, that immediateness, that intimacy of conviction which delivers us from fear. "Now we believe, not because of thy saying: for we have heard him ourselves, and know that this is indeed the Christ, the Saviour of the world."

The Bible, then, is right at the central point; it is right in its account of Jesus; it has validated its principal claim. Here, however, a curious phenomenon comes into view. Some men are strangely ungrateful. Now that we have Jesus, they say, we can be indifferent to the Bible. We have the present Christ; we care nothing about the dead documents of the past. You have Christ? But how, pray, did you get Him? There is but one answer; you got Him through the Bible. Without the Bible you would never have known so much as whether there be any Christ. Yet now that you have Christ you give the Bible up; you are ready to abandon it to its enemies; you are not interested in the findings of criticism. Apparently, then, you have used the Bible as a ladder to scale the dizzy height of Christian experience, but now that you are safe on top you kick the ladder down. Very natural! But what of the poor souls who are still battling with the flood beneath? They need the ladder too. But the figure is misleading. The Bible is not a ladder; it is a foundation. It is buttressed, indeed, by experience; if you have the present Christ, then you know that the Bible account is true. But *if* the Bible *were* false, your faith would go. You cannot, therefore, be indifferent to Bible

criticism. Let us not deceive ourselves. The Bible is at the foundation of the Church. Undermine that foundation, and the Church
will fall. It will fall, and great will be the fall of it.

Two conceptions of Christianity are struggling for the ascend-
ency to-day; the question that we have been discussing is part
of a still larger problem. The Bible against the modern preacher!
Is Christianity a means to an end, or an end in itself, an improvement of the world, or the creation of a new world? Is sin a
necessary stage in the development of humanity, or a yawning
chasm in the very structure of the universe? Is the world's good
sufficient to overcome the world's evil, or is this world lost in sin?
Is communion with God a help toward the betterment of humanity, or itself the one great ultimate goal of human life? Is
God identified with the world, or separated from it by the infinite
abyss of sin? Modern culture is here in conflict with the Bible.
The Church is in perplexity. She is trying to compromise. She
is saying, Peace, peace, when there is no peace. And rapidly she
is losing her power. The time has come when she must choose.
God grant she may choose aright! God grant she may decide for
the Bible! The Bible is despised — to the Jews a stumbling-
block, to the Greeks foolishness — but the Bible is right. God
is not a name for the totality of things, but an awful, mysterious,
holy Person, not a "present God," in the modern sense, not a God
who is with us by necessity, and has nothing to offer us but what
we have already, but a God who from the heaven of His awful
holiness has of His own free grace had pity on our bondage, and
sent His Son to deliver us from the present evil world and receive
us into the glorious freedom of communion with Himself.

CHAPTER XIV

# The Modern Use of the Bible

The "modern use of the Bible,"* as Dr. Fosdick sets it forth, consists first in a somewhat naïve application of the evolutionary point of view, and second in a separation between "abiding experiences" and the temporary "mental categories" in which those experiences were expressed. These two closely related aspects of the book may be considered briefly in turn.

In the first place, then, our author applies to the Bible the evolutionary point of view; the Bible, he insists, must not be treated as though it lay all on the same plane, but on the contrary "the new approach to the Bible saves us from the necessity of apologizing for immature stages in the development of the Biblical revelation."[1]

From the purely scientific point of view this (the arrangement of the documents of the Bible in their approximately chronological order) is an absorbingly interesting matter, but even more from the standpoint of practical results its importance is difficult to exaggerate. It means that we can trace the great ideas of Scripture in their development from their simple and elementary forms, when they first appear in the earliest writings, until they come to their full maturity in the latest books. Indeed, the general soundness of the critical results is tested by this fact that as one moves up from the earlier writings toward the later he can observe the development of any idea he chooses to select, such as God, man, duty, sin, worship[2] . . . No longer can we think of the Book as on a level, no longer read its maturer messages back into its earlier sources. We know now that every

* *The Modern Use of the Bible*, By HARRY EMERSON FOSDICK, D. D., Morris K. Jessup Professor of Practical Theology, Union Theological Seminary, New York. New York: The Macmillan Company, 1924. p. 291
1. p. 27.
2. pp. 7 f.

idea in the Bible started from primitive and childlike origins and, with however many setbacks and delays, grew in scope and height toward the culmination in Christ's Gospel. We know now that the Bible is the record of an amazing spiritual development.[3]

We have called this evolutionary view of the Bible "naïve" for several reasons. In the first place it does not do justice to the possibility of retrogression as well as advance — a possibility which certainly exists if history be looked at from the naturalistic point of view. It is true that Dr. Fosdick speaks of the roadway that leads any religious and ethical idea of the Bible "to its climax in the teaching of Jesus" as a roadway that is "often uneven;"[4] it is true that he speaks of "setbacks and delays" that occurred in the development. But despite these admissions it seems fairly clear that the fact of progress is a dogma with Dr. Fosdick. Yet we are inclined to doubt whether that dogma is in such complete accord with the findings of modern science as our author seems to suppose.

In the second place, Dr. Fosdick does not seem to see that the chronological arrangement of the Biblical sources upon which the evolutionary reconstruction depends is itself based upon that elimination of supernatural revelation which it in turn is made to support. As it stands, of course, the Biblical history does not fall into the evolutionary scheme, but involves supernatural interpositions of God in miracle and in revelation; and if, after the sources are first arranged at will in the order that will show a regular development from crude beginnings to a higher spiritual religion, the rearranged Bible shows that beautifully regular development which is the goal of the rearrangement, the result can scarcely be called significant. The truth is that the critical reconstruction itself presupposes the naturalistic principle which it is made to demonstrate. The whole argument moves in a vicious circle.

But we have not yet commented on the most astonishing thing about Dr. Fosdick's presentation of the modern use of the Bible.

---

3. pp. 11f.
4. p. 8.

The most astonishing thing is that in exalting the historical method of approach our author displays so little acquaintance with that to which he himself appeals. It would be difficult to discover a book which exhibits less understanding than this book does for the historical point of view.

It is not merely misinformation in detail to which we refer. Such misinformation is indeed at times surprising. It is somewhat surprising, for example, to find a modern man, professor in Union Theological Seminary, writing about textual criticism as though it were "a powerful help in correcting obscure and perverted renderings," and as though it enabled us to select "the more ancient or more sensible renderings."[5] What has textual criticism, which concerns, as Dr. Fosdick himself says, the task of getting back as nearly as possible to "the original autograph copies of the Scriptures," to do with the selection of the more ancient or more sensible "renderings" — that is, translations? The reader is almost tempted to doubt whether our author has any clear understanding of what textual criticism is.

But what is far more important than all such confusions in detail is the rejection of historical method at the central point — that is in the presentation of the teaching of Jesus and of the apostles. Our author is very severe upon the ancient allegorizers who read their own ideas into the Biblical writings; but what he does not seem to see is that he has made himself guilty, in a far more extreme form, of the fault which he blames in them. It would be difficult to discover a more complete abandonment of grammatico-historical exegesis, in fact though not in theory, than that which is to be found in the present book.

The prerequisite of grammatico-historical exegesis is a sharp separation between the question what the modern reader could have wished the Biblical writers to say and the question what the writers actually did say. This method has been practised, we believe, best of all by those scholars who have themselves been

5. pp. 39f.

willing to learn from the Bible, who have been willing to mould their own views of God and the world and salvation upon the views which the Biblical writers present. But it has also been practised with considerable success by many modern scholars who have not at all accepted for themselves the teachings of the Biblical writers and yet have honestly endeavored to present those teachings as they are without admixture of their own modern predilections. In Dr. Fosdick's case, however, such historical method is abandoned, and the teachings of Jesus and of the apostles are presented not as the sources — even the critically reconstructed sources — show them to have been, but as the modern author would have liked to have them be.

We do not mean that our author is entirely unaware of the fact that the apostles and even Jesus taught things that he himself cannot believe to be true; he does, for example, face in passing the possibility that Jesus shared the apocalyptic ideas of His people, which "the modern man" of course rejects. He does, moreover, deal incidentally with the question of the Messianic consciousness. But at this point he finds refuge in an extreme skepticism about the Gospels which few even of modern naturalistic historians have been willing to share; he is doubtful whether Jesus ever presented himself as the Messiah — a view which makes the origin of the Church an insoluble enigma. At other points he takes refuge in a total ignoring of the problems. One could read Dr. Fosdick's presentation of the teaching of Jesus and not have the slightest inkling of the central place which Jesus gave, for example, to that theistic view of God which Dr. Fosdick so vigorously rejects, and to the awe-inspiring doctrine of heaven and hell which runs all through the words of Jesus and is at the very foundation of the terrible earnestness of His ethical demands. These central characteristics of Jesus' teaching are for Dr. Fosdick as though they did not exist; he does not even face the problem which they present to the "modern man." Very different is the attitude of real (however radical) scholarship like that of Dr.

McGiffert, who in his *God of the Early Christians*,[6] despite a false limitation of the sources, has presented, though of course not explicitly, as devastating a refutation of Dr. Fosdick's anti-historical account of Jesus as any refutation which we might undertake.

Our author's abandonment of historical method appears at many points; it appears, for example, as has already been observed, in his ignoring of Jesus' theism and of His teaching about future rewards and punishments. But it appears most crassly of all, perhaps, in his complete failure to recognize the factual or dispensational basis of all the New Testament teaching. The plain fact of history, a fact which must be recognized by all impartial historians, is that Jesus was conscious of standing at the threshold of a new era which was to be begun by a catastrophic event, and that the apostles were conscious of looking back upon that event and of having had its meaning revealed to them by God. In Dr. Fosdick's book this central feature of the New Testament is consistently or almost consistently ignored. The result appears in exegetical monstrosities like the following:[7]

In the second place, having thus appealed to the Old Testament against the clever and sophistical interpretations that had been fathered (?) on it, he (Jesus) distinguished in the Old Testament between significant and negligible elements. He rated ceremonial law low and ethical law high. The Mosaic laws of clean and unclean foods were plainly written in the Book, but Jesus abolished them from the category of the ethical . . .

In the third place, having appealed from the oral law to the written law, and within the written law having appealed from ceremonial elements to ethical principles, he went on to recognize that some ethical principles in the written law had been outgrown . . . His whole Sermon on the Mount, starting with its assurance that the old law is to be fulfilled and not destroyed, is a definite endeavor to see that it is fulfilled, carried to completion, with its outgrown elements superseded and its abiding ideals crowned and consummated.

What the Master did, in a word, was to plunge deep beneath the sophisticated exegesis of his time, the timid literalisms, which bound men by a text instead of liberating them by a truth, and in the abiding experiences

6. Cf. PRINCETON THEOLOGICAL REVIEW, Vol. xxiii (October 1924), pp. 544 ff.

7. pp. 91 ff.

and principles of the Old Testament find a revelation of God that was fruitful and true.

Let it be clearly noted that this attitude of Jesus involved the recognition of the fact that the Scriptures did contain outgrown elements.

Let us then frankly take our stand with the Master on this basic matter!
Of course there are outgrown elements in Scripture. How could it be
otherwise in a changing world? . . .

A similar method of treatment is applied even to Paul:

In this (that is, in "translating the formula back into the life out of
which it came") they (the modern liberals) are like Paul. Brought up a
Jew, indoctrinated in the strictest sect of Hebrew orthodoxy, he discovered that much of the religious framework in which he had trusted was
for him untenable. He gave up his old interpretation of the Scripture,
dropped circumcision, clean and unclean foods, and the burden of ceremonial requirement. He gave up his old view of worship and left the
temple behind. A more radical transition in mental framework and practical religious expression it would be hard to find. Paul, however, did not
give up religion. He went deeper into it. His casting off of old forms
sprang from the positive expansion of his religious experience. Cramped
and prisoned in Judaism, he sought more room for his enlarging life. He
became a liberal, from the standpoint of his older thinking, not because he
was less religious, but because he was more religious. He struck out for
air to breathe and he found it in the central regenerative experiences which
lie at the heart of the Gospel. And when he was through he was sure that
he understood the depths of the Old Testament as he had never understood them before . That is the very genius of liberalism. Its first step is to
go through old formulas into the experiences out of which all religious
formulas must come. In Phillips Brooks' figure, it beats the crust back into
the batter.[8]

Such is Dr. Fosdick's presentation of Jesus and of Paul. Both
Jesus and Paul appear, according to our author, to have been
pragmatists of the most approved modern kind. But of course
such a presentation has nothing in the world to do with history;
it increases our knowledge of the agnostic Modernism of the
present day, but as an account of those who lived in the first
century it is nothing short of absurd.

To the historian, as distinguished from the propagandist, it
should be abundantly plain that when Jesus opposed His stupendous "I say unto you" to the requirements of the Old Testament

8. pp. 186 ff.

He was not appealing to a general right of man as man to take the commands of God with a grain of salt — to penetrate (if we may borrow from the very common misuse of 2 Cor. iii. 6) behind the "letter" to the "spirit"; but He was appealing to His own exalted right, as Messiah, to legislate for the new age which His coming was to usher in. Certainly He was not holding that the requirements of the Old Testament had been "outgrown" (what a really astonishing departure from historical method is involved in our author's repeated use, as expository of Jesus, of that word!); but He was announcing the beginning of an entirely new dispensation which was to be opened by an act of His which was also an act of God the Father.

So also it is an historical blunder of the crassest kind to represent Paul as though he were a "liberal" who rejected the ceremonial parts of the Old Testament law because of "the positive expansion of his religious experience." On the contrary the teaching of Paul is based, not upon a lax, but the strictest possible understanding of the law. And, to speak precisely, he did not "give up" the ceremonial law at all; circumcision, just as truly as love and mercy, he believed, was a command of God. But it was a command intended for the old dispensation, and by the death and resurrection of Christ a new dispensation had been ushered in. The freedom of Paul was supported not by an appeal from positive commands to inner experiences, but by an exhibition of the epoch-making significance of the Cross of Christ. It was not an anticipation of modern liberalism but the diametrical opposite of it.

The whole of the New Testament centres in an event, the redeeming work of Christ in His death and resurrection. To that event Jesus Himself in the days of His flesh pointed forward; to it the apostles looked back. But both in Jesus and in the apostles the "gospel" did not consist in the setting forth of what always had been true, but in the proclamation, whether in advance or in retrospect, of something that happened. When that central feature of the New Testament is ignored, true historical exegesis is impossible. And ignored it is in Dr. Fosdick's book from beginning to end. The author of this book displays little acquaintance with scientific historical study of the New Testament.

Before we turn from the first aspect of the book, it may be well to point out that the Christian, as well as the naturalistic historian, has a conception of progress in revelation, though a very different conception. The Christian thinks of the progress as being due to the unfolding of a gracious plan of redemption on the part of the transcendent God. That conception is certainly not wanting in grandeur. And it has the advantage, as compared with the naturalistic conception, of being true.

The other principal aspect of "the modern use of the Bible" as Dr. Fosdick sets it forth, is the separation between "abiding experiences" and the "mental categories" in which those experiences were expressed. "All doctrines," he says, "spring from life," and peace can be attained in the midst of controversy if the doctrines will only be translated back into the life from which they came; the theologies of various ages (including the "mental categories" contained in the New Testament) are merely codes in which experience is expressed, and if these codes become obsolete all that we have to do is to decode the underlying experience and start fresh. It is true that according to Dr. Fosdick even modern liberalism cannot do without theology; it must seek to clothe the religious experience which it shares with Jesus and other men of Bible times in the forms of thought that are suited to the modern age. But in doing so it incurs the disadvantage of establishing a new orthodoxy, which in some future generation will have to give place to a new liberalism,[9] and so on (we suppose) *ad infinitum.*

Dr. Fosdick places this theologizing which he thinks modern liberals must undertake in parallel with the creedmaking labors

---

9. p. 190.

of the historic Church. But of course the difference is profound. It is not merely that the results of the activity are different in the two cases, but that the whole nature of the activity is different. The greatest difference between the doctrine which our author thinks that modern liberalism must produce and the great creeds of the Church is not that the historic creeds differ from the new doctrine in this detail or that, and it is not even that they differ from the new doctrine in *all* details. But the real difference is that the authors or compilers of the historic creeds meant their creeds to be true, whereas the authors of these proposed Modernist compendia of belief do not believe their own assertions to be true but only believe them to be useful, as symbolic expressions of a really ineffable experience. But if theologizing is no more than that, we venture to think it is the most useless waste of time in which an able-bodied man could possibly engage. Very different were the great creeds of the Church, which were efforts to set forth what was not merely useful but also true.

There is no doubt that we have at this point the very centre and core of Dr. Fosdick's teaching. The assertion that "all doctrines spring from life" recurs like a refrain in the present work, and the changes are rung upon it in many different connections. But it involves of course the most radical skepticism that could possibly be conceived. It means simply that abandoning objective truth in the religious sphere, our author falls back upon pure positivism. Prior to all questions about God and creation and the future world, our lives can be changed, he holds, by the mere contemplation of the moral life of Jesus; we can enter into the experience which Jesus had. Then, Dr. Fosdick holds further, that experience into which Jesus leads us finds symbolic expression in doctrines like the divinity of Christ. Men used to apply the word "divinity" to a transcendent God, Maker and Ruler of the world. In such a God the Modernists no longer believe. But the word "God" or the word "divinity" is useful to express our veneration for the highest thing that we know; and the highest thing that Modernists know is the purely human Jesus of modern critical reconstruction.

At no point then does Dr. Fosdick's hostility to the Christian religion appear more clearly than in his assertion of the divinity of Christ. "Let us," he urges his readers, "say it abruptly: *it is not so much the humanity of Jesus that makes him imitable as it is his divinity.*"[10] There we have Modernism in a nutshell — the misleading use of Christian terminology, the blatancy of human pride, the breakdown of the distinction between God and man, the degradation of Jesus and the obliteration of the very idea of God.

In view of the underlying pragmatist skepticism of our author it hardly seems worth while to examine his teaching in detail. Since he does not believe in the objective truth of his own teaching, but regards it only as the temporary intellectual form in which an experience is expressed, we might be pardoned if we failed to be interested in it. He might affirm every jot and tittle of the Westminster Confession, for example; yet, since he would be affirming it merely as useful and not as true, he would be separated by a tremendous gulf from the Reformed Faith. As a matter of fact, however, the system of belief which Dr. Fosdick does set forth (as the temporary intellectual form in which his experience is expressed) is somewhat as follows.

God, according to Dr. Fosdick, is to be thought of as the "ideal-realizing Capacity in the universe or the creative Spirit at the heart of it,"[11] and he quotes with approval[12] words of John Herman Randall that set forth the ancient pagan *anima mundi* view of God: "The universe as we see it is God's body; then God is the soul of the universe, just as you are the soul of your body." The transcendence of God, which is at the root of all the ethical glories of the Christian religion, is by this preacher vigorously

---

10. p. 270. The italics are Dr. Fosdick's.
11. p. 161.
12. p. 266.

denied; Dr. Fosdick's whole teaching, in marked contrast to that of Jesus — even the reduced Jesus to whom he appeals — is passionately antitheistic. He has a "live cosmos," but has given up the living God.

Equally opposed to Christianity is his view of man, the root of which is found in his rejection of any real consciousness of sin. "I believe in man," Dr. Fosdick thinks, according to a recent sermon and according to the plain implications of this book, ought to be a fundamental article in our creed. Here we have the thoroughgoing paganism — the thoroughgoing confidence in human resources — which runs all through this preacher's teaching.

But if Dr. Fosdick is opposed to the Christian view of both these presuppositions of the Gospel, he is also opposed to the Christian view of the Book in which the gospel is set forth:

> Men have always gone to any sacred Scriptures they possessed primarily that they might find out how to live. That the Bible is "the infallible rule of faith and practise" is one of the most familiar statements which the church has ever framed, but in the historical development of our religion in the Old Testament the second item of that statement came first. The primary use of Scripture was to guide conduct, not to control belief . . . When, therefore, among the Hebrews we see the canon of sacred Scripture growing, when Josiah swore the people to a solemn league and covenant — the first example of a formal Hebrew Bible that we know — or when Ezra pledged the nation's loyalty to the keeping of the Levitical law, the Bible which thus was coming into being was primarily a book of divine requirements. It told the people what they ought to do . . .[13]

Now it is true that according to Dr. Fosdick Jesus broke with this legalism of the Old Testament. But He did so, the author holds, not at all because He restored truth to the primary place as over against conduct, but because He substituted "a form of conduct, a quality of spirit"[14] for detailed rules. Thus according to our author the New Testament as well as the Old Testament is valuable primarily as setting forth a way of life and not as recording facts.

---

13. pp. 235 ff.
14. p. 240.

But the Christian view is the exact opposite: the Bible according to the Christian first sets forth truth — both eternal truth regarding God and also redemptive facts of history — and upon that truth grounds its ethical demands. That is the case with the Old Testament as well as with the New Testament. Dr. Fosdick is quite wrong in thinking that the Old Testament law is, like the ethics of skeptical Modernism, left hanging in the air; on the contrary it is grounded throughout in the nature of God. Law in the Old Testament is always rooted in doctrine: the Ten Commandments are preceded by the words, "I am the Lord thy God, which have brought thee out of the land of Egypt, out of the house of bondage" (Ex. xx. 2); and the law of love in Deuteronomy is based upon the great *Sh'ma*, "Hear, O Israel: The Lord our God is one Lord" (Deut. vi. 4). Similar is the case with regard to the New Testament. The "practical" parts of the Epistles are always based upon the great doctrinal passages that precede them; and the ethical demands of Jesus are always based upon His presentation of the facts not only about God but about His own person and about heaven and hell.

Thus the *Shorter Catechism* is true to the Bible from beginning to end in the order which it observes in the answer to the question, "What do the Scriptures principally teach?" "The Scriptures principally teach," it says quite correctly, *"what man is to believe concerning God* and what duty God requires of man." The reversal of the order, or rather the virtual elimination of the former part of the answer, by Dr. Fosdick, exhibits the great gulf which exists between his teaching on the one side and the Christian religion on the other. Christianity, in accordance with the whole Bible but unlike Dr. Fosdick, founds morality upon truth, and life upon doctrine.

Of course, in speaking of Dr. Fosdick's view of the Bible it would be easy to point out the vast sections of Scripture which he holds to be directly untrue. He does not indeed make the matter always perfectly clear to the unsophisticated reader, and his failure to do so is from the ethical point of view one of the most disappointing features of the book. If this writer stated in plain language, which the lay reader could understand, his critical views about the New Testament, for example, the favor which he now enjoys among many misinformed but devout persons in the Church would at once be lost. But such frankness is not his; he prefers to undermine the faith of the Church by an entirely different method — more immediately effective, perhaps, but ethically far inferior.

But if Dr. Fosdick is opposed to the presuppositions of the Christian message and the Christian view of the Book in which the message is set forth, he is also opposed to the Christian view of the Person whose redeeming work forms the substance of the message. Jesus, according to Dr. Fosdick, is simply the fairest flower of humanity, divine in the sense in which all men are divine, the culmination of a process not the entrance of a creative interposition of God. "That differential quality in Jesus," he says, "is the most impressive spiritual fact that this earth has seen. It is the best we know. It is the fairest production that the race has to show for its millenniums of travail."[15] What an abysmal distance there is between this view of Christ as "the fairest production that the race has to show" and the Christian view of the eternal Son of God who entered freely into the world for our redemption!

Certainly the difference is not diminished but only exhibited in the clearer light when in the passage that has just been quoted the author speaks of the "differential quality in Jesus" as being "a revelation of creative reality." For here we have in striking form the degradation of the word "creative" which runs all through the book and which is involved in the passionate anti-theism which is a central characteristic of the Modernism of the present day.

---

15. p. 260.

The plain fact, of course, is that Dr. Fosdick eliminates from the pages of history all the miracles in the New Testament account of Jesus from the virgin birth to the empty tomb, as well as all the miracles in the Bible as a whole. He does speak, it is true, of miracles of Jesus that he accepts; but these "miracles," it turns out, are miracles which we also can experience. The miracles that show Jesus to have been unique are of course gone; what we have here is the elimination of the whole supernatural content of the Word of God. And how indeed can it be otherwise? There can be no supernatural interposition of a transcendent God if no transcendent God exists — if "God," like ourselves, is bound to the course of this world.

Corresponding to this degraded *view* of Jesus is the author's *attitude* toward Jesus. There is not the slightest evidence in this book that Dr. Fosdick has ever exercised faith in Jesus or indeed has the slightest notion of what faith in Jesus means. Jesus is to him a leader whom he loves, but never really a Saviour whom he trusts. "Say 'Jesus' to a medieval Christian [rather, we should put it, to *any* Christian] and he instinctively would think of a king sitting on his throne or coming in the clouds of heaven. Say 'Jesus' to a man of to-day and he instinctively thinks of that gracious and courageous Nazarene who lived and worked and taught in ancient Palestine."[16] Here we have the contrast between the Christian attitude to Christ and Dr. Fosdick's attitude: the Christian thinks of the Christ now living in glory, Dr. Fosdick thinks of the Christ who instituted a type of religious life long ago; Dr. Fosdick calls Christ "the Master," the Christian calls Him "the Lord." The difference is profound, and it is a difference of the heart and of the inner life fully as much as of the head. Dr. Fosdick speaks of a personal Saviour "with whom to fall in love;"[17] the Christian thinks of Christ as one who first

16. p. 220.
17. p. 231.

loved us. Dr. Fosdick *loves* the reconstructed Jesus of modern naturalism; the Christian *trusts* as well as loves the Jesus to whom is given all power in heaven and on earth.

In view of what has already been said, it is quite needless to point out our author's scorn for the gospel itself — the account of the redeeming work of Christ in His death and resurrection. *"The historic Jesus,"* he says, *"has given the world its most appealing and effective exhibition of vicarious sacrifice."*[18] Here the Cross of Christ is treated as a mere member of a series of acts of self-sacrifice, and so it is treated in the book throughout. But to the Christian such words about the tenderest and holiest thing in the Christian religion seem so blasphemous that even in quotation he can hardly bear to take them on his lips.

In reply to such an estimate of Dr. Fosdick as that which has here been made, the exponents of naturalistic Modernism in the creedal Churches, who themselves are just as much opposed to Christianity as this author is, are accustomed to point to individual utterances in the book, torn from their context — individual utterances in which Christian terminology is used. But that use of Christian terminology only serves to set in sharper light the divergence between this preacher and the whole tendency of Christianity; for it involves a certain carelessness about plain straightforwardness of speech, which would be thoroughly abhorrent to any one who appreciated the Christian point of view. The truth is that the similarity between Dr. Fosdick and the Christian religion is largely verbal; both in thought and in feeling (so far as the latter can be revealed by words) the divergence, despite undoubted influences of Christianity upon Dr. Fosdick in certain spheres, is profound.

In closing, a word of explanation may be due as to the reason why we have treated this book at such great length. It is because the author is representative of a very large body of persons in the modern world. He himself has asserted that theological views

---

18. p. 229. The italics are Dr. Fosdick's.

similar to his are held by hundreds of ministers in the Presbyterian Church, and certainly similar conditions prevail in most
other ecclesiastical bodies. The author of this book represents in
fairly typical, and certainly in very popular, fashion the attack
upon Christianity which is being carried on with such vigor at
the present time.

It cannot be said that this fact reflects credit upon the intellectual standard of the day; on the contrary it is only one among
many instances of the intellectual decadence which has set in
with such force. It is just the faults of Dr. Fosdick, as much as
his undoubted gifts, which make him popular. The disinclination
of this writer to clear definitions, the use of Christian terminology
to veil a totally alien meaning, the lack of that breadth of mind
which leads a man to enter at least into some sort of comprehen-
sion of the thing against which he is directing his attack — these
faults, distressing as they may be to thoughful persons, make
the book typical of the present age, and hence contribute no
doubt very largely to the popularity which the author enjoys.

But this is not the first period of decadence through which the
world has passed, as it is not the first period of desperate conflict
in the Church. God still rules, and in the midst of the darkness
there will come in His good time the shining of a clearer light.
There will come a great revival of the Christian religion; and
with it there will come, we believe, a revival of true learning:
the new Reformation for which we long and pray may well be
accompanied by a new Renaissance.

CHAPTER XV

## The Christian and Human Relationships

*"For I long to see you, that I may impart unto you some spiritual gift, to the end ye may be established; That is, that I may be comforted together with you by the mutual faith both of you and me"* (Romans 1:11,12).

INTO the communion of the early church were called not many wise according to the flesh, not many mighty, not many noble; yet it is a great mistake to suppose on that account that the early church was characterized by anything like vulgarity. In almost every country, and at almost every time, there are among the uneducated classes individuals, who by a native fineness of perception and delicacy of feeling fully atone for the lack of the acquired refinements of culture and education. Especially was this the case with the class of the poor in the land of Israel at the time of Christ, to which many of the early disciples of Jesus belonged. True, into those humble circles had not penetrated to any great extent the philosophy or learning of Greece; yet those peasants were possessed of an exquisite delicacy of thought and feeling, which through its poetical expression in the hymns of the first chapter of Luke, has been the wonder of the civilized world. Similar is the conclusion from the New Testament writings in general. It is true that the language is for the most part not the approved language of literature, even of a degenerate stage of the Greek tongue, but is rather the language of daily life; yet after all, language is primarily valuable merely as the expression of thought, and behind the plainness of the mere outward dress, we can clearly discern not merely a greatness of spiritual truth but also an exquisite fineness of mold in the form in which that truth is conceived and presented. We are not really following out the practice of the New Testament, if we imagine that any form of expression will do, if only real spiritual truth lies back of it. A study of the New Testament should make us rather more cautious in taking up new religious phrases, than are many of our modern religious teachers. To receive spiritual truth, faith alone is sufficient, but to give that truth adequate expression, to mold a religious phraseology, one must also have good taste. With that gift, as well as with other still greater ones, the New Testament writers were richly endowed.

Take Paul for example. It is rather remarkable that the man who so powerfully emphasized the absolute transcendence of the Christian life, so that he could say that there can be neither bond nor free, no male and female; for ye are all one man in Christ Jesus — it is rather remarkable that this same Paul, who more than any other emphasizes the absolute independence of the Christian of earthly conditions, should yet show himself to be such an accurate student of human relationships. Paul does not address a king in the same way that he addresses one who is his equal in station — though he regards him as just as much a sinner in the sight of God. He does not, according to Acts, address the philosophers of Athen in the same way as the Jews of Pisidian Antioch. He does not write to Christians whom he had never seen in quite the same tone as his own spiritual children. There is the same gospel for all; all human distinctions are subordinate and secondary; and yet these human distinctions are carefully to be observed. Paul was a man of tremendous spiritual power; but he was also a man of admirable tact.

As an example of this, take the verses which I have just read. Paul says, "For I long to see you, that I may impart unto you some spiritual gift, to the end ye may be established." With that an ordinary man might well have been content. Paul was in a position to impart spiritual good to others; he felt himself to be the recipient of revelation from God. Yet he seems to detect a possible objection for he half corrects himself: "that is, that I may be comforted together with you by the mutual faith both of you and me." A coarser nature would have seen no reason to make the correction; but Paul had that ability to put himself in the other man's place which is the essence of true courtesy. He wished to remove all possibility that his hearers might feel hurt, in supposing that Paul meant to regard them as men who could receive only and had no power to give. He gives his readers full credit for all that could by any possibility be theirs; it is a charming bit of fine discernment and delicate courtesy.

But like all true courtesy, it is based not on hypocrisy but on truth. It results simply from the clear discernment and generous recognition of conditions that really exist. When Paul says that he hopes to receive spiritual benefit from his association with them, he shows that he was really capable of friendship with other men; and wonderfully does his whole life bear this out. So we have two sides to the life of Paul: a supreme devotion to Christ and the things of the other world in which all outward conditions are held to be comparatively valueless; and a delicate tact in the various relationships of this life; in union with a wonderful intensity in affections for other men. How are the two things to be reconciled? We have here brought before us the great question of the position of Christianity with regard to human relationships.

In the history of the Church, three answers to the question have been given.

In the first place (our order is not the order of time), there is the worldly tendency in the Church. Christians find themselves living in a world where their social needs seem after all to be pretty well satisfied. Their time is so much taken up with their human friends that their Saviour is thrust into a secondary place. Usually, this process has been unconscious merely — men have gradually without knowing it drifted away from their first enthusiasm. But today we see this worldly tendency openly defended by professing Christians. Men say, Yes, Christianity is good, but it must be kept in its proper place; it must not be allowed to interfere with those natural relations between man and man which have been ordained by God Himself. Religion occupies merely one part of our nature; it should not be neglected just as the physical and the intellectual sides of our nature should not be neglected; but (this is really implied at least) it should not be allowed to encroach on those other spheres. Who has not heard Y.M.C.A. speeches that amount to little more than that? And then, it is said, of course, we should send missionaries to foreign lands; but we should caution them to be very careful not to create trouble. If they find that the preaching and the acceptance of the gospel begins to go too much below the surface, so as to break up ancient customs or families, or worst of all to affect the healthy development of commerce — then by all means let them desist. Religion is thus degraded to a mere part of our life or to a mere means to an end.

It scarcely requires argument to show that this conception of the position of Christianity with regard to human relations is sharply opposed to the teaching of Him who said, If any man cometh after me and hateth not his own father, and mother, and wife, and children, and brethren, and sisters, yea and his own life also, he cannot be my disciple; of Him who represented the beginning of the Christian life, not as the development of any one side of our nature, but as a new birth, as a new beginning for the entire life.

Not less harmful in its effects, though possessing more of fundamental Christian truth, is the second answer to our question —namely the answer of ascetics of various degrees of strictness. Since the relation to Christ is the supreme relation in which we stand, therefore we should seek to give it free room, by lopping off all other affections. We should seek to avoid not only love of self, but also love for our friends. The latter stands higher than the former, but even it must make way for the supreme devotion to Christ. Natural affections, not only under special conditions, but of necessity in themselves are regarded as entangling alliances with the world. Now in the Presbyterian Church we do not seem to be much troubled with asceticism; the error seems at first sight to lie all in the opposite extreme; yet I am not sure but that some ministers do not in principle err in this way also. I do not refer to exaggerated opposition to certain forms of pleasure; but to a negative attitude towards human relationships. I know some preachers who are very good men, and very devoted to Christ, who seem somehow to let their Christianity make them cold and dead to all the movings of friendship. They do not outwardly lead the lives of hermits; on the contrary, their greatest joy is to be serving Christ by preaching His word, Yet somehow there is an impenetrable barrier between them and other men. You alway have the feeling that whenever they speak to you it is out of a stern sense of duty, in order that they may do you some good. They have no spontaneous affection for individual men — all men are to them alike for all alike simply form a field for preaching. The consequence is their sermons always sound as though they were coming out of a phonograph. In order to prevent your words from being sounding brass or tinkling cymbal, two kinds of love are necessary — love to God and love to your hearers. It will not do to let your hearers say, Yes, the preacher loves Christ devotedly, but he cares not one cent for me.

It is pretty evident, as a matter of homiletics and pastoral theology, then, that there is something wrong with this second answer to our question. Nor does our New Testament desert us here; for we have, for instance, the example of Paul. Paul saw as clearly as anyone the truth which the ascetics emphasize — he is very clear with regard to the absolute independence of the Christian life of all earthly relationships, and the absolute supremacy of the place which Christ holds as over against all earthly affections — and yet, somehow, he avoids admirably the error which seems to lie so near. For so far is he from living a calm sort of life away from the world, in a kind of cold isolation, that it is hard to find in all history any man of intenser affection than he. The affection which he feels for his spiritual children is not something that he has to force upon himself as a Christian duty; but springs spontaneously right out of the depths of a warm heart. Nor is his affection confined to Christians alone. Read, for example, the touching expression of his patriotism in Romans 9, "For I could wish that myself were accursed from Christ for my brethren, my kinsman according to the flesh." Paul was no stranger to natural affection — his becoming a Christian did not make him any the less a man.

In opposing the ascetic answer to our question, we can claim not only the testimony of experience, but the example of an apostle and the authority of Scripture. We have, therefore, concluded (1) that natural affections are not to be allowed to choke our affection for Christ and (2) that neither are they to be rooted out. This brings us to the third and correct solution of the problem. Human relationships are not to be broken off, but they are to be consecrated. They are to be regarded as one of the means which God has given us for serving Him. They therefore should not only not be neglected, but should be furthered in every possible way. Far from seeking to isolate ourselves from our friends, we should seek, by every means in our power, to strengthen the bonds which unite us with them, for thus shall we be better enabled to serve Christ.

The difficulty of reconciling human relations with absolute devotion to Christ disappears the minute we see that the two things lie in different spheres. Of course, if our devotion to Christ is not different in kind from our feelings for our friends, then in a certain sense it comes into competition with them, but, in that case, it is not really a religious feeling. It may be a very enobling sentiment, but it is not truly religious. When we become

Christians, the true statement of the case is not that we substitute for our human affections the love of Christ, but rather that we set Christ up in a place in our lives which has really been vacant, whether we were aware of it or no — the place which can be filled only by God. If we tear out of our heart our natural affections, we are not, except under certain conditions, making room for Christ; but we are simply making ourselves less efficient servants of His. Love for Christ and love for our fellowmen are different in kind; and need not under healthy conditions come into competition. It is possible for one to be developed to the highest extent, without affecting the other.

True, it is not always easy to carry on this work of consecration — it requires the help and guidance of the Spirit of God. Very often it seems simpler and easier and safer to break off absolutely all connection with the world; and sometimes God uses a great sorrow in order, by depriving the Christian of human solace, to cast him back more completely upon Christ. But for us to withdraw ourselves from the world is usually to usurp the disciplinary function which is the prerogative of God alone. It is a lesser sin of the same kind as suicide.

Undoubtedly the hardest kind of worldly relation to consecrate to the service of Christ, is a relation with one who is not a Christian. Suppose I have a friend, who is an out-and-out opponent of the Christian faith; who yet is very dear to me and from whom I have received a great deal of moral aid. Does it not seem as though the help which I receive from such a man and the joy I have in his friendship must of necessity weaken the feeling of absolute devotion to Christ? It seems so until you bethink yourself who Christ is. Christ is God, and God has created the world and all the men in it. It was He who endowed my friend with those noble qualities which have been such a help to me on the pathway of life; what I owe to my friend I owe also to my God, and to Him I can give thanks.

And if we Christians should break off relations with our non-Christian friends, or if we should put between us and them a hidden wall — what hope would there be that the world would ever be brought to Christ? If we have Christ's cause at heart, we ought to rejoice that the bonds that bind us to other men are ever so strong and enter ever so deeply into the depths of the heart. For it is through the instrumentality of these real bonds of friendship that God will draw them into His fold. Without such friendship, any persuasion that we may attempt will usually be mere empty words.

But far easier is the course of affairs when our friends are Christians, and far more important. Christian fellowship is not only an aid to Christian service; it is a necessity for Christian life. It is not only a necessity for the weak, for even the great Paul, the strongest of Christians, felt the need to strengthen his faith by communion with his weaker brethren. There is none so strong that he does not need help from his fellows, there is none so weak that he may not help the strongest. No wonder that the Church is a divine institution; it satisfies a universal need.

If any one of us has ever known what it is to be helped on upon the path of life by an older and stronger Christian, if he knows by experience that calm pardon of the worst sin, that unselfish sympathy, that desire to help, by which the true disciple reveals the great Master — if any one of us has had that experience he will never be inclined to undervalue the Church. For the activities of the Church are manifold; she performs her office not merely by public services but by all kinds of intercourse between Christians, and for the formation of these we have special opportunities at the Seminary.

Now I know perfectly well that friendships cannot be made to order — it is far too subtle a thing for that — it has its roots too deep down in the human soul. All that we can do is to remove obstacles that may stand in its way.

The first of such obstacles — and one that stands in the way not only of intimate friendship but also of all Christian intercourse — is intolerance. I am not speaking so much of intolerance for different views on questions of theology — though where there is a real religious devotion to Christ, the Son of God and the Saviour of the world, tolerance is certainly a virtue — but rather of intolerance for different ways of giving expression to the common Christian faith. One man can give day and hour of his conversion, and loves to have the name of Jesus always on his lips; to another, Christian experience seems a deep and holy mystery, which must not be breathed except to sympathetic ears. One can conceive of no Christian activity other than that of preaching the gospel, and regards as part of the wisdom of this world which is foolishness with God the researches of the Christian scholar; another is filled with a deep longing for knowledge as to the way things actually happened in the time of Christ and the apostles, and is inclined to look rather askance upon the more emotional temperament of the evangelists. To one, Christianity seems a thing that is diametrically opposed to the arts; another loves to give his faith poetical expression, to bring it into some kind of connection with literature. This diversity will be a stumbling block until we remember Paul's words about a diversity of gifts but the same Spirit. We must learn to thank God that he did not make all men alike; especially that he did not make all men like us. Let us do our own work, in the special sphere and in the special way for which our gifts may fit us; but let us not disparage the work of that other man of entirely different habits of thought. Christ came to save not only the ignorant man but the scholar; not only the scholar but the ignorant man. Let us thank God that He raises up various instruments to accomplish His infinitely various work.

The second obstacle to Christian friendship is that old enemy selfishness. It takes some time to help the other man, as well as perform our own work; and we are often so much engrossed in our own affairs that we are unwilling to go out of our way. We have our eyes so steadily fixed upon some great work of our own that we are to do in the future, that we do not step aside to help in work for which we shall get no credit.

But I really believe the greatest obstacle in the way of our receiving the greatest benefit from our association with our brother Christians is not selfishness but pride. Selfishness makes us unwilling to give aid, pride makes us unwilling to receive it. We all love to think of ourselves as standing firm on our own feet, without leaning upon anyone but Christ. Let us remember the words of Paul — "That is, that I may be comforted together with you by the mutual faith both of you and me."

# CHAPTER XVI

## The Church in the War

IN MANY CASES the church has done nobly in the war. There have no doubt been many chaplains, many Y.M.C.A. secretaries, and many soldiers in the ranks who have proclaimed the gospel of Christ faithfully and humbly and effectively to dying men. Any discouraging estimate of the situation is subject to many noble exceptions. But, in general, in view of the manifest estrangement between the church and large bodies of men, there is at least some plausibility for the common opinion that the church has failed.

Fortunately, if the church has failed, it is at least perfectly clear why she has failed. She has failed because men have been unwilling to receive, and the church has been unwilling to preach, the gospel of Christ crucified. Men have trusted for their own salvation and for the hope of the world in the merit of their own self-sacrifice rather than in the one act of sacrifice which was accomplished some nineteen hundred years ago by Jesus Christ. That does not mean that men are opposed to Jesus. On the contrary, they are perfectly ready to admit Him into the noble company of those who have sacrificed themselves in a righteous cause. But such condescension is as far removed as possible from the Christian attitude. People used to say, "There was no other good enough to pay the price of sin." They say so no longer. On the contrary, any man, if only he goes bravely over the top, is now regarded as plenty good enough to pay the price of sin.

Obviously this modern attitude is possible only because men have lost sight of the majesty of Jesus' person. It is because they regard Him as a being altogether like themselves that they can compare their sacrifice with his. It never seems to dawn upon them that this was no sinful man, but the Lord of glory who died on Calvary. If it did dawn upon them, they would gladly confess, as men used to confess, that one drop of the precious blood of Jesus is worth more, as a ground for the hope of the world, than all the rivers of blood which have flowed upon the battle-fields of France.

But how may this Christian conception of the majesty of Jesus' person be regained?

Some people think it may be regained simply by more knowl-edge. If people would only read the gospels more, we are told, they would come to know Jesus, and, knowing him, they would revere him. But knowledge, important though it is, is not suf-ficient. Many men knew Jesus in the days of his flesh — in-telligent men, too — who never became His disciples. Who then were those who did come to reverence Him? The answer is plain. During the earthly life-time of Jesus and all through the centuries the men who really understood the majesty of Jesus' person were the men who were convicted of their sin. Peter was one — who said, "Depart from me, for I am a sinful man, O Lord." The dying thief was another; he knows more about Jesus to-day than many a modern preacher who has the name of Jesus forever on his lips. Paul was another — a brave, clean man he was, too, as the world looks on it, even before he found forgiveness in Christ. The real reason why men no longer understand the majesty of Jesus' person is that they do not contrast his holiness with their own sinfulness; they are without the conviction of sin.

The leading characteristic of the present age is a profound satisfaction with human goodness. The popular war-literature, for example, is redolent of such satisfaction. Get beneath the rough exterior of men, we are told, and you find sufficient self-sacrifice in order to found upon that self-sacrifice the hope of the world.

What has produced such a spirit of self-satisfaction?

In the first place, the war has provided us with a convenient scapegoat. In war-time, men have been interested in the sins of others; they have been called upon to fight in hot indignation against injustice and oppression on the part of the Germans. Such indignation has been necessary. But it has not been without its moral dangers. In attending to the sins of others, men have sometimes lost sight of their own sins.

In the second place, the sense of sin has sometimes been blunted by the consciousness of a great achievement. Certainly the achievement is very great; the men who march in triumph up Fifth Avenue deserve not less but more of honor than they are receiving from their fellow-citizens. But honor from men can be received with perfect satisfaction only where it is joined, as it is joined in the case of many and many a Christian soldier, with utter humility in the presence of God.

But the roots of modern self-satisfaction lie far deeper than the war. During the past century a profound spiritual change has been produced in the whole thought and life of the world — no less a change than the substitution of paganism for Christianity as the dominant principle of life. We are not here using "paganism" as a term of reproach; ancient Greece was pagan, but it was glorious. What we mean by "paganism" is a view of life which finds its ideal simply in a healthy and harmonious and joyous development of existing human faculties. Such an ideal is the exact opposite of Christianity, which is the religion of the broken heart.

We would not be misunderstood. In saying that Christianity is the religion of the broken heart, we do not mean that Christianity ends in the broken heart; we do not mean that the characteristic Christian attitude is a continual beating of the breast and a continual crying of "Woe is me." On the contrary, the Christian should not be always "laying again the foundation of repentance from dead works"; sin is dealt with once for all, and then a new and joyous life follows. There is thus in Christianity a higher humanism. The trouble with the humanism of ancient Greece, as with the humanism of modern times, lay not in the superstructure, which was glorious, but in the foundation, which was rotten. Sin was never really dealt with and removed; there was always something to cover up. In the higher Christian humanism there is nothing to cover up; the guilt has been removed once for all by God, and the Christian may now proceed without fear to develop every faculty which God has given him.

But if Christianity does not end with the broken heart, it does begin with it. The way to Christ lies through the conviction of sin.

Unfortunately, the fact is not always recognized. Modern preachers are inclined to suggest some easier way. They are saying to men in effect this: "You men are very good and very self-sacrificing, and we take pleasure in revealing your goodness to you. Now, since you are so good, you will probably be interested in Christianity, especially in the life of Jesus, which we believe is good enough even for you." Such preaching is very attractive — much more attractive than the preaching of the cross. But it is quite useless. It is useless to try to call the righteous to repentance.

But it is hard for men to give up their pride. How shall we find the courage to require it of them? How shall we preachers find courage to say, for example, to the returning soldiers, rightly conscious as they are of a magnificent achievement: "You are sinners like all other men, and like all other men you need a Saviour." It looks to the world like a colossal piece of impertinence. Certainly we cannot find the courage in any superior goodness of our own. But we can find the courage in the goodness and in the greatness of Christ.

Certainly the gospel does put a tremendous strain upon Jesus of Nazareth. The gospel means that instead of seeking the hope of the world in the added deeds of goodness of the millions of the human race throughout the centuries, we seek it in one act of one Man of long ago. Such a message has always seemed foolish to the wise men of this world. But there is no real reason to be ashamed of it. We may feel quite safe in relinquishing every prop of human goodness in order to trust ourselves simply and solely to Christ. The achievements of men are very imposing. But not in comparison with the Lord of glory.

> *When I survey the wondrous cross*
> *On which the Prince of glory died,*
> *My richest gain I count but loss,*
> *And pour contempt on all my pride.*

CHAPTER XVII

# Facing the Facts Before God

IN THE nineteenth chapter of the Second Book of Kings, we are told how Hezekiah, King of Judah, received a threatening letter from the Assyrian enemy. The letter contained unpalatable truth. It set forth the way in which the King of Assyria had conquered one nation after another — and could the feeble kingdom of Judah escape?

When Hezekiah received the letter, there were three things that he could do with it.

In the first place, he could obey its behest; he could go out and surrender his kingdom to the Assyrian enemy.

In the second place, he could refuse to read the letter; he could ignore its contents. Like another and worse king, with a far better communication than that, he could take out his king's penknife and cut it up and throw it bit by bit contemptuously into the fire.

As a matter of fact, Hezekiah did neither of these two things. He took the letter with all its unpalatable truth, and read it from beginning to end; he did not close his eyes to any of its threatening. But then he took the letter, with all the threatening that it contained, spread it open in the presence of Almighty God, and asked God to give the answer.

Now we too, believers in the Bible and in the blessed gospel that it contains, have received a threatening letter. It is not a letter signed by any one potentate, like the King of Assyria; but it is a collective letter signed by the men who are dominating the world of today and dominating to an increasing extent the visible Church. It is a letter breathing out threatenings of extinction to those who hold to the gospel of Jesus Christ as it is set forth in God's Word.

That letter is signed by the men who are dominating increasingly the political and social life of the world. That was not true fifty years ago, at least not in English-speaking countries. Then, to a considerable extent, in those countries at least, public opinion was in favor of the gospel of Christ. Today, almost all over the world, public opinion is increasingly against the gospel of Christ.

The letter of threatening against the gospel is signed also by the men who are dominating the literary and intellectual life of the world. To see that that is true, one needs only to read the popular magazines and the magazines that appeal to persons of literary and intellectual taste; or one needs only to read the books of the day or listen to what comes "over the air."

The threatening letter is also signed, alas, by the men who are in control of many of the larger branches of the Protestant Church. In the Presbyterian Church in the U. S. A., for example, to which the writer of this article belongs, four out of eight ministerial members of the Permanent Judicial Commission, which is practically the supreme guardian of the doctrine of the Church, are actually signers of a formal document commonly called the "Auburn Affirmation" which declares to be nonessential even for the ministry the virgin birth of our Lord and four other great verities of the Christian faith; and very slight indeed is the representation of any clear-cut and outspoken evangelicalism in the boards and agencies of the Church. In many other ecclesiastical bodies, the situation, from the Christian point of view, is even worse than it is in ours.

But it is in the colleges and universities and theological seminaries that the threatening letter against the gospel of Christ has been most generally signed. In the faculties of some of our great universities today, you can count almost on the fingers of your two hands the men who believe in the gospel in any definite and outspoken way, and in the student bodies individual believers often seem to themselves to be standing nearly alone.

When we receive this threatening letter, there are three things that we may do with it.

In the first place, we may obey its behest; we may relinquish our belief in the truth of the Bible; we may simply drift with the current of the times. Very many students in colleges and universities and theological seminaries have made that choice. They came from Christian homes; they are the subject of the prayers of godly parents. But the threatenings and persuasions of the unbelieving world have apparently been too strong for them. They have been unwilling to adopt the unpopular course. And so they have made shipwreck of their faith.

In the second place, we may refuse to read the threatening letter; we may close our eyes to the unpalatable truth that the letter contains. We may say, as so many are saying today, that the Protestant churches of our own country and of the other countries of the world are "fundamentally sound"; we may cry "Peace, peace; when there is no peace"; we may dig our heads like ostriches in the sand; we may refuse to attend to the real situation in the Church and in the world.

I pray God that we may never adopt this method of dealing with the letter of threatening; for if there is one thing that is preventing true prayer today, it is this foolish optimism with regard to the state of the times, this refusal of Christian people to face the true seriousness of the situation in which we stand.

But there is a third choice that we may make when we receive the threatening letter against the gospel of Christ. We may take the letter and read it from beginning to end, not closing our eyes to the threatening that it contains, and then lay the letter, with all its threatenings, open in the presence of Almighty God.

It is to that third choice that the League of Evangelical Students, by its Constitution, is irrevocably committed. The Prologue to the Constitution reads as follows:

"Inasmuch as mutually exclusive conceptions of the nature of the Christian religion exist in the world today and particularly in theological seminaries and other institutions of higher learning; and since it is the duty of those who share and cherish the evangelical faith to witness to it and to strive for its defense and propagation; and in view of the value for this end of common counsel, united effort and Christian fellowship:

"We, the undersigned representatives of Students' Associations in Theological Seminaries and Schools for the Training of Christian Workers, do hereby from a league organized upon the following principles. . . "

There we have a clear facing of the situation as it actually is and a brave willingness, despite that situation, to stand for the defense and propagation of the gospel of Christ.

Certain objections are sometimes raised against this method of dealing with the letter of threatening that has come to us today from a hostile world.

In the first place, we are sometimes told, it will discourage the faith of timorous souls if we tell them thus plainly that the world of today is hostile to the gospel of Christ; it will offend Christ's little ones, men say, if we bid them open their eyes to the real strength of unbelief in the modern world.

But our Lord, at least, never used this method of raising false hopes in those whom He called to be His disciples. He told those who would follow Him to count the cost before they took that step, not to be like a man who starts to build a tower before he has funds to complete it or like a man who puts his hand to the plow and then draws back. He never made it easy, in that sense, to be a disciple of Him (though in another and higher sense His yoke was easy and His burden light); and any faith in the Lord Jesus Christ which is based upon the vain hope that a man can be a disciple of Christ and still have the favor of the world is a faith that is based on shifting sand. No, it is a poor religion which makes a man willing only to walk in golden slippers in the sunshine; and such a religion is bound to fail in the time of need.

In the second place, however, men say that if we face the real condition of the times, we shall be guilty of stirring up controversy in the Church.

No doubt the fact may be admitted. If we face the real situation in the Church and in the world, and decide, despite that situation, to stand firmly for the gospel of Christ, we shall be very likely indeed to find ourselves engaged in controversy. But if we are going to avoid controversy, we might as well close our Bibles; for the New Testament is a controversial book practically from beginning to end. The New Testament writers and our Lord Himself presented truth in sharp contrast with error, and indeed that is the only way in which truth can be presented in any clear and ringing way.

I do not know all the things that will happen when the great revival sweeps over the Church, the great revival for which we long. Certainly I do not know *when* that revival will come; its coming stands in the Spirit's power. But about one thing that will happen when that blessing comes I think we can be fairly sure. When a great and true revival comes in the Church, the present miserable, feeble talk about avoidance of controversy on the part of the servants of Jesus Christ will all be swept away as with a mighty flood. A man who is really on fire with his message never talks in that feeble and compromising way but proclaims the gospel plainly and boldly in the presence of every high thing that is lifted up against the gospel of Christ.

If we do adopt this method of dealing with the present situation in the Church and in the world, if we spread the threatening letter of the adversaries unreservedly before God, there are certain things that God tells us for our comfort. When Hezekiah adopted that method in his day, God sent him Isaiah the son of Amoz, greatest of the prophets, with a message of cheer. But He has His ways of speaking also to us.

In the first place, he tells us for our comfort that this is not the first time of discouragement in the history of the Church. Often the gospel has seemed to superficial observers to be forever forgotten, yet it has burst forth with new power and set the world aflame. Sometimes the darkest hour has just preceded the dawn. So it may be in our time.

In the second place, He tells us that even in this time of unbelief there are far more than seven thousand that have not bowed the knee to the gods of the hour. In these days of doubt and defection and hostility, there are those who love the gospel of Jesus Christ. And how sweet and precious is our fellowship with them in the presence of a hostile world!

It is to be God's instrument in giving that comfort that the League of Evangelical Students exists. It is founded to say to students on many a campus who are tempted to think that they are standing alone in holding to the gospel of Christ: "No, brethren, you are not alone; we too hold humbly to the truth of God's Word, and we hold to it not through a mere shallow emotionalism but because to hold to it is a thoroughly reasonable thing, of which a real student need not for one moment be ashamed."

In the third place, God tells us not to be too much impressed by the unbelieving age in which we are living now. Do you think that this is a happy or a blessed age? Oh, no, my friends. Amid all the pomp and glitter and noise and tumult of the age, there are hungry hearts. The law of God has been forgotten, and stark slavery is stalking through the earth — the decay of free institutions in the State and a deeper slavery still in the depths of the soul. High poetry is silent; and machinery, it almost seems, rules all. God has taken the fire of genius from the world. But something far more than genius is being lost — the blessing of a humble and virtuous life. There was a time, twenty-five years ago, when we might have thought that Christian living could be maintained after Christian doctrine was given up. But if we ever made that mistake, we must abandon it today. Where is the sweetness of the Christian home; where is the unswerving integrity of men and women whose lives were founded upon the Word of God? Increasingly these things are being lost. Even men of the world are coming to see with increasing clearness that mankind is standing over an abyss.

I tell you, my friends, it is not altogether an argument *against* the gospel that this age has given it up; it is rather an argument *for* the gospel. If *this* be the condition of the world without Christ then we may well turn back, while yet there is time, to that from which we have turned away.

That does not mean that we should despise the achievements of the age; it does not mean that we should adopt the "Touch not, taste not, handle not" attitude toward the good things or the wonders of God's world which Paul condemned in his day; it does not mean that we should consecrate to God an impoverished man, narrowed in interests, narrowed in outlook upon the marvellous universe that God has made. What it does mean is that we should pray God to make these modern achievements not the instruments of human slavery, as increasingly they are threatening to become, but the instruments of that true liberty which consists in the service of God.

But the deepest comfort which God gives us is not found even in considerations such as these: it is not found in reflections upon God's dealings during the past history of the Church; it is not found in our fellowship with those who love the gospel that we love; it is not found in observation of the defects of this unbelieving age. Valuable are all these considerations, and great is the assurance that they give to our souls. But there is one consideration that is more valuable, and one assurance that is greater still. It is found in the overwhelming glory of the gospel itself.

When we attend to that glory, all the pomp and glitter of an unbelieving age seems like the blackness of night. How wonderful is the divine revelation in God's Word! How simple, yet how majestic its presentation of the being of God; how dark its picture of the guilt of man; how bright against that background its promise of divine grace! And at the centre of all in this incomparable Book there stands the figure of One in whose presence all wisdom seems to be but folly and all goodness seems to be but filthy rags. If we have His favor, little shall we care henceforth for the favor of the world, and little shall we fear the opposition of an unbelieving age.

That favor is ours, brethren, without merit, without boasting, if we trust in Him. And in that favor we find the real source of our courage in these difficult days. Our deepest comfort is found not in the signs of the times but in the great and precious promises of God.

# CHAPTER XVIII

# Westminster Theological Seminary: Its Purpose and Plan

WESTMINSTER THEOLOGICAL SEMINARY, which opens its doors to-day, will hardly be attended by those who seek the plaudits of the world or the plaudits of a worldly church. It can offer for the present no magnificent buildings, no long-established standing in the ecclesiastical or academic world. Why, then, does it open its doors; why does it appeal to the support of Christian men?

The answer is plain. Our new institution is devoted to an unpopular cause; it is devoted to the service of One who is despised and rejected by the world and increasingly belittled by the visible church, the majestic Lord and Saviour who is presented to us in the Word of God. From him men are turning away one by one. His sayings are too hard, his deeds of power too strange, his atoning death too great an offense to human pride. But to him, despite all, we hold. No Christ of our own imaginings can ever take his place for us, no mystic Christ whom we seek merely in the hidden depths of our own souls. From all such we turn away ever anew to the blessed written Word and say to the Christ there set forth, the Christ with whom then we have living communion: "Lord, to whom shall we go? Thou hast the words of eternal life."

The Bible, then, which testifies of Christ, is the center and core of that with which Westminster Seminary has to do. Very different is the attitude of most theological institutions today.

Most seminaries, with greater or lesser clearness and consistency, regard not the Bible alone, or the Bible in any unique sense, but the general phenomenon of religion as being the subject-matter of their course. It is the duty of the theological student, they maintain, to observe various types of religious experience, attested by the Bible considered as a religious classic, but attested also by the religious conditions that prevail to-day, in order to arrive by a process of comparison at that type of religious experience which is best suited to the needs of the modern man. We believe, on the contrary, that God has been pleased to reveal himself to man and to redeem man once for all from the guilt and power of sin. The record of that revelation and that redemption is contained in the Holy Scriptures, and it is with the Holy Scriptures, and not merely with the human phenomenon of religion, that candidates for the ministry should learn to deal.

There is nothing narrow about such a curriculum; many and varied are the types of intellectual activity that it requires. When you say that God has revealed himself to man, you must in the first place believe that God is and that the God who is is one who can reveal himself, no blind world-force, but a living Person. There we have one great division of the theological course. "Philosophical apologetics" or "theism," it is called. But has this God, who might reveal himself, actually done so in the way recorded in the Scriptures of the Old and New Testaments? In other words, is Christianity true? That question, we think, should not be evaded; and what is more, it need not be evaded by any Christian man. To be a Christian is, we think, a truly reasonable thing; Christianity flourishes not in obscurantist darkness, where objections are ignored, but in the full light of day.

But if the Bible contains a record of revelation and redemption, what in detail does the Bible say? In order to answer that question, it is not sufficient to be a philosopher: by being a philosopher you may perhaps determine, or think you can determine, what the Bible ought to say; but if you are to tell what the Bible does say, you must be able to read the Bible for yourself. And you cannot read the Bible for yourself unless you know the languages in which it was written. We may sometimes be tempted to wish that the Holy Spirit had given us the Word of God in a language better suited to our particular race, in a language that we could easily understand; but in his mysterious wisdom he gave it to us in Hebrew and in Greek. Hence if we want to know the Scriptures, to the study of Greek and Hebrew we must go. I am not sure that it will be ill for our souls. It is poor consecration indeed that is discouraged by a little earnest work; and sad is it for the church if it has only ministers whose preparation for their special calling is of the customary superficial kind.

We are not conducting a school for lay workers at Westminster Seminary, useful though such a school would be, but a theological seminary; and we believe that a theological seminary is an institution of higher learning whose standards should not be inferior to the highest academic standards that anywhere prevail.

If, then, the students of our seminary can read the Bible not merely in translations, but as it was given by the Holy Spirit to the church, then they are prepared to deal intelligently with the question what the Bible means. There we have the great subject of Biblical exegesis or Biblical interpretation. I hesitate to use that word "interpretation"; for it is a word that has been the custodian of more nonsense, perhaps, than any other word in the English language today. Every generation, it is said, must interpret the Bible and the creeds of the church in its own way. So it is said in effect by many modern leaders of the church: "We accept the Apostles' Creed, but we must interpret the Apostles' Creed in a way that will suit the modern mind. So we repeat the assertion of the Creed. 'The third day he rose again from the dead,' but we interpret that to mean, 'The third day he did not rise again from the dead.' "

In the presence of this modern business of interpreting perfectly plain assertions to mean their exact opposite, do you know what I verily believe? I verily believe that the new Reformation, for which we long, will be like the Reformation of the sixteenth century in that it will mean a return to plain common honesty and common sense. At the end of the middle ages the Bible had become a book with seven seals; it had been covered with the rubbish of the four-fold sense of Scripture and all that. The Reformation brushed that rubbish away. So again today the Bible has been covered with an elaborate business of "interpretation" that is worse in some respects than anything that the middle ages could produce. The new Reformation will brush all that away. There will be a rediscovery of the great Reformation doctrine of the perspicuity of Scripture; men will make the astonishing discovery that the Bible is a plain book addressed to plain men, and that it means exactly what it says.

In our work in exegesis at Westminster Seminary, at any rate, we shall seek to cultivate common sense. But common sense is not so common as is sometimes supposed, and for the cultivation of it true learning is not out of place. What a world of vagaries, what a sad waste of time, could be avoided if men would come into contact with the truly fine exegetical tradition of the Christian church! Such contact with the devout and learned minds of the past would not discourage freshness or originality. Far from it; it would help to shake us out of a rut and lead us into fields of fruitful thinking.

In true Biblical exegesis, the Bible must be taken as God has been pleased to give it to the church. And as God has been pleased to give it to the church, it is not a mere text-book of religion written all at one time and in one way. On the contrary, it is composed of sixty-six books written at widely different times and by the instrumentality of widely different men. Let us not regret that fact. If the Bible were a systematic text-book on religion, it would, indeed, possess some advantages: it would presumably be easier to interpret; for much of our present difficulty of interpretation comes from the fact that the Biblical books are rooted in historical conditions long gone by.  But if the Bible, under those circumstances, would be easier to interpret, it would speak far less powerfully to the heart of man.  As it is, God has been very good.  He has given us no cold text-book on religion, but a Book that reaches every heart and answers to every need. He has condescended to touch our hearts and arouse our minds by the wonderful variety and beauty of his Book.

When we have learned to read that Book aright, we can trace the history of the revelation that it sets forth.  When we do so, we are engaging in an important part of the theological curriculum. "Biblical theology," it is called.  Whether it is set forth in a separate course, or whether it is interwoven, as will probably be done in Westminster Seminary, with the work of the Old and New Testament departments, in either case it is a vital part of that with which we have to deal.  "God, who at sundry times and in divers manners spake in time past unto the fathers by the prophets, hath in these last days spoken unto us by his Son" — there is the program of Biblical theology; it traces the history of revelation through Old and New Testament times.

But Biblical theology is not all the theology that will be taught at Westminster Seminary; for systematic theology will be at the very center of the Seminary's course.  At that point an error should be avoided: it must not be thought that systematic theology is one whit less Biblical than Biblical theology is.  But it differs from Biblical theology in that, standing on the foundation of Biblical theology, it seeks to set forth, no longer in the order of the time when it was revealed, but in the order of logical relationships, the grand sum of what God has told us in his Word.  There are those who think that systematic theology on the basis of the Bible is impossible; there are those who think that the Bible contains a mere record of human seeking after God and that its teachings are a mass of contradiction which can never be resolved.  But to the number of those persons we do not belong.  We believe for our part that God has spoken to us in his Word, and that he has given us not merely theology, but a system of theology, a great logically consistent body of truth.

That system of theology, that body of truth, which we find in the Bible, is the Reformed Faith, the Faith commonly called Calvinistic, which is set forth so gloriously in the Confession and Catechisms of the Presbyterian Church. It is sometimes referred to as a "man-made creed." But we do not regard it as such. We regard it, in accordance with our ordination pledge as ministers in the Presbyterian Church, as the creed which God has taught us in his Word. If it is contrary to the Bible, it is false. But we hold that it is not contrary to the Bible, but in accordance with the Bible, and true. We rejoice in the approximations to that body of truth which other systems of theology contain; we rejoice in our Christian fellowship with other evangelical churches; we hope that members of other churches, despite our Calvinism, may be willing to enter into Westminster Seminary as students and to listen to what we may have to say. But we cannot consent to impoverish our message by setting forth less than what we find the Scriptures to contain; and we believe that we shall best serve our fellow-Christians, from whatever church they may come, if we set forth not some vague greatest common measure among various creeds, but that great historic Faith that has come through Augustine and Calvin to our own Presbyterian Church. Glorious is the heritage of the Reformed Faith. God grant that it may go forth to new triumphs even in the present time of unbelief!

Systematic theology, on the basis of Holy Scripture, is the very center of what we have to teach; every other theological department is contributory to that; that department gives a man the message that he has to proclaim. But we have already spoken of the heritage of the Reformed Faith, and of a glorious tradition that has come down to us in the church. And that brings us to speak of another department of the theological curriculum, the department that deals with the history of the Christian church. Our message is based, indeed, directly upon the Bible; we derive the content of it not from the experience of past ages, but from what God has told us in his Word. But it would be a mistake to ignore what past generations, on the basis of God's Word, have thought and said and done. Into many other fields of theological study the study of church history casts a beneficent light. Church history should make us less enthusiastic about a modernity which is really as old as the hills; and amid the difficulties of the present time it should give us new hope. God has brought His church through many perils, and the darkest hour has often preceded the dawn. So it may be in our day. The gospel may yet break forth, sooner than we expect, to bring light and liberty to mankind. But that will be done, unless the lesson of church history is altogether wrong, by the instrumentality, not of theological pacifists who avoid controversy, but of earnest contenders for the faith. God give us men in our time who will stand with Luther and say: "Here I stand, I cannot do otherwise, God help me. Amen."

Thus the minister who goes forth from Westminster Seminary will, we hope, be a man with a message. He will also, we hope, be a man who can so deliver his message as to reach the hearts and minds of men; and to help him do that, the department of homiletics and practical theology has an important place. It cannot, indeed, itself teach a man how to preach; that he must learn, if at all, by the long experience of subsequent years. But at least it can help him to avoid errors and can start him in the right way; it can start him out in that long course in homiletics which is provided by all the rest of life.

Such, very feebly and imperfectly presented, is the program of Westminster Theological Seminary; it is far better set forth in the fine article which Dr. Oswald T. Allis has recently contributed to *The Sunday School Times.* Many things are omitted from this brief summary of ours. Some of them are omitted because of the imperfections of the speaker or from lack of time. But others are omitted of deliberate purpose. There are many things — many useful things, too — with which a theological seminary should not attempt to deal. Let it never be forgotten that a theological seminary is a school for specialists. We are living in an age of specialization. There are specialists on eyes and specialists on noses, and throats, and stomachs, and feet, and skin; there are specialists on teeth — one set of specialists on putting teeth in, and another set of specialists on pulling teeth out — there are specialists on Shakespeare and specialists on electric wires; there are specialists on Plato and specialists on pipes. Amid all these specialties, we at Westminster Seminary have a specialty which we think, in comparison with these others, is not so very small. Our specialty is found in the Word of God. Specialists in the Bible — that is what Westminster Seminary will endeavor to produce. Please do not forget it; please do not call on us for a product that we are not endeavoring to provide. If you want specialists in social science or in hygiene or even in "religion" (in the vague modern sense), then you must go elsewhere for what you want. But if you want men who know the Bible and know it in something more than a layman's sort of way, then call on us. If we can give you such men, we have succeeded; if we cannot give them to you, we have failed. It is a large contract indeed, a contract far too great for human strength. But at least, by God's grace, we shall do our best.

Such is the task of Westminster Theological Seminary. It is a task that needs especially to be undertaken at the present time. Fifty years ago many colleges and universities and theological seminaries were devoted to the truth of God's Word. But one by one they have drifted away, often with all sorts of professions of orthodoxy on the part of those who were responsible for the change. Until May, 1929, one great theological seminary, the Seminary at Princeton, resisted bravely the current of the age. But now that seminary has been made to conform to the general drift. Signers of the Auburn Affirmation, a formal document which declares that acceptance of the virgin birth and of four other basic articles of the Christian faith is non-essential even for ministers, actually sit upon the new governing Board. And they do so apparently with the acquiescence of the rest. Not one word of protest against the outrage involved in their presence has been uttered, so far as I know, by the other members of the Board; and a formal pronouncement, signed by the President of the Seminary and the President of the Board, actually commends the thirty-three members of the Board as men who have the confidence of the church. Surely it is quite clear, in view of that pronouncement, as well as in view of the personnel of the Board, that under such a governing body, Princeton Seminary is lost to the evangelical cause.

At first sight it might seem to be a great calamity; and sad are the hearts of those Christian men and women throughout the world who love the gospel that the old Princeton proclaimed. We cannot fully understand the ways of God in permitting so great a wrong. Yet good may come even out of a thing so evil as that. Perhaps the evangelical people in the Presbyterian Church were too contented, too confident in material resources; perhaps God has taken away worldly props in order that we may rely more fully upon Him; perhaps the pathway of sacrifice may prove to be the pathway of power.

That pathway of sacrifice is the pathway which students and supporters of Westminster Seminary are called upon to tread. For that we can thank God. Because of the sacrifices involved, no doubt many have been deterred from coming to us; they have feared the opposition of the machinery of the church; some of them may have feared, perhaps, to bear fully the reproach of Christ. We do not judge them. But whatever may be said about the students who have not come to us, one thing can certainly be said about those who have come — they are real men.

No, my friends, though Princeton Seminary is dead, the noble tradition of Princeton Seminary is alive. Westminster Seminary will endeavor by God's grace to continue that tradition unimpaired; it will endeavor, not on a foundation of equivocation and compromise, but on an honest foundation of devotion to God's Word, to maintain the same principles that the old Princeton maintained. We believe, first, that the Christian religion, as it is set forth in the Confession of Faith of the Presbyterian Church, is true; we believe, second, that the Christian religion welcomes and is capable of scholarly defense; and we believe, third, that the Christian religion should be proclaimed without fear or favor, and in clear opposition to whatever opposes it, whether within or without the church, as the only way of salvation for lost mankind. On that platform, brethren, we stand. Pray that we may be enabled by God's Spirit to stand firm. Pray that the students who go forth from Westminster Seminary may know Christ as their own Saviour and may proclaim to others the gospel of his love.

# CHAPTER XIX

## Consolations in the Midst of Battle

As you go forth into the gospel ministry, we cannot tell you that you will have an easy time. There are two reasons why we cannot tell you that. In the first place, it would not be true; and, in the second place, you would not believe us even if we endeavored to deceive. The world today is opposed to the faith that you profess, and the visible Church, too often, has made common cause with the world.

Our Lord Himself, when He was on earth, never made it easy to be a disciple of Him. He called upon men to count the cost before they would be called by His name. He warned them not to be like the man who starts to build a tower and is unable to complete it, nor like the man who puts his hand to the plough and turns back.

So we at Westminster Seminary, humble followers of Christ, never desire to bring men to this place under the false pretence that if they come to us they will be popular with the world. We are not seeking mere numbers in our student body. Rather are we seeking men like you, the members of this second graduating class, who are ready to bear the reproach of Christ and who are not afraid of earnest labor in the study of God's Word.

As you go forth to face the opposition of the world, and also, alas, the opposition of a worldly Church, there are certain things that we can tell you for your comfort and strength.

In the first place, we can tell you that one possession, at least, you will always have. It is not a possession that would be valued highly by the world. But we think that it will truly be valued by you. It is the affection and prayers of the little company of men, unpopular with the world, whom you have called your teachers. We are comrades with you in trial and in testimony, and comrades also in the exuberant joy of the gospel of Christ. Our affection will go with you to the ends of the earth. And with us, brethren, there stand today far more than seven thousand who have not bowed the knee to Baal. God has not left Himself without a witness even in this unbelieving age.

In the second place, we can tell you that this is not the first time of discouragement in the history of the Christian Church. Again and again the gospel has seemed to be forever forgotten; yet always it has burst forth with new power and the world has been set aflame. So it may be in our day. God's Spirit is all-powerful, and He can still bring men to the Saviour of their souls.

But what I desire particularly to tell you is not to be too greatly impressed by the pomp and power of this unbelieving age. With all the noise and boasting of the age in which we are living, there are some things that the age has lost.

About one week ago I stood on the one hundred and second story of the great Empire State Building in the city of New York. From there I looked down upon a scene like nothing else upon this earth. I watched the elevated trains, which from that distance seemed to be like slow caterpillars crawling along the rails; I listened to the ceaseless roar of the city ascending from a vast area to that great height. And I looked down upon that strange city which has been created on Manhattan Island within the last five or ten years — gigantic, bizarre, magnificently ugly. It seemed like some weird, tortured imagination of things in another world. I came down from that building very greatly impressed.

But as I reflected upon what I had seen, there came into my mind the memory of other buildings that I had contemplated in the course of my life. I thought of an English cathedral rising from the infinite greenness of some quiet cathedral close and above the ancient trees. I thought of the west façade of some continental cathedral, produced at a time when gothic architecture was not what it is today, imitative and cold and dead, but a living expression of the human soul; when every carving in every obscure corner, never perhaps to be seen by human eye, was an act of worship of Almighty God.

As I revived these memories, certain thoughts came into my mind. The modern builders, I thought, can uplift the body; they uplifted my body in express elevators twelve hundred and forty feet in record time. But whereas the modern builders, in an age of unbelief, can uplift the body, the ancient builders, in an age of faith, could uplift the soul. As one stands before the tower of a medieval cathedral — with one century laying the foundation there below, another century contributing its quota in the middle distance, and another century bringing the vast conception to its climax in a spire that seems to point upward to the skies — one is uplifted to a height far greater than the twelve hundred and forty feet of the Empire State Building; one is uplifted, not by some rebellious tower of Babel seeking to reach unto heaven by human pride, but rather on the wings of faith, up and up until one seems to stand in the very presence of the infinite God.

I am no medievalist, my friends; and I do not want you to be medievalists. I rejoice with all my heart in the marvellous widening of our knowledge of this mysterious universe that has come in modern times; I rejoice in the wonderful technical achievements of our day. I trust that you, my brethren, will never fall into the "Touch not, taste not, handle not" attitude which Paul condemned in his time; I hope you will never fall into that ancient heresy of forgetting that this is God's world and that neither its good things nor its wonders should be despised by those upon whom, through God's bounty, they have been bestowed. I trust that you will consecrate to God not an impoverished man, narrowed in interests, narrowed in mind and heart, but a man with all God-given powers developed to the full.

Moreover, I cherish in my soul a vague yet glorious hope — the hope of a time when these material achievements, instead of making man the victim of his own machines, may be used in the expression of some wonderous thought. There may come a time when God will send to the world the fire of genius, which He has taken from it in our time, and when He will send something far greater than genius — a humble heart finding in His worship the highest use of all knowledge and of all power. There may come a time when men will wonder at their former obsession with these material things, when they will see that these modern inventions in the material realm are in themselves as valueless as the ugly little bits of metal type in a printer's composing room, and that their true value will be found only when they become the means of expressing some glorious poem.

Meanwhile, however, we are living in a drab and empty age. The law of God has been forgotten or despised, and dreary slavery is the result. Do you think that this is a happy or a blessed age? Oh, no, my friends. Amid all the noise and shouting and power and machinery, there are hungry hearts — hearts thirsting for the living water, hearts hungry for the bread that is bread indeed.

That hunger you alone can still. You can do so not by any riches of your own, but as humble ministers of the Lord Jesus Christ. How wonderfully rich you are, my brethren, rich with riches greater by far than all the wealth and power of this world, rich with the inexhaustible riches of God's Word! Oh, may you use those riches! May this graduation day be only the beginning of your study of the Word; may you learn ever to bring forth out of that treasure things new and old! May you be no adherents of some strange new sect; may you maintain your contact with the grand and noble scholarly tradition of the Christian Church; may your sermons be born in earnest study and in the agony of your souls! When you come forth into your pulpits, be they great or obscure, may you come forth out of a place of labor and meditation and prayer!

Perhaps it may be objected that that would be a new kind
of preaching. Yes, but this is a new seminary, and a new seminary
may hope to bring forth some things that are new — new at
least to this age. Who can say, my brethren? Perhaps you may
be the humble instruments, by the use of whatever talents God
has given you, of lifting preaching out of the rut into which too
often it has fallen, and of making it again, by God's grace, a
thing of power.

Remember this, at least — the things in which the world is
now interested are the things that are seen; but the things that are
seen are temporal, and the things that are not seen are eternal.
You, as ministers of Christ, are called to deal with the unseen
things. You are stewards of the mysteries of God. You alone can
lead men, by the proclamation of God's word, out of the crash
and jazz and noise and rattle and smoke of this weary age into
the green pastures and beside the still waters; you alone, as
ministers of reconciliation, can give what the world with all its
boasting and pride can never give — the infinite sweetness of the
communion of the redeemed soul with the living God.

# CHAPTER XX

## Servants of God or Servants of Men

YOU WILL notice that I have written what I shall say to you upon these few sheets of paper that I hold in my hand. That does not mean that what I shall say does not come from the heart. It does not mean that when in deep affection I bid you Godspeed in my own name and in the name of my colleagues in the Faculty I desire to place any cold medium of a written page between my heart and yours. But it means that I am conscious of standing here in a very great crisis in the history of the Presbyterian Church in U. S. A. On such an occasion it is incumbent upon a man to weigh his words, and to keep precise record of what he says. I am speaking, indeed, without consultation of my colleagues. I alone am responsible for what I shall say. But I am aware of the momentous issues involved, and I have sent a copy of this little address, insignificant though it be in itself, to the Stated Clerk of the General Assembly of the Presbyterian Church in the U. S. A., and to the stated clerks of the Presbyteries of New Brunswick and Philadelphia.

You are seeking entrance into the Christian ministry. At such a time it is proper for you to count the cost; it is proper for you to ask just what being a Christian minister means. There is just one thing that I want to say to you in answer to that question. The thing that I want to say to you is that you cannot be a Christian minister if you proclaim the word of man; you can be a Christian minister only if you proclaim, without fear or favor, the Word of God.

In the twenty-second chapter of the Second Book of Kings, we read how a messenger who was sent to call the prophet Micaiah the son of Imlah coached him as to what he should say. "Behold now," he said, "the words of the prophets declare good unto the king with one mouth; let thy word, I pray thee, be like the word of one of them, and speak that which is good." But Micaiah said: "As the Lord liveth, what the Lord saith unto me, that will I speak."

You, my brethren, must be like Micaiah the son of Imlah; you too must say: "As the Lord liveth, what the Lord saith unto me that will I speak." The Lord does not, indeed, speak to you in the manner in which He spoke to Micaiah. He does not speak to you by direct supernatural revelation. You are not prophets. But He speaks to you through the supernatural Book. It is only when you proclaim the words of that Book that you are a true minister of Jesus Christ. Only then can you say: "Thus saith the Lord."

The congregations for which you labor may, as the world looks upon them, be but insignificant groups of humble people. But never forget that those insignificant and humble groups are the Church of the living God, and that you as their ministers must proclaim to them the awful and holy and blessed Word.

If you obtain your message from any other authority than the Word of God, if you obtain it from the pronouncements of presbyteries or General Assemblies, then you may wear the garb of ministers, but you are not ministers in the sight of God. You are disloyal to the Lord Jesus Christ: you have betrayed a precious trust.

The temptation to you to be disloyal is coming to you in insistent fashion just at the present moment. It is coming to you through the words of cultured and well-meaning gentlemen, and it is coming to you through the unwarranted acts of ecclesiastical councils and courts. In the Presbytery of Baltimore, at a recent meeting, it came through the Stated Clerk of the General Assembly. The following passage from a letter of the Stated Clerk of the General Assembly to the Stated Clerk of that Presbytery was read in open session:

> If and when any students from Westminster Seminary come before your Presbytery, they should be informed that the Presbytery will neither license nor ordain them until they have given a written pledge that they will support the official agencies of the Church as a part of their pledge of loyalty to the government and discipline of the Church.

The Presbytery of New Brunswick, acting, earlier, on the same principle, and in violation of the Constitution of the Presbyterian Church in the U. S. A., has placed in its manual a provision that no one shall be received into the Presbytery without being subjected to an examination as to his willingness to support the regularly appointed Boards and Agencies.

I feel compelled to say to you, my brethren, with the utmost plainness, that if you sign the pledge demanded of you in that letter of Dr. Mudge and practically implied in that action of the Presbytery of New Brunswick, if you obtain your licensure or ordination in that way, then, quite irrespective of the question whether the Boards and Agencies are or are not faithful at this moment or at any particular moment, you have become servants of men and are not in the high Biblical sense servants of the Lord Jesus Christ. If you promise to adapt your message to shifting majorities in church councils or to the mandates of church officials, if you promise to commend one kind of missions this year and an opposite kind next year, as the General Assembly, newly elected every year, may direct, if you thus take the Bible from your pulpits and place the Minutes of the General Assembly in its place, if you thus abandon the Reformation and do despite to all the blood and tears that it cost, if you thus abandon the high liberty guaranteed you by the Constitution of the Presbyterian Church in the U. S. A., and if (as, alas, you do if you abandon that liberty) you abandon your allegiance to the Lord Jesus Christ by putting fallible men into the place of authority that belongs only to Him, then the ministry has become, as far as you are concerned, merely a profession, and rather a contemptible profession too. You may, by taking such a step, obtain high ecclesiastical preferment, but never can you be ministers of the New Covenant, never can you be ambassadors of God.

If, on the other hand, you choose, as indeed you have already shown very nobly that you have chosen, to obey God rather than men, then you may look to the future with unconquerable joy. If any one door be closed to you by the usurped authority of human councils or officials, be assured that some other and greater door will be opened to you in God's own way. But above all remember that that Captain is worthy whose service you are thus preferring to the favor of men. He is worthy because of His infinite power and glory. But He is also worthy because of something else. There are other things besides the effulgence of His royal majesty which mark Him as our Lord:

> *Hath He marks to lead me to Him,*
> *If He be my Guide?*
> *"In His feet and hands are wound-prints,*
> *And His side."*
>
> *Is there diadem, as Monarch,*
> *That His brow adorns?*
> *"Yea, a crown, in very surety,*
> *But of thorns."*
>
> *If I find Him, if I follow,*
> *What His guerdon here?*
> *"Many a sorrow, many a labor,*
> *Many a tear."*
>
> *If I still hold closely to Him,*
> *What hath He at last?*
> *"Sorrow vanquished, labor ended,*
> *Jordan passed."*

*If I ask Him to receive me,*
   *Will He say me nay?*
*"Not till earth and not till heaven*
   *Pass away."*

*Finding, following, keeping, struggling,*
   *Is He sure to bless?*
*"Saints, apostles, prophets, martyrs,*
   *Answer, 'Yes.'"*

"Ye were bought with a price," my brethren; "be not ye the servants of men."

# CHAPTER XXI

## Does Fundamentalism Obstruct Social Progress?

THE TERM "Fundamentalism" in the title of our discussion is evidently to be taken in a broad sense, not to designate "Premillennialists" but to include all those who definitely and polemically maintain a belief in supernatural Christianity as over against the Modernism of the present day. In what ways has "Fundamentalism," defined thus broadly to include men like ourselves, been held to be inimical to social progress?

In the first place, it has been held to be inimical to social progress because it maintains unchanged certain root convictions in the sphere of history. It is opposed to social progress, we are told, because it is opposed to all progress. It maintains a traditional view of what Jesus was and what Jesus did in the first century of our era, and therefore, we are told, it is opposed to the advance of science. If we no longer hold to the chemistry or physics of the sixteenth century or the fourth century or the first century, why should we hold to the account which those past ages gave of what Jesus said and did?

This objection ignores the peculiarity of history as over against the experimental sciences. A thing that has happened can never be made by the passage of the years into a thing that has not happened; all history is based upon a thoroughly static view of facts. Progress can never obliterate events.

It is a great mistake to suppose that the evangelical Christian is opposed to the discovery of new facts: on the contrary he welcomes the discovery of new facts with all his mind and heart. But he is a Christian because he maintains certain facts which

244

have been known for many hundreds of years. In particular he believes that on a certain morning some nineteen hundred years ago, the body of Jesus of Nazareth emerged from the tomb in which it had been laid. That belief involves the most far-reaching consequences in every sphere of thought and of conduct; the Christian risks the whole of his life upon his conviction as to the resurrection of Christ.

If indeed that conviction should prove to be ill-grounded, it would certainly have to be given up. The Christian ought to welcome to the full the investigation of the resurrection of Christ by all the methods of scientific history. But the point is that that investigation seems to him only to result in a confirmation of his belief. And if it results in a confirmation of his belief, then to relinquish that belief is not progress but retrogression. The grounding of life upon falsehoods is inimical to progress; but the grounding of it upon facts is a necessary condition of any true advance.

In the second place, Christianity is held to hinder social progress because it maintains a pessimistic view of human nature as at present constituted. This charge is sometimes evaded; and the Christian religion is represented as though it were a kind of sweet reasonableness based upon confidence in human goodness. But the evasion reverses the true character of our religion. Confidence in human resources is paganism — or modernism — whereas Christianity begins with the consciousness of sin, and grounds its hope only in the regenerating power of the Spirit of God.

It is no wonder that the advocates of the modernist program regard Christians as opponents of social progress. Men who refuse to go with the current and who rebuke the easy self-confidence of their time have always been regarded as enemies of the human race. But this antipathy is well founded only if the pessimism that is objected to is out of accord with the facts. The physician who comforts the patient by a false diagnosis is pleasing for the moment; but the true friend and helper is the one who designates the disease by its true name.  So it may turn out to be with the Bible and with the Christian preacher who brings the Bible message to the modern world.  Modern social science has erected an imposing building; it has in many respects improved the mechanical aspect of human life: and Christianity certainly has nothing to say against its achievements.  But, unless we mistake the signs of the times, there is among the social architects of the present day a vague sense of uneasiness.  There is abroad in the world an ill-defined but nonetheless disconcerting sense of futility.  The work on the social edifice still goes on, but rifts are beginning to appear in the walls and underneath there are intimations of dreadful things.  Shall the trouble with the foundations continue to be ignored?  If it is ignored, the enthusiasm of the architects may for a time be maintained, but all the greater will be the crash when at last it comes.  Utilitarianism, in other words, is proving to be a quite inadequate basis for the social edifice, and there are those — despised and abused as the enemies of progress and the race — who insist upon facing the underlying facts of personal life. In these men the hope of society really rests.  The edifice erected by social science need not be destroyed if the foundations be strengthened in time.  And the strengthening is provided by the Christian faith.

In the third place, historic Christianity is thought to be inimical to social progress because it is individual rather than social.  The older evangelism, it is said, seeks to win individuals; it invites men to come forward to the mourners' bench, receive salvation, and so escape from this wicked world.  The newer and better evangelism, on the other hand — thus the claim runs — instead of rescuing individuals and leaving the world to its fate, seeks so to improve the physical conditions of life and the relations between man and man as to set up what may be called the "Kingdom of God" here upon this earth.

This objection depends partly upon a caricature of the Christian religion. It is not true that the Christian gospel offers individual men a selfish escape from the world and leaves society to its fate. On the contrary, Christianity is social as well as individual. Even the relation of the individual to his God is not individual but social, if God exists; certainly it is not regarded by anyone who experiences it as a selfish thing. But the Christian also sustains relationships to his fellow men, and his religion is far from discouraging those relationships. When a man is rescued inwardly from the world, he is not, according to Christian teaching, allowed to escape from the world into a place of mystic contemplation, but is sent forth again into the world to battle for the right.

Nevertheless, despite onesidedness, the assertion of modern social workers to the effect that historic Christianity is individual rather than social has in it a large element of truth. It is true that Christianity as over against certain social tendencies of the present day insists upon the rights of the individual soul. We do not deny the fact; on the contrary we glory in it. Christianity, if it be true Christianity, must place itself squarely in opposition to the soul-killing collectivism which is threatening to dominate our social life; it must provide the individual soul with a secret place of refuge from the tyranny of psychological experts; it must fight the great battle for the liberty of the children of God.

The rapidly progressing loss of liberty is one of the most striking phenomena of recent years. At times it makes itself felt in blatant ways, as in the notorious Lusk laws for the licensing of teachers in the State of New York, or in the Oregon school law now being tested in the United States courts. Liberty still has some bulwarks; but even those bulwarks are threatened. In Nebraska, for example, where the study of languages other than English was forbidden and thus literary education was made a crime, all outer defenses were broken through and the enemy was checked only by that last bulwark of liberty, the United States

Supreme Court. But unless the temper of the people changes. that bulwark also will fall. If liberty is to be preserved against the materialistic paternalism of the modern state, there must be something more than courts and legal guarantees; freedom must be written not merely in the constitution but in the people's heart. And it can be written in the heart, we believe, only as a result of the redeeming work of Christ. Other means in the long run will fail. Sometimes, it is true, self-interest will accomplish beneficent results. The Lusks laws, for example, which attacked liberty of speech in the State of New York, were opposed partly by the socialists against whom the laws were originally aimed. But the trouble is that socialism, if it were ever put into effect, would mean a physical, intellectual and spiritual slavery more appalling than that which prevailed under the worst despotisms that the world so far has ever known. The real defenders of liberty are those who are devoted to it for its own sake, who believe that freedom of speech means not only freedom for those with whom they are agreed but also freedom for those to whom they are opposed. It is such a defense of liberty which is favored by the true followers of Christ.

But at this point an objection may arise. "Fundamentalism," it is said, "is a synonym of intolerance: and the writer of the present article desires to cast out of the ministry of his church those who hold views different from his own. How can such a person pretend to be a lover of liberty?"

The objection ignores the distinction between voluntary and involuntary organizations. The state is an involuntary organization, an organization to which a man is forced to belong whether he will or no. For such an organization to prescribe any one type of education for its members is an intolerable interference with liberty. But the Church is a purely voluntary organization, and no one is forced to enter its ministry. For such an organization to prescribe terms of admission and to insist that its authorized teachers shall be in agreement with the creed or message for the propagation of which the Church exists involves not the slightest interference with liberty, but is a matter of plain common honesty and common sense. Insistence on fundamental agreement within a voluntary organization is therefore not at all inconsistent with insistence upon the widest tolerance in the state. Indeed the two things are not merely consistent, but are connected logically in the closest possible way. One of the essential elements in civil and religious liberty is the right of voluntary association — the right of individuals to associate themselves closely for the propagation of anything that they may desire, no matter how foolish it may seem to others to be. This right is being maintained by "Fundamentalists," and it is being combated subtly but none the less dangerously by some of their opponents. The most serious danger to liberty in America today is found in the widespread tendency towards a centralized state monopoly in education — the tendency which has manifested itself crassly and brutally in the Oregon school law, and which manifests itself more subtly in the proposed development of a Federal department of education, which will make another great addition to the vast Washington bureaucracy, the bureaucracy which with its discouragement of spiritual initiative is doing so much to drain the life-blood of the people. The same tendency manifests itself also in the advocacy of anti-theological and anti-evangelical propaganda under the guise of "character-building" in monopolistic public schools. Under these circumstances, it has come about — paradoxical though it may seem — that one of the chief defenders of American liberty is the Roman Catholic Church. Catholics and "Fundamentalists," despite their immense differences, are at least agreed, in America, in their insistence upon the right of voluntary association; and such insistence is the very foundation of civil and religious liberty. To *persuade* Catholic parents to send their children to non-Catholic schools is no doubt in many cases wise; to *force* them to do so, no matter how high the motive of the compulsion, is tyranny. The end, we hold, does not justify the means, and violation of sacred rights will in the long run, through the retributive justice of God, bring ruin.

The last objection to historic Christianity is that it is doctrinal rather than practical. There is so much misery in the world, it is said — so many crowded tenements, so many starving children — that there is no time to engage in theological or historical discussions about the death and resurrection of Christ. This objection, we are constrained to believe, betokens a singular narrowness of mind. It seems to be assumed that the Church has to choose between examining the basis of her faith and relieving the physical distress of men. As a matter of fact she ought to do both. Neglect of either one will certainly bring disaster. And to-day the danger lies altogether in the neglect, not of the physical, but of the intellectual and spiritual task. The truth is that the present age is characterized by an unparalleled intellectual and spiritual decline.

The growth of ignorance — certainly in America and probably elsewhere as well — is appalling; poetry is silent; and even the appreciation of fine and noble things seems almost to be lost. Certainly a generation that follows Mr. H. G. Wells in his contemptuous neglect of all the higher ranges of the human mind, or deserts Milton for Van Loon, can hardly convince any thinking man that it is an infallible judge of what is beautiful or good.

We do not therefore seek to evade this last objection, but we meet it squarely in the face. We are opposed with all our might to the passionate anti-intellectualism of the Modernist Church; we refuse to separate religion sharply from science; and we believe that our religion is founded not upon aspirations but upon facts. Of course if the intellectual defense of our faith causes us to neglect our duty to the poor, we have made ourselves guilty of a great sin. And in that case may God pity us and set us back into the pathway of duty and love! But relief of physical distress, important as it is, is not all that the Church has to do. And even that task, we believe, cannot be accomplished if we neglect the intellectual basis of our faith. False ideas are responsible even for the physical evils in the world; the machinery of the world's business will not perform its task if we neglect the soul of man; the best of engines will not run if it is not producing a spark.

Thus we maintain that far from being inimical to social progress, "Fundamentalism" (in the broad, popular sense of the word) is the only means of checking the spiritual decadence of our age. Some men are satisfied with the thought of the time when the physical conditions of life will so be improved by the advance of science that there shall be no poverty and no disease, and when vain aspirations will so be conquered by reason that death will lose its terrors and men will be able to part from their loved ones without a pang. But would such a rule of reason represent an advance over the present state of mankind? For our part, we think not. The deadening of spiritual aspirations and the abolition of individual liberty may bring about a diminution of pain, but they will also bring about the destruction of all that makes life worth while. We do not for one moment discourage the relief of distress and the improvement of the physical condition of the race; indeed these things have obtained their real impetus from the "Fundamentalism" of the past. But if these things prove to be all, then mankind will have sunk to the level of the beasts.

The process of decadence has been going on apace, and it is high time to seek a way of rescue if mankind is to be saved from the abyss. Such a way of rescue is provided by the Christian religion, with its supernatural origin and supernatural power. It is a great mistake to represent us who are adherents of historic Christianity as though we were clinging desperately to the past merely because it is old, and as though we had no message of hope. On the contrary, our eyes are turned eagerly to the future. We are seeking no mere continuation of spiritual conditions that now exist but an outburst of new power; we are looking for a mighty revival of the Christian religion which like the Reformation of the sixteenth century will bring light and liberty to mankind. When such a revival comes, it will destroy no fine or unselfish or noble thing; it will hasten and not hinder the relief of the physical distress of men and the improvement of conditions in this world. But it will do far more than all that. It will also descend into the depths — those depths into which utilitarianism can never enter — and will again bring mankind into the glorious liberty of communion with the living God.

CHAPTER XXII

# What Fundamentalism Stands For Now

THE TERM "Fundamentalism" is distasteful to the present writer and to many persons who hold views similar to his. It seems to suggest that we are adherents of some strange new sect; whereas in point of fact we are conscious simply of maintaining the historic Christian faith and of moving in the great central current of Christian life. That does not mean that we desire to be out of touch with our own time, or that we live in a static world without variety and without zest. On the contrary, there is nothing more varied and more interesting than the effect of the Christian religion upon different races and different ages; there is no more absorbing story than that of the relations between Christianity and its changing environment.

But what we do mean is that despite changes in the environment, there is something in Christianity which from the very beginning has remained the same.

This historic continuity of the Christian religion is based upon its appeal to a body of facts — facts about God, about man, and about the way in which, at a definite point in the world's history, some nineteen hundred years ago, a new relationship was set up between God and man by the work of Jesus Christ. There is one advantage about facts — they "stay put." If a thing really happened, it can never possibly be made by the passage of time or by the advance of science into a thing that has not happened. New facts may be discovered, and certainly we Christians welcome the discovery of new facts with all our heart; but old facts, if they be really facts, will remain facts beyond the end of time.

This sheer factual basis of the Christian religion is denied by a large body of persons in the modern Church; indeed at this point we find what is really perhaps the most fundamental divergence in the religious world at the present day. More fundamental than differences of opinion about this truth or that is the difference of opinion about truth as such. When historic Christianity maintains that the Christian religion is based upon a body of truth, a body of doctrine, which will remain true beyond the end of time, it is opposed by a very widespread pragmatism, which maintains that doctrine is merely the necessarily changing expression of an inner experience.

Doctrine, the pragmatist admits, is indeed necessary, but in the very nature of the case it cannot be permanent; it is the mere attempt to express the Christian life in the forms of thought proper to any one generation, and in another generation a different expression will necessarily be in place. Thus according to the logic of the pragmatist position, two contradictory doctrines may be equally good; one may serve for one generation or for one class of persons, and another may serve for another generation or another class of persons.

Obviously this attitude involves the most bottomless skepticism; for to say that doctrines which are contradictory to each other are equally true is just the same as saying that the two doctrines are equally false, and that permanent, objective truth in the sphere of religion can never be attained. To such pragmatist skepticism the believer in historic Christianity is sharply opposed; against the passionate anti-intellectualism of a great section of the modern Church he maintains the primacy of the intellect; he holds that God has given to man a faculty of reason which is capable of apprehending truth, even truth about God.

That does not mean that we finite creatures can find out God by our own searching; but it does mean that God has made us capable of receiving the information which He chooses to give. I cannot possibly evolve an account of China out of my own inner consciousness, but I am perfectly capable of understanding the account which comes to me from travellers who have been there themselves. So our reason is certainly insufficient to tell us about God unless He reveals Himself, but it is capable (or would be capable if it were not clouded by sin) of receiving revelation when once it is given.

God's revelation of Himself to man embraces, indeed, only a small part of His being; the area of what we know is infinitesimal compared with what we do not know. But partial knowledge is not necessarily false knowledge; and our knowledge of God, on the basis of His revelation, is, we hold, true as far as it goes.

Christianity then on our view is not a life as distinguished from a doctrine, or a life of which doctrine is the symbolic intellectual expression; but — just the other way around — it is a life founded upon a doctrine. We refuse therefore to abandon to the student of natural science the entire realm of fact, in order to reserve to religion merely a realm of ideals; on the contrary, theology, we hold, is just as much a science as is chemistry. The two sciences, it is true, differ widely in their subject matter, and in particular they differ widely in the qualifications required of the investigator; but they are both concerned with the acquisition and orderly arrangement of truth.

The body of truth upon which the Christian religion is based may be divided into three parts. There is first the doctrine of God (or theology proper), second the doctrine of man, and third the doctrine of the relationship between God and man. These three divisions may now be considered briefly in turn.

The basis of the Christian view of God — by no means all of it, but the basis of it — is simply theism, the belief, namely, that the universe was created and is now upheld by a personal Being upon whom it is dependent but who is not dependent upon it. This view is opposed to all forms of the prevalent pantheism, which either makes "God" merely a collective name for the world process itself, or else regards Him as related to the world process as the soul of man is related to his body.

All forms of pantheism differ from theism in denying the transcendence of God, the separateness of God from the world. But the transcendence of God, what the Bible calls the "holiness" of God, is at the very root of the Christian religion. God is indeed, according to the Christian view, immanent in the world, but He is also personally distinct from the world and from the finite creatures that He has made.

The Christian doctrine of man is partly involved in the Christian doctrine of God; theism, with its distinction between God and the world, humbles man as creature under the almighty hand of God, while the current pantheism exalts man because his life is regarded as being a part of all the God there is. But another difference of opinion is more important still; it appears in divergent views of moral evil. According to historic Christianity, all mankind are under the just condemnation of God, and are utterly helpless because of the guilt and power of sin; according to another very widespread type of belief, human resources are sufficient for human needs, and self-development, especially the development of the religious nature, is the Christian ideal. This type of belief is optimistic about human nature as it is at present constituted, while historic Christianity regards all mankind as being in itself hopelessly lost.

Many preachers seek to arouse man's confidence in himself; "I believe in Man" is one of the cardinal articles of their creed; but the preacher of historic Christianity tries first of all to destroy man's confidence in himself and to arouse in his soul the dreadful consciousness of sin.

God enveloped in a terrible righteousness, man an offender against His law and under His just wrath — these are the two great presuppositions of the historic Christian gospel. But on the basis of these terrible presuppositions, the Christian preacher comes with a message of hope. The hope is found not at all in any attenuation of the facts about God and man, not at all in any effort to take lightly the curse of God's law, but simply and solely in an account of what God Himself has done.

We deserved eternal death, but the Son of God, who was Himself God, came into this world for our redemption, took upon Himself the just punishment of our sins, died instead of us on the cross, and finally completed His redeeming work by rising from the tomb in a glorious resurrection. There and there alone is found the Christian gospel, the piece of "good news" upon which all our hope is based.

That gospel, as indeed the term "news" implies, is an account, not of something that always was true, but of something that happened; Christianity is based not merely on ethical principles or on eternal truths of religion, but also on historical facts.

The redeeming facts upon which the Christian hope is based were things done by the Lord Jesus Christ, and those facts involve the entrance into the course of this world of the creative power of God; in other words, they involve the supernatural.

Acceptance of the supernatural does not, as is often supposed, destroy the basis of science; it does not introduce an element of arbitrariness which would make impossible any exhibition of regular sequences in nature. On the contrary, a miracle, according to the Christian view, is not an arbitrary or purposeless event, but proceeds from the very source of all the order that there is in the world, namely from the will of God.

God is the author of nature, and we Christians are willing to trust Him not to destroy that orderly system in which it is His will that we should live. Indeed the believer in the supernatural is in some respects kinder to the scientist than the scientist ventures to be to himself; for in order to maintain the distinctness of the supernatural from the natural we are obliged to hold that there is a real order of nature — not a mere observed set of sequences but a really existent order. Only, that order of nature, though really existent, is not self-existent; it was created by the fiat of God's will, and He has never abandoned His freedom in the presence of His world.

We are not saying that while miracles were accomplished by God ordinary events are not accomplished by Him, but only that in the case of ordinary events He uses means or "second causes," while in the case of miracles He puts forth His creative power. A miracle then is an event wrought by the immediate, as distinguished from the mediate power of God; it is not a work of providence but a work of creation.

The outstanding miracle narrated in the New Testament is the emergence of the body of Jesus from the tomb; upon that miracle the Christian Church was founded, and the evidence for it is of a singularly varied and cumulative kind. But that event is not isolated; it is connected with a consistent representation of Jesus in the New Testament as a supernatural Person — not the fairest flower of humanity, the finest thing the world has to show, not divine only because divinity courses through all things, not God only because He was the highest development of man, but the eternal Son of God who came voluntarily into the world for our redemption.

Acceptance of this New Testament account of Jesus involves a certain attitude toward Him which is widely different from the attitude assumed by many persons in the Church today. Jesus to us was not only a teacher and example (though He was all that), but He was, and is, our Saviour and Lord; He was not the first Christian, the initiator of a new type of religious life, but He stood in a far more fundamental and far more intimate relationship to Christianity than that, because he was the One who made Christianity possible by His redeeming work.

At no point does our attitude appear in more characteristic fashion than just here: many persons hold up their hands in amazement at our assertion that Jesus was not a Christian; we regard it as the very height of blasphemy to say that he was a Christian. "Christianity" to us is a way of getting rid of sin; and therefore to say that Jesus was a Christian would be to deny His perfect holiness.

"But," it is said, "do you mean to tell us that if a man lives a life like the life of Jesus he is not a Christian even though he rejects the doctrine of the redeeming work of Christ in His death and resurrection?" The question is often asked, but the answer is very simple. Of course if a man really lives a life like the life of Jesus, all is well; such a man is indeed not a Christian, but he is something better than a Christian; he is a being who has never lost his high estate of sonship with God.

But our trouble is that our lives, to say nothing of the lives of those who thus so confidently appeal to their own similarity to Jesus, do not seem to be like the life of Jesus; we are sinners, hence we become Christians; we are sinners, and hence we accept with thankfulness the redeeming love of the Lord Jesus Christ, who had pity on us and made us right with God, through no merit of our own, by His atoning death.

Thus we make Jesus not merely an example for faith, but primarily the object of faith. In doing so, we have the whole New Testament on our side; the Jesus who preached "a religion of Jesus" and not "a religion about Jesus" never really was heard of until modern times; the Jesus of all the Gospels presented Himself not merely as teacher but also as Lord and as Redeemer.

This redeeming work of Christ which is at the center of the Bible is applied to the individual soul, according to our view, by the Holy Spirit; we find no permanent hope for society in the mere "principles of Jesus" or the like; but we find it in the new birth of individuals souls. Important indeed are the social applications of Christianity; but as Francis Shunk Downs has well said there can be no applied Christianity unless there is a Christianity to apply, and there can be no Christianity to apply unless there are Christian men. And men are made Christian by the Spirit of God.

But the means which the Spirit of God uses in making men Christians is faith; and faith is the response of the human soul to the gospel message. A man becomes convicted of sin; he sees himself as God sees him; he is in despair. And then the Lord Jesus is offered to him in the gospel — in the good news that the guilt of sin has been blotted out by the wonderful sacrifice which God Himself provided, in His mysterious love for sinners, on Calvary. The acceptance of that message is faith, faith in the Lord Jesus Christ; through faith a man becomes a child of God; and then follows a new life, with a victorious battle against sin.

Such is the way of salvation as it is set forth in the Bible and in historic Christianity. It seems to those who have followed it to be the most blessed thing in all the world; who can measure the peace and joy that have been found at the foot of the Cross? But to others the message seems strange and full of offence.

The offence comes — and has come ever since the very first days of the Christian Church — from the inveterate insistence and exclusiveness of the Christian message. What causes offence is not that we present this way of salvation, but that we present it as the only way. The world according to our view is lost in sin; the gospel provides the only way of escape; and the blackest guilt into which any Christian can fall is to deceive dying souls into thinking that some other way will answer as well.

If our views are wrong, they should be refuted; but what is ethically indefensible is to ask us to hold those views and then act as though we did not hold them. If those views are true, they must determine our every action, in our capacity both as men and as ministers in the Church. God has placed us in the world as witnesses, and we cannot, in the interests of ecclesiastical harmony or for any other reason allow our witness to become untrue; we cannot consent to deceive men into thinking that they can be saved in any other way than through the gospel that is set forth in the Word of God.

# CHAPTER XXIII

# Christianity and Liberty

WHEN I was honored by an invitation to contribute an article to The Forum, it could only be because the Editor is broadminded enough to accord a hearing to a humble representative of a very unpopular cause. To be an adherent today of that redemptive religion that has always hitherto been known as Christianity, and to be at all in earnest about the logical consequences of that conviction, is to stand sharply at variance not only with the world at large but also with the forces that dominate most of the larger Protestant churches. These churches, many of them, instead of engaging in the sweet and gentle ministrations to the human soul in which they formerly engaged, have made themselves political lobbies or agencies of the police. Church organizations, already proud of their bigness, have sought to unite themselves in the gigantic monopoly of one Protestant body. Amid the rattle of all this machinery, amid the bustle of all this efficiency, there is little sympathy for the man who asks what it is at bottom that the Church is in the world to do. The churches often profess belief, indeed, in the Bible and in the ancient creeds; but for an individual in the churches to believe in the Bible and in the creeds and to be at all earnest about the logical consequences of such belief — this is regarded as an unpardonable ecclesiastical crime.

Whatever may be thought of such an unpopular step as that, it can hardly be any unworthy motives of self-interest that lead a man to take it. It is not easy to stand against the whole current of an age, and the sacrifice which is involved in doing so is far from being light. Why then do we adherents of the religion of the

Bible insist on being so peculiar; why do we resist in such perverse fashion the pronouncements of the "modern mind"?

Perhaps, for one thing, it is because we do not think so highly as some persons do of the modern mind — of the modern mind and of the modern world that that modern mind has produced.

It is not the incidental defects of the modern mind of which I am thinking just now. Those incidental defects are surely plain enough even to the most enthusiastic modernity.

I suppose my experience is similar to the experience of a good many men. When I was a student in Europe in 1905-1906, the argument from modern authority seemed to me to be a very powerful argument against the supernaturalistic Christianity in which I had been brought up. I was living in an environment where that Christianity had long been abandoned, where it was no longer regarded even as being worthy of debate. It was a very stimulating environment indeed, dominated by men whom I enthusiastically admired then and whom I still admire. And the world in general might have seemed to a superficial observer to be getting along very well without Christ. It was a fine comfortable world — that godless and Christless European world prior to 1914. And as for anything like another European war, that seemed to be about as well within the bounds of possibility as that medieval knights should don their armor and set their lances again in rest. The international bankers obviously would prevent anything so absurd. But we discovered our mistake. Our comfortable utilitarian world proved to be not so comfortable after all.

In some directions, indeed, there was advance even in warfare, over conditions that had prevailed before. Antiseptic surgery no doubt had accomplished much. But in other directions there was a marked decline. The notion of the nation in arms, that redoubtable product of the French Revolution, was carried out to something approaching its logical result. Even more logical and even more damnable, no doubt, will be its results in the next war.

Modern scientific utilitarianism, in other words, did not produce the millennium prior to 1914; and there is not the slightest evidence that it has produced the millennium since that time or that it ever will produce the millennium in the ages to come.

In further incidental indictment of the age in which we are living, I might point to the brutal injustices and enormities of the peace that followed upon a war which was supposed to be waged for justice and liberty. And I might point also to the appalling spiritual decline which has come over the world within the last fifty years. High poetry, for the most part, is silent; art is either imitative or bizarre. There is advance in material things; but in the higher ranges of the human mind an amazing sterility has fallen on the world. Very extra-ordinary is the complacency of such an age; indeed that complacency is perhaps the most appalling indication of decadence that could possibly be conceived.

But serious as are such incidental defects of the age in which we are living, it is not those incidental defects of which I am thinking just now. After all, there has been advance in some directions to balance the retrogression in others. Humanitarian effort has no doubt accomplished much; war has been declared against the mosquito and the germ, and some day we may be living in a world without disease. I doubt it, for my part; but at any rate the possibility cannot altogether be denied.

What, then, if it is not found in incidentals — even so stupendous an incidental as the world war — is the real indictment against the modern world? The answer seems clear enough to some of us. The real indictment against the modern world is that by the modern world human liberty is being destroyed.

At that point, no doubt, many readers will only with difficulty repress a smile. The word "liberty" today has a decidedly archaic sound. It suggests G. A. Rnety, flag-waving, the boys of '76, and the like. Twentieth-century intellectuals, it is thought, have long

ago outgrown all such childishness as that.  So the modern historians are writing "liberty" in quotation marks, when they are
obliged to use the ridiculous word: no principle, they are telling
us, for example, was involved in the American Revolution; economic causes alone produced that struggle; and Patrick Henry was
indulging in cheap melodrama when he said: "Give me liberty
or give me death."  Certainly, at any rate, whatever our estimate
of history, liberty is out of date in modern life.  Standardization
and efficiency have very largely taken its place.

Even nature is being made to conform to standard.  In the
region that I have visited in Maine off and on for the past thirty
years, I have seen the wild exuberance of woods and streams gradually giving place to the dreary regularities of a National Park.  It
seems almost as though some sweet, delicate living creature were
being ruthlessly destroyed.

But that is only a symbol of what is also going on today in the
higher sphere of human life; the same ruthless standardization
of human souls.  That is particularly true in the all-important
field of education.  If, it is said, we allow all sorts of queer private
schools and parochial schools to confuse the mind of youth, what
will become of the welfare of the State?  How can we have a unified nation without a standardized school?

I know that this process of standardization has recently been
checked in America here and there.  The supreme Court of the
United States declared unconstitutional the Oregon school law
that simply sought to wipe all private schools and Christian schools
out of existence in that State, and it also declared unconstitutional
the Nebraska language law (similar to laws in other States) that
made literary education even in private schools a crime.  The
abominable Lusk laws in the State of New York, one of which
placed private teachers under State supervision and control, were
repealed.  The bill establishing a Federal department of education, despite the powerful interests working in behalf of it, has
not yet become a law.  The misnamed "Child Labor Amendment"

to the Constitution of the United States, which would have placed the youth of the country under centralized bureaucratic control, has not yet received the requisite ratification from the States. But I fear that these set-backs to the attack on liberty, unless the underlying temper of the people changes, are but temporary, and that the process of standardization and centralization will go ruthlessly on.

In some spheres, no doubt, standardization is a good thing. It is a good thing, for example, in the making of a Ford car. But it does not follow that it should be applied to human beings; for a human being is a person and a Ford car is a machine.

The typical modern experts deny this distinction, and that is our fundamental quarrel with the "modern mind." I know that there are those who tell us that this tendency to which we object is merely incidental to a change in the physical conditions of life. The liberty of the individual, they tell us, has always had to be limited somehow in the interests of the community and of the race; and the limitation, as life becomes more complex, merely has to appear in somewhat more intricate form. We may be passing through a period just now when the pendulum between individualism and collectivism has swung too much to the latter extreme; but it will swing back, and all will be well.

I should like to think that this view of the situation is correct, but I am unable to think so. The trouble is not that the modern world has been unsuccessful in an effort to preserve liberty, but that it is not seeking to preserve liberty at all. Mussolini is thought to be a benefactor of the race, because, although liberty of speech is destroyed in Italy, the streets of Italian cities are clean. The Soviet tyrants in Russia are said not to be efficient; but it never seems to occur to modern critics that they would be far more dangerous tyrants if they were. Mankind, in other words, has become willing to buy material benefits at any price. I do not know how the bargain will turn out in detail. But in the bargain something at any rate will have been lost. We may have gained the whole world, but we are in danger of losing our own soul.

What sort of world is it to which we are tending today? What is really the modern ideal? I suppose it is a world in which the human machine has arrived at the highest stage of efficiency. Disease, I suppose, may be abolished; and as for death, although we shall not have abolished it, we shall at least have abolished its terrors. Vague, childish longings, pre-scientific speculations as to a hereafter, will all be gone; and we shall have learned, as reasonable and scientific men, to stand without a pang at the grave of those whom in a less-scientific age we should have been childish enough to love.

What is to be thought of such a mechanistic world? I will tell you what we think of it; we think it is a world in which all zest, all glory, all that makes life worth living will have been destroyed. It will no doubt have its advantages. In it, no doubt, the span of our life may be extended far beyond the previously alloted period of threescore years and ten. Experts appointed by the State will always be by our side to examine our physical and mental condition and keep us alive upon the earth. Perhaps they may be successful in keeping us alive upon the earth. But what will be the use? Who would want to live longer in a world where life is so little worth living?

From such a slavery, which is already stalking through the earth in the materialistic paternalism of the modern State, from such a world of unrelieved drabness, we seek escape in the high adventure of the Christian religion. Men call us, indeed, devotees of a Book. They are right. We are devotees of a Book. But the Book to which we are devoted is the Magna Charta of human liberty — the Book which alone can make men free.

At that point I am particularly desirous of not being misunderstood. I do not mean for one moment that a man ever became a real Christian merely through the desire to attain civil or political freedom or even the very highest of worldly ends. Valuable are the by-products of Christianity, and one of them is the civil liberty of the race. But if a man carries on this undertaking for the sake of the by-products, the undertaking and the by-products are both sure to be lost. Jesus said indeed: "Seek ye first the Kingdom of God and His righteousness, and all these things shall be added unto you;" but if a man seeks the Kingdom of God and His righteousness in order that all these things may be added unto him, he will miss the Kingdom of God and those other things as well.

But what I do mean is that the defects of the modern world, though they will never make a man a Christian in themselves, may yet lead him to a consideration of far profounder needs. He may begin by seeking escape from mechanism and go on to seek escape from sin. In the Christian religion, we find a liberty that is far deeper than the civil and religious liberty of which we have spoken. It is a liberty that enters into the depths of the soul.

In the Bible, we find, in the first place, God. Back of the stupendous mechanism of the world there stands, as the Master of it and not as its slave, no machine but a living person. He is enveloped, indeed, in awful mystery; a dreadful curtain veils His being from the gaze of men. But unlike the world, He is free, and He has chosen in His freedom to lift the veil and grant us just a look beyond. In that look we have freedom from the mechanism of the world. God is free, and where He is there is liberty and life.

In the Bible, in the second place, we find man; we regain that birthright of freedom which had been taken from us by the modern mind. It is a dreadful birthright indeed. For with freedom goes responsibility, and with responsibility, for us, there goes the awful guilt of sin. That conscience awakens which makes cowards of us all. Gone for us Christians is the complacency of the modern mind; gone is the lax, comforting notion that crime is only a disease; gone is the notion that strips the ermine from the judge and makes him but the agent of a utilitarian society; gone is the blindness that refuses to face the moral facts. The Christian world, unlike the modern world, is a world of nameless terrors; the Christian views man as standing over a bottomless abyss. Such a view will find little sympathy from the experts of the present day; they will doubtless apply to it their usual method of dealing with a thing that they do not understand — they will give it a long name and let it go. But is their judgment really to be trusted? There are some of us who think not. There are some of us who think that the moral judgments of us sinners, even when they are the judgments of experts, are not always to be trusted, and that the real pathway of advance for humanity lies through a rediscovery of the law of God.

In the third place, in the Bible we find redemption. Into this vast universe, into this world of sin, there came in God's good time a divine Redeemer. No mere teacher is He to us, no mere example, no mere leader into a larger life, no mere symbol or embodiment of an all-pervading divinity. No; we stand to Him, if we be really His, in a relationship far dearer, far closer than all that. For us He gave His precious life upon the cross to make all well between us sinners and the righteous God, by whose love He came.

At that point, I despair of finding words to tell the readers fully what I mean. Perhaps we may tell you what we think; but it is harder to tell you what we feel. You may dismiss it all as "theory of the atonement," and fall back upon the customary commonplaces about a principle of self-sacrifice exemplified in the Cross of Christ or the culmination there of a universal law or a revelation of the love of God or the hallowing of suffering or the similarity between Christ's death and the death of soldiers who gave themselves for others in the World war. And then, by God's grace, there may come, when you least expect it, a flash of light into your soul, and all will be as clear as day. Then you will say with Paul, as you contemplate the Saviour upon the cross: "He loved me and gave Himself for me." Thus will the ancient burden fall from our back; then do we become true moderns at last. "Old things are passed away; behold; they are become new." Then and then only will you have true freedom. It will be a freedom from mechanism; but the freedom from mechanism will be rooted in a freedom from sin.

At this point I think I know what some of the readers may say. Do we not agree, they may say, with much that has been said? Do we not reject behaviorist psychology; do we not believe in the freedom of the soul? do we not believe in God? But need such beliefs be connected with such very doubtful conclusions in the sphere of external history; may we not believe in the eternal worth of the human soul, and enter into communion with God, without insisting upon the external miracles of the Bible? May we not have a true Christian experience without believing in the empty tomb?

This attitude lies at the basis of what may be called, by a very unsatisfactory and question-begging term, "Liberalism" in the Church. It is a very imposing phenomenon. I hope I do not approach it without sympathy. I have listened to many of its representatives during the last twenty-five years with high admiration — ever since I sat in Herrmann's classroom at Marburg and obtained some impression of the fervor and glow of that remarkable man. I can quite understand how men desire to escape if they can the debate in the field of science; I quite understand how they seek to avoid disputing about what happens or has happened in the external world and fall back upon an internal world of the soul into which scientific debate cannot enter. It seems to be such a promising solution of our apologetic difficulties just to say that science and religion belong in two entirely different spheres and can never by any chance come into conflict. It seems to be so easy for religion to purchase peace by abandoning to science the whole sphere of facts in order to retain for itself merely a sphere of feelings and ideals.

But in reality these tactics are quite disastrous. You effect thus a strategic retreat; you retreat into a Hindenburg line, an inner line of defense whence you think that science can never dislodge you. You get down into your pragmatist dugout and listen comfortably to the muffled sound of the warfare being carried on above by those who are old-fashioned enough to be interested in truth; you think that whatever creedal changes, whatever intellectual battle there may be, you at least are safe. You have your Christian experience; and let science and Biblical criticism do what they will!

But do not comfort yourself. The enemy in this warfare is good at mopping up captured trenches; he has in his mechanistic psychologists a very efficient mopping-up squad. He will soon drive you out of your refuge; he will destroy whatever decency and liberty you thought you had retained; and you will discover, too late, that the battle is now lost, and that your only real hope lay not in retreating into some anti-intellectualistic dugout but in fighting bravely to prevent the initial capture of the trench.

No, the battle between naturalism and supernaturalism, between mechanism and liberty, has to be fought out sooner or later; and I do not believe that there is any advantage in letting the enemy choose the ground upon which it shall be fought. The strongest defense of the Christian religion is the outer defense; a reduced and inconsistent Christianity is weak; our real safety lies in the exultant supernaturalism of God's Word.

And is the case for that supernaturalism really so weak? There are many things that lead us to think that it is not; but if you want to learn of one of them, just read the four Gospels for yourselves. Do not study them this time, important though it is to study them at other times. Just read them; just let the stupendous figure of Jesus stand before your eyes. Has not that figure the marks of truth? Could that figure ever have been produced in impersonal fashion to satisfy the needs of the primitive Church? No, the figure of Jesus in the Gospels possesses an individuality that is irreducible, a shining, startling vividness against which criticism will ultimately fail. Yet criticism has had its beneficent results; it has shown with increasing clearness that the picture of Jesus in the New Testament is essentially one. Gone is the day when men thought that a few miracles could be removed from the Gospels to leave a "liberal Jesus," a mere preacher of the "fatherhood of God and the brotherhood of man."

Recent New Testament criticism has tended strongly against any such easy solution of the problem as that. Increasingly the great alternative is becoming clearer; give Jesus up, and confess that His portrait is forever hidden in the mists of legend; or else accept Him as a supernatural Person, as He is presented by all the four Gospels and by Paul.

We have chosen the latter alternative for ourselves; and we believe that only in that alternative are true progress and true liberty to be attained for mankind.

# CHAPTER XXIV

# The Responsibility of the Church in Our New Age

THE QUESTION of the Church's responsibility in the new age involves two other questions: (1) What is the new age? (2) What is the Church?

The former question is being answered in a number of different ways; differences of opinion prevail, in particular, with regard to the exact degree of newness to which the new age may justifiably lay claim. There are those who think that the new age is so very new that nothing that approved itself to past ages can conceivably be valid now. There are others, however, who think that human nature remains essentially the same and that two and two still make four. With this latter point of view I am on the whole inclined to agree. In particular, I hold that facts have a most unprogressive habit of staying put, and that if a thing really happened in the first century of our era, the acquisition of new knowledge and the improvement of scientific method can never make it into a thing that did not happen.

Such convictions do not blind me to the fact that we have witnessed astonishing changes in our day. Indeed, the changes have become so rapid as to cause many people to lose not only their breath but also, I fear, their head. They have led many people to think not only that nothing that is old ought by any possibility to remain in the new age, but also that whatever the new age favors is always really new.

Both these conclusions are erroneous. There are old things which ought to remain in the new age; and many of the things, both good and bad, which the new age regards as new are really as old as the hills.

In the former category are to be put, for example, the literary and artistic achievements of past generations. Those are things which the new age ought to retain, at least until the new age can produce something to put in their place, and that it has so far signally failed to do. I am well aware that when I say to the new age that Homer is still worth reading, or that the Cathedral of Amiens is superior to any of the achievements of the *art nouveau,* I am making assertions which it would be difficult for me to prove. There is no disputing about tastes. Yet, after all, until the artistic impulse is eradicated more thoroughly from human life than has so far been done even by the best efforts of the metallic civilization of our day, we cannot get rid of the categories of good and bad or high and low in the field of art. But when we pay attention to those categories, it becomes evident at once that we are living today in a drab and decadent age, and that a really new impulse will probably come, as it has come so many times before, only through a rediscovery of the glories of the past.

Something very similar needs to be said in the realm of political and social science. There, too, something is being lost — something very precious, though very intangible and very difficult of defense before those who have not the love of it in their hearts. I refer to civil and religious liberty, for which our fathers were willing to sacrifice so much.

The word "liberty" has a very archaic sound today; it is often put in quotation marks by those who are obliged to use the ridiculous word at all. Yet, despised though liberty is, there are still those who love it; and unless their love of it can be eradicated from their unprogressive souls, they will never be able to agree, in their estimate of the modern age, with those who do not love it.

To those lovers of civil and religious liberty I confess that I belong; in fact, civil and religious liberty seems to me to be more valuable than any other earthly thing — than any other thing short of that truer and profounder liberty which only God can give.

What estimate of the present age can possibly be complete that does not take account of what is so marked a feature of it — namely, the loss of those civil liberties for which men formerly were willing to sacrifice all that they possessed? In some countries, such as Russia and Italy, the attack upon liberty has been blatant and extreme; but exactly the same forces which appear there in more consistent form appear also in practically all the countries of the earth. Everywhere we have the substitution of economic considerations for great principles in the conduct of the state; everywhere a centralized state, working as the state necessarily must work, by the use of force, is taking possession of the most intimate fields of individual and family life.

These tendencies have proceeded more rapidly in America than in most other countries of the world; for if they have not progressed so far here as elsewhere, that is only because in America they had a greater handicap to overcome. Thirty years ago we hated bureaucracy and pitied those countries in Europe that were under bureaucratic control; today we are rapidly becoming one of the most bureaucratic countries of the world. Setbacks to this movement, such as the defeat, for the present at least, of the misnamed "child-labor amendment," the repeal of the Lusk laws in New York placing private teachers under state supervision and control, the invalidation of the Nebraska language law making literary education even in private schools a crime, the prevention so far of the establishment of a Federal department of education — these setbacks to the attack on liberty are, I am afraid, but temporary unless the present temper of the people changes.

The international situation, moreover, is hardly such as to give encouragement to lovers of liberty, especially in view of the recent proposal of Premier Herriot that a policy of conscription, inimical as it is to liberty as well as to peace, shall be made general and permanent. Everywhere in the world we have centralization of power, the ticketing and cataloguing of the individual by irresponsible and doctrinaire bureaus, and, worst of all, in many places we have monopolistic control of education by the state.

But is all that new? In principle it is not. Something very much like it was advocated in Plato's *Republic* over two thousand years ago. The battle between collectivism and liberty is an age-long battle; and even the materialistic paternalism of the modern state is by no means altogether new. The technique of tyranny has, indeed, been enormously improved; a state-controlled compulsory education has proved far more effective in crushing out liberty than the older and cruder weapons of fire and sword, and modern experts have proved to be more efficient than the dilettante tyrants of the past. But such differences are differences of degree and not of kind, and essentially the battle for freedom is the same as it always has been.

If that battle is lost, if collectivism finally triumphs, if we come to live in a world where recreation as well as labor is prescribed for us by experts appointed by the state, if the sweetness and the sorrows of family relationships are alike eliminated and liberty becomes a thing of the past, we ought to place the blame for this sad denouement — for this sad result of all the pathetic strivings of the human race — exactly where it belongs. And it does not belong to the external conditions of modern life. I know that there are those who say that it does belong there; I know that there are those who tell us that individualism is impossible in an industrial age. But I do not believe them for one moment. Unquestionably, industrialism, with the accompanying achievements of modern science in both the physical and the social realm, does constitute a great temptation to destroy freedom; but temptation is not compulsion, and of real compulsion there is none.

No, my friends, there is no real reason for mankind to surrender to the machine. If liberty is crushed out, if standardization has its perfect work, if the worst of all tyrannies, the tyranny of the expert, becomes universal, if the finer aspirations of humanity give way to drab efficiency, do not blame the external conditions in the world today. If human life becomes mechanized, do not blame the machine. Put the blame exactly where it belongs — upon the soul of man.

Is it not in general within that realm of the soul of man that the evils of society have their origin today? We have developed a vast and rather wonderful machinery — the machinery of our modern life. For some reason, it has recently ceased to function. The experts are busily cranking the engine, as I used to do with my Ford car in the heroic days when a Ford was still a Ford. They are wondering why the engine does not start. They are giving learned explanations of its failure to do so; they are adducing the most intricate principles of dynamics. It is all very instructive, no doubt. But the real explanation is much simpler. It is simply that the driver of the car has forgotten to turn on the switch. The real trouble with the engine of modern society is that it is not producing a spark. The real trouble lies in that unseen realm which is found within the soul of man.

That realm cannot be neglected even in a time of immediate physical distress like the present. I do not know in detail how this physical distress is to be relieved. I would to God that I did. But one thing I do know; it will never be relieved if, in our eagerness to relieve it, we neglect the unseen things. It is not practical to be merely practical men; man cannot successfully be treated as a machine; even the·physical welfare of humanity cannot be attained if we make that the supreme object of our pursuit; even in a day when so many material problems are pressing for our attention, we cannot neglect the evils of the soul.

But if that be so, if the real trouble with the world lies in the soul of man, we may perhaps turn for help to an agency which is generally thought to have the soul of man as its special province. I mean the Christian Church. That brings us to our second question: What is the Church?

About nineteen hundred years ago, there came forth from Palestine a remarkable movement. At first it was obscure; but within a generation it was firmly planted in the great cities of the Roman Empiré and within three centuries it had conquered the Empire itself. It has since then gone forth to the ends of the earth. That movement is called the Christian Church.

What was it like in the all-important initial period, when the impulse which gave rise to it was fresh and pure? With regard to the answer to that question, there may be a certain amount of agreement among all serious historians, whether they are themselves Christians or not. Certain characteristics of the Christian Church at the beginning stand out clear in the eyes both of friends and of foes.

It may clearly be observed, for example, that the Christian Church at the beginning was radically doctrinal. Doctrine was not the mere expression of Christian life, as it is in the pragmatist skepticism of the present day, but — just the other way around — the doctrine, logically though not temporally, came first and the life afterward. The life was founded upon the message, and not the message upon the life.

That becomes clear everywhere in the primary documents. It appears, for example, in the First Epistle to the Thessalonians, which is admitted by all serious historians, Christian and non-Christian, to have been really written by a man of the first Christian generation — the man whose name it bears. The Apostle Paul there gives us a summary of his missionary preaching in Thessalonica — that missionary preaching which in Thessalonica and in Philippi and elsewhere did, it must be admitted, turn the world upside down. What was the missionary preaching like? Well, it contained a whole system of theology. "Ye turned to God," says Paul, "from idols to serve the living and true God, and to wait for His Son from heaven, whom He raised from the dead, even Jesus, which delivereth us from the wrath to come." Christian doctrine, according to Paul, was not something that came after salvation, as an expression of Christian experience, but it was something necessary to salvation. The Christian life, according to Paul, was founded upon a message.

The same thing appears when we turn from Paul to the very first church in Jerusalem. That too was radically doctrinal. In the First Epistle to the Corinthians — again one of the universally accepted Epistles — Paul gives us a summary of what he had received from the primitive Jerusalem Church. What was it that he had received; what was it that the primitive Jerusalem Church delivered over unto him? Was it a mere exhortation; was it the mere presentation of a program of life; did the first Christians in Jerusalem say merely: "Jesus has lived a noble life of self-sacrifice; we have been inspired by Him to live that life and we call upon you our hearers to share it with us?" Not at all. Here is what those first Christians said: "Christ died for our sins according to the Scriptures: He was buried; He has been raised on the third day according to the Scriptures." That is not an exhortation, but a rehearsal of facts; it is couched not in the imperative but in the indicative mood; it is not a program, but a doctrine.

I know that modern men have appealed sometimes at this point from the primitive Christian Church to Jesus Himself. The primitive Church, it is admitted, was doctrinal; but Jesus of Nazareth, it is said, proclaimed a simple gospel of divine Fatherhood and human brotherhood, and believed in the essential goodness of man. Such an appeal from the primitive Church to Jesus used to be expressed in the cry of the so-called "Liberal" Church, "Back to Christ!" But that cry is somewhat antiquated today. It has become increasingly clear to the historians that the only Jesus whom we find attested for us in our sources of information is the supernatural Redeemer presented in the four Gospels as well as in the Epistles of Paul. If there was back of this supernatural figure a real, non-doctrinal, purely human prophet of Nazareth, his portrait must probably lie forever hidden from us.

Such, indeed, is exactly the skeptical conclusion which is being reached by some of those who stand in the van of what is called progress in New Testament criticism today.

There are others, however — and to them the present writer belongs — who think that the supernatural Jesus presented in all of our sources of information was the real Jesus who walked and talked in Palestine, and that it is not necessary for us to have recourse to the truly extraordinary hypothesis that the intimate friends of Jesus, who were the leaders of the primitive Church, completely misunderstood their Master's person and work.

Be that as it may, there is, at any rate, not a trace of any non-doctrinal preaching that possessed one bit of power in those early days of the Christian Church. It is perfectly clear that that strangely powerful movement which emerged from the obscurity of Palestine in the first-century of our era was doctrinal from the very beginning and to the very core. It was totally unlike the ethical preaching of the Stoic and Cynic philosophers. Unlike those philosophers, it had a very clearcut message; and at the center of that message was the doctrine that set forth the person and work of Jesus Christ.

That brings us to our second point. The primitive Church, we have just seen, was radically doctrinal. In the second place, it was radically intolerant. In being radically intolerant, as in being radically doctrinal, it placed itself squarely in opposition to the spirit of that age. That was an age of synchronism and tolerance in religion; it was an age of what J. S. Phillimore has called "the courtly polygamies of the soul." But with that tolerance, with those courtly polygamies of the soul, the primitive Christian Church would have nothing to do. It demanded a completely exclusive devotion. A man could not be a worshiper of the God of the Christians and at the same time be a worshiper of other gods; he could not accept the salvation offered by Christ and at the same time admit that for other people there might be some other way of salvation; he could not agree to refrain from proselytizing among men of other faiths, but came forward, no matter what it might cost, with a universal appeal. That is what I mean by saying that the primitive Christian Church was radically intolerant.

In the third place, the primitive Church was radically ethical. Religion in those days, save among the Jews, was by no means closely connected with goodness. But with such a non-ethical religion the primitive Christian Church would have nothing whatever to do. God, according to the primitive Christians, is holy; and in His presence no unclean thing can stand. Jesus Christ presented a life of perfect goodness upon earth; and only they can belong to Him who hunger and thirst after righteousness. Christians were, indeed, by no means perfect; they stood before God only in the merit of Christ their Saviour, not in their own merit; but they had been saved for holiness, and even in this life that holiness must begin to appear. A salvation which permitted a man to continue in sin was, according to the primitive Church, no matter what profession of faith it might make, nothing but a sham.

These characteristics of primitive Christianity have never been completely lost in the long history of the Christian Church. They have, however, always had to be defended against foes within as well as without the Church. The conflicts began in apostolic days; and there is in the New Testament not a bit of comfort for the feeble notion that controversy in the Church is to be avoided, that a man can make his preaching positive without making it negative, that he can ever proclaim truth without attacking error. Another conflict arose in the second century, against Gnosticism, and still another when Augustine defended against Pelagius the Christian view of sin.

At the close of the Middle Ages, it looked as though at last the battle were lost — as though at last the Church had become merged with the world. When Luther went to Rome, a blatant paganism was there in control. But the Bible was rediscovered;

the ninety-five theses were nailed up; Calvin's *Institutes* was written; there was a counter-reformation in the Church of Rome; and the essential character of the Christian Church was preserved. The Reformation, like primitive Christianity, was radically doctrinal, radically intolerant, and radically ethical. It preserved these characteristics in the face of opposition. It would not go a step with Erasmus, for example, in his indifferentism and his tolerance; it was founded squarely on the Bible, and it proclaimed, as providing the only way af salvation, the message that the Bible contains.

At the present time, the Christian Church stands in the midst of another conflict. Like the previous conflicts, it is a conflict not between two forms of the Christian religion but between the Christian religion on the one hand and an alien religion on the other. Yet — again like the previous conflicts — it is carried on within the Church. The non-Christian forces have made use of Christian terminology and have sought to dominate the organization of the Church.

This modern attack upon the Christian religion has assumed many different forms, but everywhere it is essentially the same. Sometimes it is frankly naturalistic, denying the historicity of the basic miracles, such as the resurrection of Jesus Christ. At other times it assails the necessity rather than the truth of the Christian message; but, strictly speaking, to assail the necessity of the message is to assail its truth, since the universal necessity of the message is at the center of the message itself. Often the attack uses the shibboleths of a complete pragmatist skepticism. Christianity, it declares, is a life and not a doctrine; and doctrine is the expression, in the thought-forms of each generation, of Christian experience. One doctrine may express Christian experience in this generation; a contradictory doctrine may express it equally well in a generation to come. That means, of course, not merely that this or that truth is being attacked, but that truth itself is being attacked.   The very possibility of our attaining to truth, as distinguished from mere usefulness, is denied.

This pragmatist skepticism, this optimistic religion of a self-sufficient humanity, has been substituted today, to a very considerable extent, in most of the Protestant communions, for the redemptive religion hitherto known as Christianity — that redemptive religion with its doctrines of the awful transcendence of God, the hopelessness of a mankind lost in sin, and the mysterious grace of God in the mighty redemptive acts of the coming and death and resurrection of Jesus Christ.   Many of the rank and file of the churches, many of the individual congregations, are genuinely Christian; but the central organizations of the churches have in many cases gradually discontinued their propagation of the Christian religion and have become agencies for the propagation of a vague type of religion to which Christianity from its very beginning was diametrically opposed.

So, in speaking about the responsibility of the Church in the new age, I want it to be distinctly understood that I am not speaking about the responsibility of the existing Protestant church organizations (unless they can be reformed), but about the responsibility of a true Christian Church.   The present ecclesiastical organizations may have their uses in the world.   There may be a need for such societies of general welfare as some of them have become; there may be a need for the political activities in which they are increasingly engaged: but such functions are certainly not at all the distinctive function of a real Christian Church.

Even in the sphere of such worldly functions, I am inclined to think that there are agencies more worthy of your attention than these Protestant church organizations, or than, for example, such an organization as the Federal Council of the Churches of Christ in America.   The trouble is that the gentlemen in control of these organizations are, though with the best and most honorable intentions in the world, in a hopelessly false position.   The churches are for the most part creedal; it is on the basis of their creeds that they have in the past appealed, and that to some extent they still appeal, for support; yet the central organizations of the churches have quietly pushed the creeds into the background and have devoted themselves to other activities and a different propaganda. Perhaps in doing so they have accomplished good here and there in a worldly sort of way. But, in general, the false position in which they stand has militated against their highest usefulness. Equivocation, the double use of traditional terminology, subscription to solemn creedal statements in a sense different from the sense originally intended in those statements — these things give a man a poor platform upon which to stand, no matter what it is that he proposes, upon that platform, to do.

But if the existing Protestant church organizations, with some notable exceptions, must be radically reformed before they can be regarded as truly Christian, what, as distinguished from these organizations, is the function of a true Christian Church?

In the first place, a true Christian Church, now as always, will be radically doctrinal. It will never use the shibboleths of a pragmatist skepticism. It will never say that doctrine is the expression of experience; it will never confuse the useful with the true, but will place truth at the basis of all its striving and all its life. Into the welter of changing human opinion, into the modern despair with regard to any knowledge of the meaning of life, it will come with a clear and imperious message. That message it will find in the Bible, which it will hold to contain not a record of man's religious experience but a record of a revelation from God.

In the second place, a true Christian Church will be radically intolerant. At that point, however, a word of explanation is in place. The intolerance of the Church, in the sense in which I am speaking of it, does not involve any interference with liberty, on the contrary, it means the preservation of liberty. One of the most important elements in civil and religious liberty is the right of voluntary association — the right of citizens to band themselves together for any lawful purpose whatever, whether that purpose does or does not commend itself to the generality of their fellow men. Now, a church is a voluntary association. No one is compelled to be a member of it; no one is compelled to be one of its accredited representatives. It is, therefore, no interference with liberty for a church to insist that those who do choose to be its accredited representatives shall not use the vantage ground of such a position to attack that for which the church exists.

It would, indeed, be an interference with liberty for a church, through the ballot box or otherwise, to use the power of the state to compel men to assent to the church's creed or conform to the church's program. To that kind of intolerance I am opposed with all my might and main. I am also opposed to church union for somewhat similar reasons, as well as for other reasons still more important. I am opposed to the depressing dream of one monopolistic church organization, placing the whole Protestant world under one set of committees and boards. If that dream were ever realized, it would be an intolerable tyranny. Certainly it would mean the death of any true Christian unity. I trust that the efforts of the church-unionists may be defeated, like the efforts of the opponents of liberty in other fields.

But when I say that a true Christian Church is radically intolerant, I mean simply that the Church must maintain the high exclusiveness and universality of its message. It presents the gospel of Jesus Christ not merely as one way of salvation, but as the only way. It cannot make common cause with other faiths. It cannot agree not to proselytize. Its appeal is universal, and admits of no exceptions. All are lost in sin; none may be saved except by the way set forth in the gospel. Therein lies the offense of the Christian religion, but therein lies also its glory and its power. A Christianity tolerant of other religions is just no Christianity at all.

In the third place, a true Christian Church will be radically ethical. It will not be ethical in the sense that it will cherish any hope in an appeal to the human will; it will not be ethical in the sense that it will regard itself as perfect, even when its members have been redeemed by the grace of God. But it will be ethical in the sense that it will cherish the hope of true goodness in the other world, and that even here and now it will exhibit the beginnings of a new life which is the gift of God.

That new life will express itself in love. Love will overflow, without questions, without calculation, to all men whether they be Christians or not; but it will be far too intense a passion ever to be satisfied with a mere philanthropy. It will offer men simple benefits; it will never pass coldly by on the other side when a man is in bodily need. But it will never be content to satisfy men's bodily needs; it will never seek to make men content with creature comforts or with the coldness of a vague natural religion. Rather will it seek to bring all men everywhere, without exception, high and low, rich and poor, learned and ignorant, compatriot and alien, into the full warmth and joy of the household of faith.

There are certain things which you cannot expect from such a true Christian Church. In the first place, you cannot expect from it any cooperation with non-Christian religion or with a non-Christian program of ethical culture. There are those who tell us that the Bible ought to be put into the public schools, and that the public schools should seek to build character by showing the children that honesty is the best policy and that good Americans do not lie nor steal. With such programs a true Christian Church will have nothing to do. The Bible, it will hold, is made to say the direct opposite of what it means if any hope is held out to mankind from its ethical portions apart from its great redemptive center and core; and character building on the basis of human experience may be character destruction; it is the very antithesis of that view of sin which is at the foundation of all Christian convictions and all Christian life.

There is no such thing, a true Christian Church will insist, as a universally valid fund of religious principles upon which particular religions, including the Christian religion, may build; "re-

ligion" in that vague sense is not only inadequate but false; and
a morality based upon human experience instead of upon the law
of God is no true morality. Against such programs of religious
education and character building, a true Christian Church will
seek from the state liberty for all parents everywhere to bring up
their children in accordance with the dictates of their conscience,
will bring up its own children in accordance with the Word of
God, and will try to persuade all other parents, becoming Christians, to bring up their children in that same Christian way.

In the second place, you cannot expect from a true Christian
Church any official pronouncements upon the political or social
questions of the day, and you cannot expect cooperation with the
state in anything involving the use of force. Important are the
functions of the police, and members of the Church, either indi-
vidually or in such special associations as they may choose to form,
should aid the police in every lawful way in the exercise of those
functions. But the function of the Church in its corporate capacity is of an entirely different kind. Its weapons against evil are
spiritual, not carnal; and by becoming a political lobby, through
the advocacy of political measures whether good or bad, the
Church is turning aside from its proper mission, which is to bring
to bear upon human hearts the solemn and imperious, yet also
sweet and gracious, appeal of the gospel of Christ.

Such things you cannot expect from a true Christian Church.
But there are other things which you may expect. If you are dissatisfied with a relative goodness, which is no goodness at all; if
you are conscious of your sin and if you hunger and thirst after
righteousness; if you are dissatisfied with the world and are seeking the living God, then turn to the Church of Jesus Christ. That
Church is not always easy to distinguish today. It does not always present itself to you in powerful organizations; it is often
hidden away here and there, in individual congregations resisting
the central ecclesiastical mechanism; it is found in groups, large
or small, of those who have been redeemed from sin and are citi-

zens of a heavenly kingdom. But wherever it is found, you must turn to that true Church of Jesus Christ for a message from God. The message will not be enforced by human authority or by the pomp of numbers. Yet some of you may hear it. If you do hear it and heed it, you will possess riches greater than the riches of all the world.

Do you think that if you heed the message you will be less successful students of political and social science; do you think that by becoming citizens of another world you will become less fitted to solve this world's problems; do you think that acceptance of the Christian message will hinder political or social advance? No, my friends. I will present to you a strange paradox but an assured truth — this world's problems can never be solved by those who make this world the object of their desires. This world cannot ultimately be bettered if you think that this world is all. To move the world you must have a place to stand.

This, then, is the answer that I give to the question before us. The responsibility of the Church in the new age is the same as its responsibility in every age. It is to testify that this world is lost in sin; that the span of human life — nay, all the length of human history — is an infinitesimal island in the awful depths of eternity; that there is a mysterious, holy, living God, Creator of all, Upholder of all, infinitely beyond all; that He has revealed Himself to us in His Word and offered us communion with Himself through Jesus Christ the Lord; that there is no other salvation, for individuals or for nations, save this, but that this salvation is full and free, and that whosoever possesses it has for himself and for all others to whom he may be the instrument of bringing it a treasure compared with which all the kingdoms of the earth — nay, all the wonders of the starry heavens — are as the dust of the street.

An unpopular message it is — an impractical message, we are told. But it is the message of the Christian Church. Neglect it, and you will have destruction; heed it, and you will have life.

## XXV

## The Necessity of the Christian School

THE CHRISTIAN SCHOOL is to be favored for two reasons. In the first place, it is important for American liberty; in the second place, it is important for the propagation of the Christian religion. These two reasons are not equally important; indeed, the latter includes the former as it includes every other legitimate human interest. But I want to speak of these two reasons in turn.

In the first place, then, the Christian school is important for the maintenance of American liberty.

We are witnessing in our day a world-wide attack upon the fundamental principles of civil and religious freedom. In some countries, such as Italy, the attack has been blatant and unashamed; Mussolini despises democracy and does not mind saying so. A similar despotism now prevails in Germany; and in Russia freedom is being crushed out by what is perhaps the most complete and systematic tyranny that the world has ever seen.

But exactly the same tendency that is manifested in extreme form in those countries, is also being manifested, more slowly but none the less surely, in America. It has been given an enormous impetus first by the war and now by the economic depression; but aside from these external stimuli it had its roots in a fundamental deterioration of the American people. Gradually the people have come to value principle less and creature comfort more; increasingly it has come to prefer prosperity to freedom; and even in the field of prosperity it cannot be said that the effect is satisfactory.

The result of this decadence in the American people is seen in the rapid growth of a centralized bureaucracy which is the thing against which the Constitution of the United States was most clearly intended to guard.

In the presence of this apparent collapse of free democracy, any descendant of the liberty-loving races of mankind may well stand dismayed; and to those liberty-loving races no doubt most of my hearers tonight belong: I am of the Anglo-Saxon race; many of you belong to a race whose part in the history of human freedom is if anything still more glorious: and as we all contemplate the struggle of our fathers in the winning of that freedom which their descendants seem now to be so willing to give up, we are impressed anew with the fact that it is far easier to destroy than to create. It took many centuries of struggle — much blood and many tears — to establish the fundamental principles of our civil and religious liberty; but one mad generation is sufficient to throw them all away.

It is true, the attack upon liberty is nothing new. Always there have been tyrants in the world; almost always tyranny has begun by being superficially beneficent, and always it has ended by being both superficially and radically cruel.

But while tyranny itself is nothing new, the technique of tyranny has been enormously improved in our day; the tyranny of the scientific expert is the most crushing tyranny of all. That tyranny is being exercised most-effectively in the field of education. A monopolistic system of education controlled by the State is far more efficient in crushing our liberty than the cruder weapons of fire and sword. Against this monopoly of education by the State the Christian school brings a salutary protest; it contends for the right of parents to bring up their children in accordance with the dictates of their conscience and not in the manner prescribed by the State.

That right has been attacked in America in recent years in the most blatant possible ways. In Oregon, a law was actually passed some years ago requiring all children to attend the public school — thus taking the children from the control of their parents and

290 What Is Christianity?

placing them under the despotic control of whatever superintendent of education might happen to be in office in the district in
which they resided. In Nebraska, a law was passed forbidding
the study of languages other than English, even in private schools,
until the child was too old to learn them well. That was really a
law making literary education a crime. In New York, one of the
abominable Lusk Laws placed even private tutors under state
supervision and control.

It is true that no one of these measures is in force at the present
time. The Lusk Laws were repealed, largely through the efforts
of Governor Alfred E. Smith. The Oregon School Law and the
Nebraska Language Law were declared unconstitutional by the
United States Supreme Court, and Justice McReynolds in the
decision in the latter case gave expression to the great principle
that in America the child is not the mere creature of the State.

Even such salutary decisions as that are not to be contemplated with unmixed feelings by the lover of American institutions.
They are based, I suppose, upon the great "Bill-of-Rights" provisions of the Constitution of the United States. But the original
intent of those provisions was that they should be a check upon
Congress, not that they should be a check upon the states. The
fundamental rights of man were to be guaranteed, it was assumed,
by the constitutions of the individual states, so far as the powers
reserved to the states are concerned. It is a sign of appalling deterioration when the Federal Supreme Court steps in to do what
the state courts ought to do. Nevertheless we cannot help rejoicing
at the result. For the present at least, such an excess of tyranny
as was put into effect in Oregon and has been seriously advocated
in Michigan and other states is postponed.

Yet the forces inimical to liberty have not been discouraged by
these temporary checks. They are at work with great persistency
just at the present time, busying themselves particularly in the
advocacy of two vicious measures, both of which concern childhood and youth.

One of these is the mis-named "child-labor amendment" to the Constitution of the United States. That amendment masquerades under the cloak of humanitarianism; it is supposed to be intended to prevent sweat-shop conditions or the like. As a matter of fact it is just about as heartless a piece of proposed legislation as could possibly be conceived. Many persons who glibly favor this amendment seem never to have read it for themselves. They have a vague notion that it merely gives power to regulate the gainful employment of children. Not at all. The word "labor" was expressly insisted on in the wording of the amendment as over against the word "employment." The amendment gives power to Congress to enter right into your home and regulate or control or prevent altogether the helpful work of your children without which there can be no normal development of human character and no ordinary possibility of true happiness for mankind.

But, someone will say, Congress will never in the world be so foolish as that; the amendment does give Congress that power but the power will never be exercised. Now, my friends, I will just say this: when I listen to an argument like that, I sometimes wonder whether the person who advances it can possibly be convinced by it himself. If these stupendous powers are never to be exercised, why should they be granted? The zeal for the granting of them, the refusal of the framers of the amendment to word the amendment in any reasonably guarded way, show plainly that the powers are intended to be exercised; and certainly they will be exercised, whatever the intention of the framers of the amendment may be. I will tell you exactly what will happen if this amendment is adopted by the states. Congress will pass legislation which, in accordance with the plain meaning of the language, will be quite unenforceable. The exact degree of enforcement will be left to Washington bureaus, and the individual family will be left to the arbitrary decision of officials. It would be difficult to imagine anything more hostile to the decency of family life and to all the traditions of our people. If there ever was a measure that looked as though it were made in Russia, it is this falsely so-called "child-labor amendment" to the Constitution of the United States. In reality, it can hardly be called an amendment to the Constitution. Rather is it the complete destruction of the Constitution; for if human life in its formative period — up to eighteen years in the life of every youth — is to be given to Federal bureaucrats, we do not see what else of very great value can remain. The old principles of individual liberty and local self-government will simply have been wiped out.

This so-called child labor amendment was originally submitted to the states a number of years ago. It was in process of being rushed right through without any more examination than other amendments received. But then fortunately some patriotic citizens in Massachusetts, especially in the organization called "the Sentinels of the Republic," informed the people of the state what was really involved in this vicious measure. Massachusetts had a strict child labor law; it might have been expected, therefore, in accordance with the customary specious argument, to need protection against states where the child labor laws are less strict. Yet in a referendum the amendment was rejected by an overwhelming vote. Other states followed suit, and it looked as though this attack upon American institution and the decencies of the American home had been repelled.

But we are living now in another period of hysteria, a period even worse than that which was found at the time of the war. So the so-called child labor amendment has been revived. State after state has adopted it, to a total number, I believe, of fourteen. It looks as though the enemies of American institutions might soon have their will, and as though the childhood and youth of our country might be turned over after all to the tender mercies of Washington bureaus. That disastrous result can only be prevented if there is an earnest effort of those who still think the preservation of the American home to be worth while.

Another line of attack upon liberty has appeared in the advocacy of a Federal department of education. Repeatedly this vicious proposal has been introduced in Congress. It has been consistently favored by that powerful organization, the National Education Association. Now without being familiar with the internal workings of that Association I venture to doubt whether its unfortunate political activities really represent in any adequate way the rank and file of its members or the rank and file of the public-school teachers of this country. When I appeared at a joint hearing before the Senate Committee on Education and Labor and the House Committee on Education in 1926, Mr. Lowrey of the House Committee asked me how it was that the resolution favoring the Federal department of education was passed unanimously by the National Education Association although he had discovered that many members of that Association were saying that they were opposed to it. Neither Mr. Lowrey nor I seemed to be able to give any very good explanation of this fact. At any rate, I desire to pay the warmest possible tribute to many thousands of conscientious men and women who are teachers in the public schools of this country. I do not believe that in the entire governmental aspect of education these teachers have any really effective representation.

The commission on the subject which President Hoover appointed, for example, was composed hardly at all of teachers, but almost exclusively of "educators". It had within its membership professors of "education," superintendents of schools and the like; but in the entire roll of its membership there was found, if I remember right, hardly a single man eminent in any branch of literary studies or of natural science. The composition of that commission was typical of one of the fundamental vices in education in America at the present time — namely, the absurd over-emphasis upon methodology in the sphere of education at the expense of content. When a man fits himself in America to teach history or chemistry, it scarcely seems to occur to him, or rather it scarcely seems to occur to those who prescribe his studies for him, that he ought to study history or chemistry. Instead, he studies merely "education." The study of education seems to be regarded as absolving a teacher from obtaining any knowledge of the subject that he is undertaking to teach. And the pupils are being told, in effect, that the simple storing up in the mind of facts concerning the universe and human life is a drudgery from which they have now been emancipated; they are being told, in other words, that the great discovery has been made in modern times that it is possible to learn how to "think" with a completely empty mind. It cannot be said that the result is impressive. In fact the untrammeled operation of the effects of this great American pedogogic discovery is placing American schools far behind the schools of the rest of the civilized world.

But that is perhaps something like a digression. Let us return to the 'educators" and their general demand either for a Federal department of education or for Federal aid to the states. Such demands are in the interests of uniformity in the sphere of education. There should be, it is said, a powerful coordinating agency in education, to set up standards and encourage the production of something like a system. But what shall we say of such an aim. I have no hestitation, for my part, in saying that I am dead opposed to it. Uniformity in education, it seems to me, is one of the worst calamities into which any people can fall.

There are, it is true, some spheres in which uniformity is a good thing. It is a good thing, for example, in the making of Ford cars. In the making of a Ford car; uniformity is the great end of the activity. That end is, indeed, not always fully attained. Sometimes a Ford car possesses entirely too much individuality. My observation was, in the heroic days before the invention of self-starters, when a Ford was still a Ford, that sometimes a Ford car would start and sometimes it would not start; and if it would not start there was no use whatever in giving it any encouraging advice. But although uniformity was not always perfectly attained, the aim, at least, was to attain it; the purpose of the whole activity was that one Ford car should be just as much like every other Ford car as it could possibly be made.

But what is good for a Ford car is not always good for a human being, for the simple reason that a Ford car is a machine while a human being is a person. Our modern pedagogic experts seem to deny the distinction, and that is one place 'where our quarrel with them comes in. When you are dealing with human beings, standardization is the last thing you ought to seek. Uniformity of education under one central governmental department would be a very great calamity indeed.

We are constantly told, it is true, that there ought to be an equal opportunity for all the children in the United States; therefore, it is said, Federal aid ought to be given to backward states. But what shall we say about this business of "equal opportunity?" I will tell you what I say about it: I am entirely opposed to it. One thing is perfectly clear — if all the children in the United States have equal opportunities, no child will have an opportunity that is worth very much. If parents cannot have the great incentive of providing high and special educational advantages for their own children, then we shall have in this country a drab and soul-killing uniformity, and there will be scarcely any opportunity for anyone to get out of the miserable rut.

The thing is really quite clear. Every lover of human freedom ought to oppose with all his might the giving of Federal aid to the schools of this country; for Federal aid in the long run inevitably means Federal control, and Federal control means control by a centralized and irresponsible bureaucracy, and control by such a bureaucracy means the death of everything that might make this country great.

Against this soul-killing collectivism in education, the Christian school, like the private school, stands as an emphatic protest. In doing so, it is no real enemy of the public schools. On the contrary, the only way in which a state-controlled school can be kept even relatively healthy is through the absolutely free possibility of competition by private schools and church schools; if it once becomes monopolistic, it is the most effective engine of tyranny and intellectual stagnation that has yet been devised.

That is one reason why I favor the Christian school. I favor it in the interests of American liberty. But the other reason is vastly more important. I favor it, in the second place, because it is necessary to the propagation of the Christian Faith.

Thoughtful people, even many who are not Christians, have become impressed with the shortcomings of our secularized schools. We have provided technical education, which may make the youth of our country better able to make use of the advances of natural science; but natural science, with its command over the physical world, is not all that there is in human life. There are also the moral interests of mankind; and without cultivation of these moral interests a technically trained man is only given more power to do harm. By this purely secular, non-moral and non-religious, training we produce not a real human being but a horrible Frankenstein and we are beginning to shrink back from the product of our own hands.

The educational experts, in their conduct of their state-controlled schools, are trying to repair this defect and in doing so are seeking the cooperation of Christian people. I want to show you — and I do not think I shall have much difficulty in showing this particular audience — why such co-operation cannot be given.

In the first place, we find proposed to us today what is called "character-education" or "character-building." Character, we are told, is one thing about which men of all faiths are agreed. Let us, therefore, build character in common, as good citizens, and then welcome from the various religious faiths whatever additional aid they can severally bring. Let us first appeal to the children on a "civilization basis" — to use what I believe is the most recent terminology — and then let the various faiths appeal to whatever additional motives they may be able to adduce.

What surprises me about this program is not that its advocates propose it; for it is only too well in accord with the spirit of the age. But what really surprises me about it is that the advocates of it seem to think that a Christian can support it without ceasing at that point to be Christian.

In the first place, when this program of character-education is examined, it will be found, I think, to base character upon human experience; it will be found to represent maxims of conduct as being based upon the collective experience of the race. But how can they be based upon the collective experience of the race and at the same time, as the Christian must hold, be based upon the law of God. By this experiential morality the reverence for the law of God is being broken down. It cannot be said that the results — even judged by "civilization" standards (if I may borrow the terminology of my opponents for a moment) — is impressive. The raging tides of passion cannot successfully be kept back by the flimsy mud-embankments of an appeal to human experience. It is a feeble morality that can say nothing better for itself than that it works well.

For that reason, character-building, as practiced in our public schools, may well prove to be character-destruction. But suppose it were free from the defect that I have just mentioned. I do not see how it can possibly be free from it, if it remains, as it must necessarily remain, secular; but just suppose it were free from it. Just suppose we could have moral instruction in our public schools that should be based not upon human experience but upon something that might be conceived of as a law of God. Could a Christian consistently support even such a program as that?

We answer that question in the negative, but we do not want to answer it in the negative in any hasty way. It is perfectly true that the law of God is over all. There is not one law of God for the Christian and another law of God for the non-Christian. May not, therefore, the law be proclaimed to men of all faiths; and may it not, if it is so proclaimed, serve as a restraint against the most blatant forms of evil through the common grace of God; may it not even become a schoolmaster to bring men to Christ?

The answer is that if the law of God is proclaimed in public schools, to people of different faiths, it is bound, in the very nature of the case, to be proclaimed with optimism; and if it is proclaimed with optimism it is proclaimed in a way radically opposed to the Christian doctrine of sin. By hypothesis it is regarded as all that good citizens imperatively need to know; they may perhaps profitably know other things, but the fundamental notion is that if they know this they know all that is absolutely essential. But is not a law that is proclaimed to unredeemed persons with such optimism at best only an imperfect, garbled law? Is it not very different from the true and majestic law of God with its awful pronouncements of eternal death upon sinful man?

The answer to these questions is only too plain. A proclamation of morality which regards itself as all that is necessary — which regards itself as being capable at the most of non-essential supplementation by additional motives to be provided by Christianity or other faiths — is very different from that true proclamation of the law of God which may be a schoolmaster to bring men to Christ. It is not merely insufficient, but it is false; and I do not see how a consistent Christian can possibly regard it as providing any part of that nurture and admonition of the Lord which it is the duty of every Christian parent to give to his children.

What other solution, then, has the public school to offer for the problem which we are considering just now? Well, many people tell us that the reading of the Bible can be put into the public schools. Every educated man, we are told, ought to know something about the Bible; and no intelligent, broad-minded person, whether a Christian or not, ought to object to the bare reading of this great religious classic. So in many places we find the Bible being read in public schools. What shall we say about that?

For my part, I have no hesitation in saying that I am strongly opposed to it. I think I am just about as strongly opposed to the reading of the Bible in state-controlled schools as any atheist could be.

For one thing, the reading of the Bible is very difficult to separate from propaganda about the Bible. I remember, for example, a book of selections from the Bible for school reading, which was placed in my hands some time ago. Whether it is used now I do not know, but it is typical of what will inevitably occur if the Bible is read in public schools. Under the guise of being a book of selections for Bible-reading, it really presupposed the current naturalistic view of the Old Testament Scriptures.

But even where such errors are avoided, even where the Bible itself is read, and not in one of the current mistranslations but in the Authorized Version, the Bible still may be so read as to obscure and even contradict its true message. When, for example, the great and glorious promises of the Bible to the redeemed children of God are read as though they belonged of right to man as man, have we not an attack upon the very heart and core of the Bible's teaching? What could be more terrible, for example, from the Christian point of view, than the reading of the Lord's Prayer to non-Christian children, as though they could use it without becoming Christians, as though persons who have never been purchased by the blood of Christ could possibly say to God. "Our Father, which art in Heaven?" The truth is that a garbled Bible may be a falsified Bible; and when any hope is held out to lost humanity from the so-called ethical portions of the Bible apart from its great redemptive core, then the Bible is represented as saying the direct opposite of what it really says.

So I am opposed to the reading of the Bible in public schools. As for any presentation of general principles of what is called "religion," supposed to be exemplified in various positive religions, including Christianity, it is quite unnecessary for me to say in this company that such presentation is opposed to the Christian religion at its very heart.  The relation between the Christian way of salvation and other ways is not a relation between the adequate and the inadequate or between the perfect and the imperfect, but it is a relation between the true and the false.  The minute a professing Christian admits that he can find neutral ground with non-Christians in the study of "religion" in general, he has given up the battle, and has really, if he knows what he is doing, made common cause with that synchronism which is today, as it was in the first century of our era, the deadliest enemy of the Christian Faith.

What, then, should the Christian do in communities where there are no Christian schools?  What policy should be advocated for the public schools?

I think there is no harm in advocating the release of public school children at convenient hours during the week for any religious instruction which their parents may provide.  Even at this point, indeed, danger lurks at the door.  If the State undertakes to exercise any control whatever over the use by the children of this time which is left vacant, even by way of barely requiring them to attend upon some kind of instruction in these hours, and still more clearly if it undertakes to give public school credits for such religious instruction, then it violates fundamental principles and will inevitably in the long run seek to control the content of the instruction in the interests of the current syncretism.  But if — as is, it must be admitted, very difficult — it can be kept free from these evils, then the arrangement of the public school schedule in such manner that convenient hours shall be left free for such religious instruction as the parents, entirely at their individual discretion, shall provide, is I think, unobjectionable, and it may under certain circumstances be productive of some relative good.

But what miserable makeshifts all such measures, even at the best, are!  Underlying them is the notion that religion embraces only one particular part of human life.  Let the public schools take care of the rest of life — such seems to be the notion — and one or two hours during the week will be sufficient to fill the gap which they leave. But as a matter of fact the religion of the Christian man embraces the whole of his life. Without Christ he was dead in trespasses and sins, but he has now been made alive by the Spirit of God; he was formerly alien from the household of God, but has now been made a member of God's covenant people. Can this new relationship to God be regarded as concerning only one part, and apparently a small part, of his life? No, it concerns all his life; and everything that he does he should do now as a child of God.

It is this profound Christian permeation of every human activity, no matter how secular the world may regard it as being, which is brought about by the Christian school and the Christian school alone. I do not want to be guilty of exaggerations at this point. A Christian boy or girl can learn mathematics, for example, from a teacher who is not a Christian; and truth is truth however learned. But while truth is truth however learned, the bearings of truth, the meaning of truth, the purpose of truth, even in the sphere of mathematics, seem entirely different to the Christian from that which they seem to the non-Christian; and that is why a truly Christian education is possible only when Christian conviction underlies not a part, but all, of the curriculum of the school. True learning and true piety go hand in hand, and Christianity embraces the whole of life — those are great central convictions that underlie the Christian school.

I believe that the Christian school deserves to have a good report from those who are without; I believe that even those of our fellow citizens who are not Christians may, if they really love human freedom and the noble traditions of our people, be induced to defend the Christian school against the assaults of its adversaries and to cherish it as a true bulwark of the State. But for Christian people, its appeal is far deeper. I can see little consistency in a type of Christian activity which preaches the gospel on the street corners and at the ends of the earth, but neglects the children of the covenant by abandoning them to a cold and un-believing secularism. If, indeed, the Christian school were in any sort of competition with the Christian family, if it were trying to do what the home ought to do, then I could never favor it. But one of its marked characteristics, in sharp distinction from the secular education of today, is that it exalts the family as a blessed divine institution and treats the scholars in its classes as children of the covenant to be brought up above all things in the nurture and admonition of the Lord.

I cannot bring this little address to a close without trying to pay some sort of tribute to you who have so wonderfully maintained the Christian schools. Some of you, no doubt, are serving as teachers on salaries necessarily small. What words can I possibly find to celebrate the heroism and unselfishness of such service? Others of you are maintaining the schools by your gifts, in the midst of many burdens and despite the present poverty and dis-tress. When I think of such true Christian heroism as yours, I count everything that I ever tried to do in my life to be pitifully unworthy. I can only say that I stand reverently in your presence as in the presence of brethren to whom God has given richly of His grace.

You deserve the gratitude of your country. In a time of spiritual and intellectual and political decadence, you have given us in America something that is truly healthy; you are to our coun-try something like a precious salt that may check the ravages of decay. May that salt never lose its savor! May the distinc-tiveness of your Christian schools never be lost; may it never give place, by a false "Americanization," to a drab uniformity which is the most un-American thing that could possibly be con-ceived!!

But if you deserve the gratitude of every American patriot, how much more do you deserve the gratitude of Christian men and women! You have set an example for the whole Christian world;

you have done a thing which has elsewhere been neglected, and the neglect of which is everywhere bringing disaster. You are like a city set on a hill; and may that city never be hid! May the example of your Christian schools be heeded everywhere in the Church! Above all, may our God richly bless you, and of His grace give you a reward with which all the rewards of earth are not for one moment worthy to be compared!

# XXVI

## Mountains and Why We Love Them

WHAT right have I to speak about mountain-climbing? The answer is very simple. I have none whatever. I have, indeed, been in the Alps four times. The first time I got up Monte Rosa, the second highest of the Alps, and one or two others of the easier Zermatt peaks. On my second visit I had some glorious days in the Grossglockner group and on a few summits in the Zillerthal Alps and also made my first visit to that beautiful liberty-loving land of South Tirol, where, as a result of a war fought to "make the world safe for democracy," Mussolini is now engaged in the systematic destruction of a language and civilization that has set its mark upon the very face of the landscape for many centuries. On my third visit, in 1913, I did my most ambitious climbing, all in the Eastern Alps, getting up the Kleine Zinne by the north face, certain of the sporty Cortina courses, and also the Campanile di Val Montanaia, which is not considered altogether easy. In 1932 I was on three of the first-class Zermatt peaks.

Why, then, have I no right to talk about mountain-climbing? For the simple reason that I did all of these climbs with good guides, safeguarded by perfectly good Alpine ropes. An Alpine guide is said to be able to get a sack of meal up the Matterhorn about as well as he can get some tourists up, and then those tourists go home and boast what great mountaineers they are. Well, I differed from the proverbial sack of meal in two particulars: (1) I am a little superior to the sack of meal in climbing ability; (2) the sack of meal is unaware of the fact that it is not a mountaineer, and I am fully aware of the fact that I am not. The man who leads on the rope is the man who has to be a real mountaineer, and I never did that. I am less than the least of the thousands of real climbers who go to the Alps every summer and climb without guides.

But although I am not a mountaineer, I do love the mountains and I have loved them ever since I can remember anything at all. It is about the love of the mountains, rather than about the mountains, that I am venturing to read this little paper today.

Can the love of the mountains be conveyed to those who have it not? I am not sure. Perhaps if a man is not born with that love it is almost as hopeless to try to bring it to him as it would be to explain what color is to a blind man or to try to make President Roosevelt understand the Constitution of the United States. But on the whole I do believe that the love of the mountains can at least be cultivated, and if I can do anything whatever toward getting you to cultivate it, the purpose of this little paper will be amply attained.

One thing is clear — if you are to learn to love the mountains you must go up them by your own power. There is more thrill in the smallest hill in Fairmount Park if you walk up it than there is in the grandest mountain on earth if you go up it in an automobile. There is one curious thing about means of locomotion — the slower and simpler and the closer to nature they are, the more real thrill they give. I have got far more enjoyment out of my two feet than I did out of my bicycle; and I got more enjoyment out of my bicycle than I ever have got out of my motor car; and as for airplanes — well, all I can say is that I wouldn't lower myself by going up in one of the stupid, noisy things! The only way to have the slightest inkling of what a mountain is is to walk or climb up it.

Now I want you to feel something of what I feel when I am with the mountains that I love. To that end I am not going to ask you to go with me to any out-of-the-way place, but I am just going to take you to one of the most familiar tourist's objectives, one of the places to which one goes on every ordinary European tour — namely, to Zermatt — and in Zermatt I am not going to take you on any really difficult climbs but merely up one or two of the peaks by the ordinary routes which modern mountaineers despise. I want you to look at Zermatt for a few minutes not with the eyes of a tourist, and not with the eyes of a devotee of mountaineering in its ultra-modern aspects, but with the eyes of a man who, whatever his limitations, does truly love the mountains.

In Zermatt, after I arrived on July 15, 1932, I secured Alois Graven as my guide; and on a number of the more ambitious expeditions I had also Gottfried Perren, who also is a guide of the first class. What Ty Cobb was on a baseball diamond and Bill Tilden is on the courts, that such men are on a steep snow or ice slope, or negotiating a difficult rock, *Ueberhang*. It is a joy as I have done in Switzerland and in the Eastern Alps, to see really good climbers at work.

At this point I just want to say a word for Swiss and Austrian guides. Justice is not done to them, in my judgment, in many of the books on climbing. You see, it is not they who write the books. They rank as professionals, and the tourists who hire them as "gentlemen;" but in many cases I am inclined to think that the truer gentleman is the guide. I am quite sure that that was the case when I went with Alois Graven.

In addition to climbing practice on the wrong side of the cocky little Riffelhorn and on the ridge of the Untergabelhorn — which climbing practice prevented me from buttoning my back collar button without agony for a week — and in addition to an interesting glacier expedition around the back side of the Breithorn and up Pollux (13,430 feet) and Caster (13,850) and down by the Fellikjoch through the ice fall of the Zwillingsgletscher, on which expedition I made my first acquaintance with really bad weather in the high Alps and the curious optical illusions which it causes — it was perfectly amazing to see the way in which near the summit of Caster the leading guide would feel with his ice-axe for the edge of the ridge in what I could have sworn to be a perfectly innocent expanse of easy snowfield right there in plain view before our feet, and it was also perfectly amazing to see the way in which little pieces of ice on the glacier were rolled by way of experimentation down what looked like perfectly innocent slopes, to see whether they would simply disappear in crevasses which I could have sworn not to be there (if they disappeared we didn't because we took the hint and chose some other way through the labyrinth) — after these various preliminary expeditions and despite the agony of a deep sore on my right foot in view of which the Swiss doctor whom I consulted told me that as a physician he would tell me to quit but that as a man he knew I would not do so and that therefore he would patch me up as well as possible, and despite the even greater agony of a strained stomach muscle which I got when I extricated myself and was extricated one day from a miniature crevasse and which made me, the following night in the Theodul hut, feel as helpless as a turtle laid on its back, so that getting out of my bunk became a difficult mountaineering feat — after these preliminary expeditions and despite these and other agonies due to a man's giving a fifty-year-old body twenty-year-old treatment, I got up three first-class Zermatt peaks: the Zinalrothorn, the Matterhorn and the Dent Blanche. Of these three, I have not time — or rather you have not time (for I for my part should just love to go on talking about the mountains for hours and Niagara would have nothing on me for running on) — I say, of these *you* have not time for me to tell about more than one. It is very hard for me to choose among the three. The Zinalrothorn, I think, is the most varied and interesting as a climb; the Dent Blanche has always had the reputation of being the most difficult of all the Zermatt peaks, and it is a glorious mountain indeed, a mountain that does not intrude its splendors upon the mob but keeps them for those who will penetrate into the vastnesses or will mount to the heights whence true nobility appears in its real proportions. I should love to tell you of that crowning day of my month at Zermatt, when after leaving the Schönbühl Hut at about 2:30 A.M. (after a disappointment the previous night when my guides had assisted in a rescue expedition that took one injured climber and the body of one who was killed in an accident on the Zmutt Ridge of the Matterhorn, opposite the hut where we were staying, down to Zermatt so that we all arrived there about 2 A. M., about the time when it had been planned that we should leave the hut for our climb) we made our way by lantern light up into the strange upper recesses of the Schönbühl Glacier, then by the dawning light of day across the glacier, across the bottom of a couloir safe in the morning but not a place where one lingers when the warmth of afternoon has affected the hanging glacier two thousand feet above, then to the top of the Wandfluh, the great south ridge, at first broad and easy but contracting above to its serrated knife-edge form, then around the "great gendarme" and around or over the others of the rock towers on the ridge, until at last that glorious and unbelievable moment came when the last few feet of the sharp snow ridge could be seen with nothing above but a vacancy of blue, and when I became conscious of the fact that I was actually standing on the summit of the Dent Blanche.

But the Matterhorn is a symbol as well as a mountain, and so I am going to spend the few minutes that remain in telling you about that.

There is a curious thing when you first see the Matterhorn on a fresh arrival at Zermatt. You think your memory has preserved for you an adequate picture of what it is like. But you see that you were wrong. The reality is far more unbelievable than any memory of it can be. A man who sees the Matterhorn standing at that amazing angle above the Zermatt street can believe that such a thing exists only when he keeps his eyes actually fastened upon it.

When I arrived on July 15, 1932, the great mountain had not yet been ascended that summer. The masses of fresh snow were too great; the weather had not been right. That is one way in which this mountain retains its dignity even in the evil days upon which it has fallen when duffers such as I can stand upon its summit. In storm, it can be almost as perilous as ever even to those who follow the despised easiest route.

It was that despised easiest route, of course, which I followed — though my guide led me to have hopes of doing the Zmutt ridge before I got through. On Monday, August 1st, we went up to the "Belvedere," the tiny little hotel (if you can call it such) that stands right next to the old Matterhorn Hut at 10,700 feet. We went up there intending to ascend the Matterhorn the next day. But alas for human hopes. Nobody ascended the Matterhorn the next day, nor the day after that, nor that whole week. On Wednesday we with several other parties went a little way, but high wind and cold and snow soon drove us back. The Matterhorn may be sadly tamed, but you cannot play with it when the weather is not right. That applies to experts as well as to novices like me. I waited at the Belvedere all that week until Friday. It is not the most comfortable of summer resorts, and I really think that the stay that I made in it was one of the longest that any guest had ever made. Its little cubby-holes of rooms are admirable as Frigidaires, but as living quarters they are "not so hot." People came and people went; very polyglot was the conversation: but I remained. I told them that I was the hermit or the *Einsiedler* of the Belvedere. At last, however, even I gave it up. On Friday I returned to Zermatt, in plenty of time for the Saturday night bath!

The next Monday we toiled again up that five thousand feet to the Belvedere, and this time all went well. On Tuesday, August 9th, I stood on what I suppose is, next to Mt. Everest, the most famous mountain in the world.

From the Belvedere to the summit is about four thousand feet. The Matterhorn differs from every other great Alpine peak that I know anything about in that when you ascend it by the usual route you do not once set foot on a glacier. You climb near the northeast ridge — for the most part not on the actual ridge itself but on the east face near the ridge. In some places in the lower part there is some danger from falling stones, especially if other parties are climbing above. There is scarcely anything that the blasé modern mountaineer calls rock climbing of even respectable difficulty; but it is practically all rock climbing or clambering of a sort, and it seems quite interesting enough to the novice. The most precipitous part is above what is called "the shoulder," and it was from near this part that the four members of Whymper's party fell 4000 feet to their death when they were descending after the first ascent in 1865. There are now fixed ropes at places in this part. You grasp the hanging rope with one hand and find the holds in the rock with the other. It took me five hours and forty minutes to make the ascent from the Belvedere. It would certainly have been no great achievement for an athlete; but I am not an athlete and never was one, and I was then fifty-one years of age and have an elevator in the building where I live. The rarefied air affected me more than it used to do in my earlier years, and the mountain is about 14,700 feet high. I shall never forget those last few breathless steps when I realized that only a few feet of easy snow separated me from the summit of the Matterhorn. When I stood there at last — the place where more than any other place on earth I had hoped all my life that I might stand — I was afraid I was going to break down and weep for joy.

The summit looks the part. It is not indeed a peak, as you would think it was from looking at the pictures which are taken from Zermatt, but a ridge — a ridge with the so-called Italian summit at one end and the so-called Swiss summit three feet higher at the other. Yes, it is a ridge. But what a ridge! On the south you look directly over the stupendous precipice of the south face to the green fields of Valtournanche. On the north you look down an immensely steep snow slope — with a vacancy beyond that is even more impressive than an actual view over the great north precipice would be. As for the distant prospect, I shall not try to describe it, for the simple reason that it is indescribable. Southward you look out over the mysterious infinity of the Italian plain with the snows of Monte Viso one hundred miles away. To the west, the great snow dome of Mont Blanc stands over a jumble of snow peaks; and it looks the monarch that it is. To the north the near peaks of the Weisshorn and the Dent Blanche, and on the horizon beyond the Rhone Valley a marvelous glittering galaxy of the Jungfrau and the Finsteraarhorn and the other mountains of the Bernese Oberland. To the east, between the Strahlhorn and Monte Rosa, the snows of the Weissthorn are like a great sheet let down from heaven, exceeding white and glistering, so as no fuller on earth can white them; and beyond, fold on fold, soft in the dim distance, the ranges of the Eastern Alps.

Then there is something else about that view from the Matterhorn. I felt it partly at least as I stood there, and I wonder whether you can feel it with me. It is this. You are standing there not in any ordinary country, but in the very midst of Europe, looking out from its very centre. Germany just beyond where you can see to the northeast, Italy to the south, France beyond those snows of Mont Blanc. There, in that glorious round spread out before you, that land of Europe, humanity has put forth its best. There it has struggled; there it has fallen; there it has looked upward to God. The history of the race seems to pass before you in an instant of time, concentrated in that fairest of all the lands of earth. You think of the great men whose memories you love, the men who have struggled there in those countries below you, who have struggled for light and freedom, struggled for beauty, struggled above all for God's Word.  And then you think of the present and its decadence and its slavery, and you desire to weep. It is a pathetic thing to contemplate the history of mankind.

I know that there are people who tell us contemptuously that always there are croakers who look always to the past, croakers who think that the good old times are the best.  But I for my part refuse to acquiesce in this relativism which refuses to take stock of the times in which we are living.  It does seem to me that there can never be any true advance, and above all there can never be any true prayer, unless a man does pause occasionally, as on some mountain vantage ground, to *try*, at least, to evaluate the age in which he is living.  And when I do that, I cannot for the life of me see how any man with even the slightest knowledge of history can help recognizing the fact that we are living in a time of sad decadence — a decadence only thinly disguised by the material achievements of our age, which already are beginning to pall on us like a new toy.  When Mussolini makes war deliberately and openly upon democracy and freedom, and is much admired for doing so even in countries like ours; when an ignorant ruffian is dictator of Germany, until recently the most highly educated country in the world — when we contemplate these things I do not see how we can possibly help seeing that something is radically wrong.  Just read the latest utterances of our own General Johnson, his cheap and vulgar abuse of a recent appointee of our President, the cheap tirades in which he develops his view that economics are bunk — and then compare that kind of thing with the state papers of a Jefferson or a Washington — and you will inevitably come to the conclusion that we are living in a time when decadence has set in on a gigantic scale.

What will be the end of that European civilization, of which I had a survey from my mountain vantage ground — of that European civilization and its daughter in America?  What does the future hold in store? Will Luther prove to have lived in vain? Will all the dreams of liberty issue into some vast industrial machine? Will even nature be reduced to standard, as in our country the sweetness of the woods and hills is being destroyed, as I have seen them destroyed in Maine, by the uniformities and artificialities and officialdom of our national parks? Will the so-called "Child Labor Amendment" and other similar measures be adopted, to the destruction of all the decencies and privacies of the home? Will some dreadful second law of thermodynamics apply in the spiritual as in the material realm? Will all things in church and state be reduced to one dead level, coming at last to an equilibrium in which all liberty and all high aspirations will be gone? Will that be the end of all humanity's hopes? I can see no escape from that conclusion in the signs of the times; too inexorable seems to me to be the march of events. No, I can see only one alternative. The alternative is that there is a God — a God who in His own good time will bring foward great men again to do His will, great men to resist the tyranny of experts and lead humanity out again into the realms of light and freedom, great men, above all, who will be the messengers of His grace. There is, far above any earthly mountain peak of vision, a God high and lifted up who, though He is infinitely exalted, yet cares for His children among men.

What have I from my visits to the mountains, not only from those in the Alps, but also, for example, from that delightful twenty-four-mile walk which I took one day last summer in the White Mountains over the whole Twin Mountain range? The answer is that I have memories. Memory, in some respects, is a very terrible thing. Who has not experienced how, after we have forgotten some recent hurt in the hours of sleep, the memory of it comes back to us on our awaking as though it were some dreadful physical blow. Happy is the man who can in such moments repeat the words of the Psalmist and who in doing so regards them not merely as the words of the Psalmist but as the Word of God.  But memory is also given us for our comfort; and so in hours of darkness and discouragement I love to think of that sharp summit ridge of the Matterhorn piercing the blue or the majesty and the beauty of that world spread out at my feet when I stood on the summit of the Dent Blanche.

# XXVII

## The Benefits of Walking

H AVING the great joy of three weeks of climbing in the Canadian Rockies, I am writing this little article to see whether I cannot help even those readers who cannot climb and cannot go to the Canadian Rockies to get some of the benefits which I am getting here.

Climbing mountains is good, in the first place for the body, and, in the second place, for the soul.

It is good for the body because of the wholesome buffeting of the body which it brings. To get such buffeting the "tired American business man" is wont, I believe, to place himself under the despotic control of some ex-prize-fighter until he comes out of the ex-prize-fighter's (very expensive) establishment feeling fit. There are, I suppose, cruel and unusual punchings of the 'bag and pulling of the chest weights most severe. I shudder' when I think of it. Such drudgery will people submit to' in order to harden their bodies and make them a little better able to undertake the duties of life. I admire people who thus recognize the fact that a soft body will not do hard work.

But there are even better ways of hardening the body, and one of these is to learn to climb. Let that tired business man get a good Swiss guide, like the one that I have here; let him be initiated into the mysteries of rock-climbing, and he will find that his softness of body will soon disappear. What a thoroughgoing twisting and pulling and bumping the body gets, at every conceivable angle and in every conceivable way, on a rock climb even of moderate difficulty! It is glorious exercise indeed.

Now I know that it is only a few people who can climb. Climbing without expert guides, unless one is oneself a real expert, is highly dangerous; and there are now, I believe, only four mountaineering guides in all of Canada. Since the Canadian Pacific Railway speaks of western Canada as "fifty Switzerlands in one," that makes just about one guide for every dozen Switzerlands — hardly enough to go around!

But the point that I am making is that many of the same benefits as those that are obtained in climbing may be obtained also without climbing and without the expense of guides. They may be secured through that cheapest and simplest of all forms of exercise — the exercise of walking.

I can testify to that from personal experience; for I have been a walker all my life. I do not, indeed, under-estimate those comparatively rare occasions when I have been able to climb. They would hardly have justified the expense involved in them if they had brought to me merely the pleasure of the moment, but as a matter of fact when the climbs have been over the benefit of them has just begun. During a period of nineteen years, when I did no climbing at all, how I used to live over again in memory those glorious days in the Eastern Alps in 1913! How eagerly did I read countless descriptions, in books and Alpine journals, of precipitous mountains of South Tirol! Then in 1932 and 1935 came the crowning joy of standing on the great Zermatt peaks. When I get discouraged I love to think of that unbelievable half hour when, after having climbed the Matterhorn by the Zmutt Ridge, we sat on the Italian summit, with our feet over Italy and our backs to a little wall of summit snow, and let our eyes drink in the marvelous beauty of the scene. What a wonderful help it is in all discouragements, what a blessed gift of God, to be able to bring before the mind's eye such a vision as that.

But, do you know, my friends, a man can have very much that same joy in much simpler ways.

The more I see of the high mountains, the more I love the simple beauty of the woods and hills, and the more I love to walk.

What a very simple amusement walking is! You do not need any elaborate equipment; you can just "up and do it" any time you like.

But perhaps you say that as a matter of fact you do *not* like it. All right, I say; but will you not learn to like it?

There are many things that man does not like at first, and yet that he comes to like. A man says, for example, that he cannot see anything at all in golf. It seems to him a very silly game. But then a friend persuades him one day to go out and have a try. He has "beginner's luck." He manages just once to hit the ball instead of the earth. To his amazement he watches that ball go. How amazingly far that little pellet will sail when you happen to hit it right! Well, the man understands the fascination at last. He plays golf and talks golf all the rest of his life. He is a hopeless victim of the well-known "hoof and mouth disease."

So when you say you do not love to walk, I do wish I could just get you to try. I do wish I could persuade you to use the old Ford this summer just to get to the edge of the woods. If you did choose that kind of a holiday it would not cost you much, shoe-leather being much cheaper than gasoline and rubber tires. And the wholesome exercise you would get, and the close contact with the beauties of nature, would be a wonderful thing "as well for the body as the soul."

# Other Related Princeton Titles

In addition to the Machen titles listed behind the title page, Solid Ground is one of the leading publishers in the world of Old Princeton titles. Many are listed below . . .

**Theology on Fire: Vols. 1 & 2** by J.A. Alexander is the two volume set of sermons by this brilliant scholar from Princeton Seminary. He was a truly gifted preacher.

**A Shepherd's Heart** by J.W. Alexander is a volume of outstanding expository sermons from the pastoral ministry of one of the leading preachers of the 19th century.

**Evangelical Truth** by Archibald Alexander is a volume of practical sermons intended to be used for Family Worship.

**The Lord of Glory** by B.B. Warfield is one of the best treatments of the doctrine of the Deity of Christ ever written. Warfield is simply masterful.

**The Power of God unto Salvation** by B.B. Warfield is the first book of sermons ever published of this master-theologian. Several of these are found nowhere else.

**The Person & Work of the Holy Spirit** by B.B. Warfield is a compilation of all the sermons, articles and book reviews by a master-theologian on a theme that should interest every child of God. Brilliant in every way!

**Grace & Glory** by Geerhardus Vos is a series of addresses delivered in the chapel to the students at Princeton. John Murray said of him, "Dr. Vos is, in my judgment, the most penetrating exegete it has been my privilege to know, and I believe, the most incisive exegete that has appeared in the English-speaking world in this century."

**Princeton Sermons:** *Chapel Addresses from 1891-92* by B.B. Warfield, W.H. Green, C.W. Hodge, John D. Davis and More. According to Joel Beeke, this is "a treasure-trove of practical Christianity delivered by some of the greatest preachers and seminary teachers America has ever known."

Call us at **1-205-443-0311**
Send us an e-mail at **mike.sgcb@gmail.com**
Visit us on line at **www.solid-ground-books.com**

CPSIA information can be obtained
at www.ICGtesting.com
Printed in the USA
LVOW07s0219161116
513160LV00012B/207/P